Teaching Thinking Through Effective Questioning

Teaching Thinking Through Effective Questioning

Francis P. Hunkins

University of Washington

Christopher-Gordon Publishers, Inc.

Boston

Christopher-Gordon Publishers, Inc.
480 Washington Street
Norwood, MA 02062

Printed in the United States of America

10 9 8 7 6 5 4 3 2 1   94 93 92 91 90 89

Brief Table of Contents

Teaching Thinking Through Effective Questioning
Francis P. Hunkins

Table of Contents

PREFACE

Teaching Thinking Through Effective Questioning is for both preservice and inservice teachers as well as supervisors, principals, and those with curriculum and instruction responsibilities. It is a book for persons who consider themselves students of questions.

The book is intentionally comprehensive in its treatment of questions. One of the book's major strengths is its comprehensiveness. Because of its depth of treatment, the book is not meant to be read in just one sitting; it is meant to be used as a valuable reference to which one will turn many times when dealing with ways to make questions and questioning within instruction dynamic and meaningful to students.

Chapter 1 sets the stage by placing questions within the educational arena and within the realm of thinking. Throughout, *Teaching Thinking Through Effective Questioning* gives detailed attention to ways to utilize questions and, more importantly, to get students to raise questions within the activity of thinking.

Chapter 2 elaborates on the complexity of the question and discusses the nature of questioning and the assumptions behind the questioning act. Chapter 3 presents information on question types as to their cognitive and affective functions. Chapter 4 deals with question types as to focus and syntax. Attention to question focus and syntax reveals that we in education have many more ways to classify questions than cognitive level. Information in this chapter should help teachers greatly to enrich the types of questions they use in the classroom.

We do not become effective questioners and skilled facilitators of students' questions without careful planning. Chapter 5 deals with ways of generating effective questions and planning productive questioning strategies. The point is developed that planning is a type of decision making, a means of thinking, in this case about questions and questioning strategies.

Chapter 6 discusses questions within the classroom with special attention to questions employed in generic teaching methods: lecture, discussion, demonstration and inquiry. Chapter 7, on the other hand, deals with specific questioning strategies for both teachers and students. These strategies will offer the reader some challenges. When taught to students, students will become skilled inquirers.

In addition to various questioning strategies, there are several questioning techniques that assist one in effectively utilizing questions: wait time, probing, clarification, elaboration, redirection and supporting techniques. Chapter 8 deals with these techniques as well as with nonquestioning options that can allow students to reflect and to question.

The key performers in the classroom should be the students. We as teachers should work to get them comfortable in planning their questions and questioning strategies and then afford them opportunities to question and assess their questions and questioning strategies. Chapter 9 addresses this topic of student involvement with questions.

The book concludes with Chapter 10 on the questioning attitude. Attention is given to questioning within innovative learning, within the active processing of information. An attempt is made to leave the reader not only with answers to the realms of effective questions and effective thinking but also with additional questions and the motivation to seek answers to them.

Questioning and thinking are complex activities; therefore, the ways in which we question and our strategies for thinking are likewise complex. The strategies included in this book have value as reinforcement and are supported by research. However, the strategies require practice.

One cannot read Chapter 7 on specific questioning strategies and expect immediate mastery. I would not encourage the reader to attempt to master all of the strategies at once. Rather, select any one and then practice it. As with any new skill, you will not be very proficient at first, but in time you will become accomplished. The strategies included in this book, if mastered, will reward you with quality teaching. In sharing this information with your students and allowing them time to practice, you will discover that they will gain control over their learning that will reap for them benefits of increased understanding.

Teaching Thinking Through Effective Questioning differs in several ways from other books on questions on the market. First, it differs in its depth of coverage; second, it differs in its range of treatment of questions. Third, it furnishes detailed information on many strategies and encourages you to select those you think most valuable in light of your skills, teaching style, philosophical orientations, and types of students. Fourth, the book relates questions to thinking and to metacognition. While several books on thinking are on the market, they do not give indepth treatment of questions and questioning. Fifth, the book contains various activities by which the reader can begin to gain ownership of this information.

In writing a book, one is always influenced by numerous people who deserve to be thanked publicly. I would like to thank Hiram Howard, President of Christopher-Gordon Publishers, Inc., who took initial interest in my idea for this book and encouraged me to pursue it. I also want to thank Susanne Canavan, Executive Vice President of Christopher-Gordon, for her assistance. Special thanks is given also to Alice Tessier, who served as copy editor.

I want also to express my thanks to William Wilen, Jay McTighe, and Esther Fusco, who reviewed the manuscript.

DEDICATION

To my children, Leah and Francis, Jr., who as young adults continue to be effective questioners and effective thinkers, I dedicate this book. I also dedicate it to the spirit of my mother, who during her life challenged life with questions and served as one of my most significant teachers.

1

Questions, Their Place Within the Educational Arena

Questions, thinking, active students, challenging lessons, dynamic instruction, metacognitive approaches—these words are frequently heard in today's education dialogue. The discussions reflect interesting educational times, frustrating times, confusing times, challenging times.

THE CURRENT EDUCATIONAL ARENA

Our educational history reveals stages in which our vision of the student has shifted between a perception of an active individual and a passive one. This vacillation has occurred despite our almost constant commitment to students as active thinkers and processors of information, as individuals whose rightful role in learning is one of self-management. This belief in the active learner in control of his or her scholarship is currently receiving new emphasis. Currently, our notion of the active student is tied to our views of the times. We recognize that the essence of the student's activeness relates to the character of that which is demanding the activity and to the context within which the activity is or is likely to occur.[1]

Getting Students Involved

Accepting students' involvement as essential for optimal learning and thinking, educators are suggesting ways they can assure students' optimal engagement in their learning. Discussions center on approaches to encourage students' inquisitiveness, which many cognitive scientists purport to be, along with certain thinking abilities, an innate feature of humans.[2]

Inquisitiveness and the ability to think are essential for functioning in the present and fast-developing information society. Naisbitt,[3] Toffler,[4] and other futurists have discussed this information age in great detail. Hallmark to this new age is the new wealth of knowhow and the strategic skills necessary for creating and managing information.

Toffler talks of constructing an info-sphere, an environment literally unknown in previous times. "We are imparting to the 'dead' environment around us not life but intelligence."[5] In creating this info-sphere, we are altering how we conceptualize our world; modifying the manner of thinking about our problems; changing our approaches to synthesizing information. Essentially, we are varying the methods by which we think and question. In the info-sphere, we are striving to enhance our mind power, to open doors to a new universe of imagination and pleasure. In short, we are in the process of redefining literacy.

While Toffler attends to the new machines of this age, he notes that in the upcoming decades human intelligence, imagination, and intuition will be far more important than the machine.[6] Mindful of this, we educators should create within educational arenas smart environments that enable students to work on their intelligence through reflecting on their mental capacities, their questions.

Toffler, quoting a neuropsychiatrist notes,

> ... kids raised in a smart, responsive environment, which is complex and stimulating, may develop a different set of skills. If kids can call on the environment to do things for them, they become less dependent on parents at a younger age. They may gain a sense of mastery or competency. And they can afford to be inquisitive, exploratory, imaginative, and to adopt a problem-solving approach to life.
> A smarter environment might make smarter people.[7]

A smart education environment contains within it variables with which students can interact, variables that can be questioned, variables about which students can think. These variables, complex and stimulating, can serve as units capable of propelling students to greater understanding of the information encountered. Obviously, time must be allowed for such thinking, for the raising of questions. Given such environments, schools can unleash within students energies that will increase those literacies essential for optimal functioning within the world's info-spheres.

While few of us would contest that schools should provide those literacies requisite for optimal functioning within current and future times, there is less agreement as to what those literacies entail. Notwithstanding this, there seems to be consensus that thinking and effective inquiry are paramount skills. The National Science Board Commission on Pre-college Education in Mathematics, Science and Technology in its report *Educating Americans for the Twenty-first Century* urged a

> ... return to basics, but the basics of the twenty-first century are not only reading, writing, and arithmetic. They include communication and higher problem-solving skills, and scientific and technological literacy—the thinking tools that allow us to understand the technological world around us.[8]

The commission presented as a fundamental goal the development of students' capacities for problem solving and critical thinking in all realms of knowing.

The National Council of Teachers of English in its publication *Essentials of English* denotes the close link between thinking and language.

> Thinking skills, involved in the study of all disciplines, are inherent in the reading, writing, speaking, listening and observing involved in the study of English. The ability to analyze, classify, compare, formulate hypotheses, make inferences, and draw conclusions is essential to the reasoning processes of all adults. The capacity to solve problems... is a way to help students cope successfully with the experience of learning.... [9]

To address the urgings of these associations successfully requires conscious changes in our functioning so that students participate in their learning. John Goodlad, in his book *A Place Called School*, reports that we are not living up to our rhetoric, not allowing our students to relinquish being passive answer-absorbers.[10] Harold Shane, more than a decade ago, sketched that we needed to switch from our traditional ways so that we go

from	*to*
Mass teaching	Personalized teaching
Single learnings	Multiple learnings
Passive answer absorbing	Active answer seeking
Training in formal skills and knowledge	Building desirable attitudes and appreciations that stimulate a questing for knowledge
Teacher initiative and direction	Child initiative and group planning
Isolated content	Interrelated content
Memorized answers	Problem awareness
Passive mastery of information	Active stimulation on/of intellect[11]

Implicit in these shifts is that we go from viewing questions as devices by which one evaluates the specifics of learning to using questions as a means for actively processing, thinking about, and using information productively. Students must be weaned from believing that questions are engaged in to attain certain answers and must be introduced to the notion that questions can elicit awareness of the diversity, complexity, and richness of knowledge. Students must advance from thinking of questions as devices for gaining certain answers to considering questions as linguistic tools that enable thinking.

Educating Students for Critical Awareness

Involved students are critically aware of their world and its organizations. Critical awareness brings forth knowing, perceiving understanding one's world; it means perceiving the avenues through which one comprehends and reflects—being cognizant of the kinds of questions possible about one's world.[12]

While the young possess a natural curiosity and a felt need to explore their physical and psychological worlds (much as they have the innate capacity at birth to walk), they require guidance to think rationally and critically, to raise questions of significance (much as they need education to advance from walking to dancing). All need instruction in ways of formulating their knowledge. Students are not sponges present for absorbing a teacher's wisdom. They are interactive entities requiring engagement with content.[13] Most of us accept the dictum that for individuals to know something, they must understand it in their own terms, at levels of rule complexity commensurate with their developmental levels.[14]

Critical awareness is essential to understanding knowledge. Asking questions is also essential. Jane Martin has suggested that understanding is essentially perceiving relationships or connections among the thing to be understood.[15] It is an activity in which one distinguishes and classifies the thing being attended. These activities, driven by one's questions, relate to concepts, to means of processing information, to one's background knowledge, to one's awareness of categories.

Accepting critical awareness as an essential goal of education means furnishing more than bits and pieces of information to students. It means structuring the educational encounter in ways that awaken our students to life. Children come to school believing that the reality they see is *the* reality. Agreeing that children are indeed curious, many of us argue that they are clear as to their object of curiosity; however, children only ask obvious questions. The young cannot without help imagine questions about aspects of realities that are only contemplated. With help, however, students can achieve perspective transformation, in which their learning is not just the addition of new layers to previously held concepts but a rearrangement of known concepts into entirely new entities.[16] Armed with critical awareness, students attain new views of previously unimagined realities.

Students so educated distinguish and classify their world utilizing particular conceptual frameworks.[17] Such students have command of questions that bring meaning to their worlds. In employing such power—such questions, to be particular—they make their knowing dynamic. Critically aware, students understand the various possible structures of knowledge, grasp approaches for processing data, and learn ways of thinking about that which they observe. Those students have the disposition to question, and question meaningfully.

Stressing critical awareness augments students' commitment to and capacity for learning.[18] Ideally, we who accept this emphasis realize that students must raise significant questions and devise means of answering them. This requires time—time to identify problems, organize questions, contemplate and carrying out solutions, generate ways to judge the worth of solutions. To students who are successful, knowledge becomes more than a textbook, more than a worksheet completed. Critically aware students realize that school learning can be linked into meaningful clusters that will trigger additional questions, additional points about which to think. These students appreciate that they can connect what they learn in school classrooms with their lives; what is gained in school has utility for their present and future lives. There are choices to be made, and it is within them to manage those choices.[19]

THE NATURE OF THINKING—
GETTING STUDENTS TO THINK

Developing critical awareness in students is essentially making them realize their potential, the richness of the world, and the necessity of being active in contemplating and thinking about the world and their place within it. Despite our support for thinking students, some confusion exists as to just what thinking is.

It is ironic that almost all people testify to understanding what thinking is but usually are hard put to explain it. Our myriad investigations into this phenomenon seem to have afforded us a rich confusion rather than a clear view. Part of our difficulty may derive from our reference to thinking in both a common and an uncommon or specialized way. From our everyday experiences, we denote as thinking what we and other people do all the time when faced with novelty in our environments.[20] Beyer, in discussing thinking, states that it is, in its most general sense, the searching for or the creation of meaning.

Thinking is also a scientific concept investigated by education specialists and psychologists. It is amusing that this community is largely responsible for the confusion and debate about thinking, indeed making the concept of thinking an enigma. While we can claim it furnishes direction to our educational efforts, to a significant degree it makes a mess of our attempts to create educational experiences that will foster it.

REFLECTION

Smart environments foster the development of critical awareness, the raising of questions. Reflect on your own classrooms. Note the ways in which your classroom environment is a smart environment.

My Classroom	Ways in which it is a smart environment	How my classroom stimulates awareness
_____	_____	_____
_____	_____	_____
_____	_____	_____
_____	_____	_____

Think of ways in which you can make your classroom even smarter. It may be productive to share your responses with a colleague—brainstorm, critique.

Part of the difficulty in explaining thinking is that only recently have we in education begun to make initial attempts at understanding the processes of the brain. Teyler notes that "we know relatively little of brain processes associated with thinking, reasoning, motivation, and other more 'cognitive' processes."[21] We do know that our brains allow us to process information, to create meaning. It is still unknown, however, how the brain is altered as a result of processing and storing information. How the brain thinks up some new questions remains a mystery. Admitting ignorance as to how the brain processes and stores information does not mean that the brain remains a total black box. Indeed, there is much current information about the potential mechanisms within the brain. Researchers have studied the changes of protein in the brain in relation to memory; they have investigated the growth of new synaptic contacts and the physical/chemical alterations within synapses.[22]

The cloudiness of our thinking about thinking has not prevented us from generating numerous definitions of it. Also, few if anyone would deny its existence. William James at the outset of this century noted "the first fact for us ... as psychologists, is that thinking of some sort goes on."[23] While we cannot view it directly, we can and do make assumptions about it from studying the visible actions of people. We also accept the fact that, whatever it is, it represents a complex, multidimensional human activity.[24]

Gagne noted that thinking most likely brings into play stimulus categorization, hypothesis formation, and decision making as the result of perceiving a problem.[25] Bourne, Ekstrand, and Dominowski in discussing thinking list several things that can be said about it: first, thinking is a way of characterizing a behaving individual; second, thinking codifies an operative potential for a certain range of behavior by an individual; third, thinking comes into play when the circumstances are problematical; fourth, the activity of thinking is minimally governed by performance standards; and fifth, thinking, as is true of all behavior, follows a rule-following model that has the components of knowledge, skill, intention, and performance levels.[26]

Beyer presents a useful model of thinking, depicting thinking as a complicated enactment of various ways of processing information, activated simultaneously or in various combinations. His model is presented in Figure 1–1.

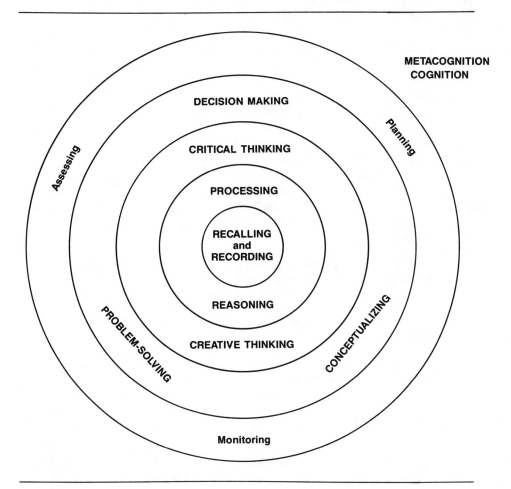

Figure 1–1
A Model of Functional Thinking[27]

Beyer's model contains two types of operations: cognitive and metacognitive. He distinguishes between these operations stating that they differ in the mental levels at which they are enacted, in the objects on which they act, and in the particulars of their procedures.[28] The cognitive functions, occupying the central portion of the model, contain those operations enacted for the purpose of making meaning. Many of these operations, at least the terms, are familiar to us in a general sense. Actually, many are subtypes of thinking, such as critical and creative thinking.

The central operations of recalling and recording relate to the initial phases of thinking when an individual perceives a situation and then organizes and makes plans to utilize past experiences to process the situation. Some argument exists that these initial operations are not thinking at all; the same can be said of processing. It does refer to operations a person employs to process information perceived in order to generate initial meaning. It also refers to the raising of particular questions in definite sequences. Questions, it should be noted, are employed in each of these various cognitive operations. How one records the observed is influenced by the questions raised either consciously or intuitively. Decision making, problem solving, and conceptualization are specialized cognitive operations, some say types of thinking; others identify them as heuristic procedures that trigger types of thinking and cognitive operations. Beyer states that problem solving, decision making, and conceptualizing are complex general strategies.

In Beyer's model, metacognition compromises the outer rim of the model and is superordinate to the cognitive operations. Essentially, metacognition refers to both an awareness or knowledge about one's own cognitive operations or processes (thinking and learning activities) and a strategic regulation of one's cognitive processes.

> Metacognition refers to one's knowledge concerning one's own cognitive processes and products or anything related to them; e.g., the learning-relevant properties of information or data. For example, I am engaging in metacognition (metamemory, metalearning, meta-attention, metalanguage or whatever) if I notice that I am having more trouble learning A than B; if it strikes me that I should double check C before accepting it as fact; if it occurs to me that I had better scrutinize each and every alternative in any multiple-choice type task situation before deciding which is the best one; if I sense that I had better make a note of D because I may forget it.... Metacognition refers among other things, to the active monitoring and consequent regulation and orchestration of these processes in relation to the cognitive objects or data on which they bear, usually in the service of some concrete goal or objective.[29]

Cognition and metacognition differ in that the former seeks to generate a product that is meaning while the latter aims at the deliberate and conscious control of cognitive operations engaged in to produce the meaning. The individual invokes strategies, termed endeavors, in order to think about thinking, to actually reflect on the means by which one has engaged in remembering, in recalling, and in processing information.[30] For example, in processing information raising particular questions, one would be conscious of the particular questions employed, the rationale for these questions, and the justification for selecting a particular sequence of questions in light of a specific learning task. In metacognition, besides being aware of the questions and their strategy, one is also cognizant of the nature of the situation and the materials being employed.

When functioning at a metacognitive level, the learner maintains in consciousness the purpose of the learning or information processing or meaning making, the procedures or thinking operations being undertaken, and the manner in which he or she is engaging in the meaning-making process. Such cognizance allows the individual to modify the approach when required by the results or the unfolding situation.

Types of Thinking

Problem Solving

Beyer notes that there are diverse thinking strategies—operations that require various and oftentimes sequential steps.[31] Most of us are familiar with the term "problem solving." Even so, it can be debated that it is really not a thinking strategy but rather a heuristic organizer that allows us to contemplate ways in which we can and perhaps should organize and reorganize knowledge in order to solve perceived difficulty. To some the term is synonymous with goal-directed thinking. Bourne, Ekstrand, and Dominowski offer a more limited interpretation—problem solving is an aspect of thinking that engages a person in both the formulating and selection of likely responses to a problematic situation.[32] Essentially, it enables the discovery of appropriate solutions. To be successful, the problem solver must know the steps: identifying a problem and its elements for possible manipulation; determine meaningful principles that will enable a solution to be attained, modify resources and techniques in new and varied ways, and judge the appropriateness of the results. Equally crucial, the problem solver must be skilled in raising questions appropriate for each stage.

Decision Making

Beyer, in his model, identifies decision making as a major thinking strategy while noting that some equate decision making with problem solving.[33] All of us make decisions, but we do not always engage in problem solving.

The hallmark of decision making is the selection of a course of action from alternatives.[34] Good decisions result from good question raising and answering. Beyer identifies the following steps for decision making: (1) define the goal, (2) identify alternatives, (3) analyze alternatives, (4) rank alternatives, (5) judge highest ranked alternatives, and (6) choose best alternatives.[35] The selection of and processing of these alternatives is to accomplish some goal. Ideally, in decision making, the person must contemplate the consequences of each of the various alternative courses of action. Judgment must be made as to whether each consequence is desirable or productive in relation to the goal. As with problem solving, the quality of one's decision is influenced by the questions raised at the various steps of the strategy.

Conceptualizing

Beyer's third thinking strategy, which can be considered a type of thinking, is conceptualizing. In a sense, conceptualizing is stating the obvious in that all behavior is conceptual. Our reactions to the world are not to the unique dimensions of our encounters but rather to the patterns, the regularities, the clusters, the clumps of experiences. Humans in their behaving usually respond to particular situations as examples of a more general case, rule, principle, or concept.[36] People attempt to take from particular situations some generalized statement or conclusion or to invent pictures (called concepts and models) to assist in making meaning of the particulars. This is thinking; this is raising questions that direct one's attention to the attributes of the situation, to the characteristics, and to the relationships between objects or situations.

Beyer lists the following steps for conceptualizing: (1) identify examples, (2) identify common attributes, (3) classify attributes, (4) interrelate categories of attributes, (5) identify additional examples and nonexamples, and (6) modify concept attributes/structure.[37]

Critical Thinking

John Dewey, defining critical thinking as "suspended judgment," placed its essence in focus. Despite such early focus, diversity of opinions still exist as to what critical thinking is. Beyer states rather specifically what it is not. It is not a strategy consisting of sequenced cognitive operations that require orderly enactment. Beyer, not denying that critical thinking has particular operations, argues that such operations can be used alone or in any particular combination depending upon the situation. He lists ten critical thinking skills or operations: (1) distinguishing between verifiable facts and value claims; (2) distinguishing relevant from irrelevant information, claims, or reasons; (3) determining the factual accuracy of a statement; (4) determining the credibility of a source; (5) identifying ambiguous claims or arguments; (6) identifying unstated assumptions; (7) detecting bias; (8) identifying logical fallacies; (9) recognizing logical inconsistencies in a line of reasons; and (10) determining the strength of an argument or claim.[38]

Researchers have furnished educators with numerous definitions of critical thinking. Paul I. Dressel and Lewis B. Mayhew conducted one of the earliest and most extensive studies of critical thinking. Essentially, they defined it as a process of analyzing a problem, examining its logical and factual bases, and arriving at warranted conclusions.[39] Despite the specificity of their listing of particular critical thinking skills, these researchers did not get much beyond labels.

Russell, in 1956, offered a definition similar to that of Dressel and Mayhew, explaining the process as the examining of both the concrete and the abstract in relation to objective evidence and arriving at some conclusions in connection with the judgment made.[40] Four years later, Russell refined his definition of critical thinking—the process of evaluation or categorization consistent with some previously selected standards.

Ennis, in 1962, purported that if students are to engage in developing critical thinking abilities, they must first be cognizant of the aspects of this thinking process. Pupils must have grasped the meaning of statements, must be able to recognize ambiguity in reasoning, must determine whether certain statements are contradictory with other statements, must determine if a particular statement logically follows another statement, must judge the reliability of statements considered, must determine whether something is an assumption, must judge the adequacy of a definition, must recognize acceptable authority, and finally must determine if a conclusion is warranted.[41]

Two decades later Ennis and colleagues had only slightly modified their considerations about critical thinking, noting that such thinking was involved in determining if (1) a statement follows from the premises, (2) something is an assumption, (3) an observation statement is reliable, (4) an alleged authority is reliable, (5) a simple generalization is warranted, (6) a hypothesis is warranted, (7) a theory is warranted, (8) an argument depends on an equivocation, (9) a statement is overly vague or overly specific, and (10) a reason is relevant.[42]

Threaded through all of these definitions is analysis and evaluation—the seeking of relationships and the judging of the validity and worth or significance of those relationships. Notwithstanding this, the educator searching for ways to elicit such thinking is left uninformed as to how to use particular questions to get at analysis and evaluation—to break down information and judge what is revealed. Left without specifics as to the questions enacted at each stage, the person who engages in critical thinking about such thinking develops an intuitive sense that there are particular questions to be raised to activate specific critical thinking skills.

Creative Thinking

The dialogue concerning thinking could lead one to assume that most thinking follows precise, well agreed upon steps arranged in a particular sequence to be followed in all situations. However, thinking is more than following steps. Beyer's model suggests that critical thinking is related to creative thinking, but he is quick to point out that they are not the same. Critical thinking is concerned with breaking down reality to arrive at some point of understanding, while creative thinking deals with combining elements of reality in novel ways to formulate new perceptions, enriched concepts, new understandings. Creativity pertains to synergism, making conclusions greater than the sum of the parts processed. Creativity involves the total person, touching the cognitive, affective and psychomotor domains.[43] David Perkins and Alan J. McCormack note that creative thinking is essentially a state of mind rather than an exactment of particular steps.[44] It is a disposition that allows one to act on the fringes, to perceive reality in novel ways and to contemplate novel uses of the results of one's creative deliberations.

Extensive reading in the area of creativity and its related creative thinking reveals, as is true with the general literature on thinking, a diversity of views as to just what it is. David Perkins notes that the entire field of creativity is messy and myth-ridden.[45]

Creative thinking, even when discussed by experts in creativity, still does not come out as a precise strategy. Perkins alludes to the fact that thinking becomes creative when it follows a creative pattern—a mix of particular strategies, skills, and dispositions toward reality.[46] Such thinking involves using questions designed to get individuals to react to situations and information so as to look at other sides of issues, possible rearrangements of data to produce novel results—to force thinkers to mind stretch; to add to the situation; to subtract from it; to rearrange it; to look for the novel, the serendipity in reality.

There appears to be no good definition of creative thinking. Many define it by using the term itself, which furnishes little help. Perkins defines creative thinking as thinking that leads to creative results.[47] One still lacks knowledge as to what it is or how to do it. Others have defined it as similar to problem solving only looking for the novel in the problem and the manner of its solution. Some have classified it as divergent production.[48]

A creative definition is furnished by George Prince:

> Creativity: An arbitrary harmony, an unexpected astonishment, a habitual revelation, a familiar surprise, a generous selfishness, an unexpected certainty, a formable stubborness, a vital triviality, a disciplined freedom, an intoxicating steadiness, a repeated initiation, a difficult delight, a predictable gamble, an ephemeral solidity, a unifying difference, a demanding satisfier, a miraculous expectation, an accustomed amazement.[49]

Prince has defined creativity by a series of what Gordon would call "compressed conflict"—a metaphorical form in which two opposite words, essentially in contradiction, describe an object. Metaphorical thinking is closely related, perhaps not separated from creativity. Perhaps creativity is a phenomenon that has to be defined continuously, something that allows for effective surprise. Whatever it is, it demands from the person a willingness to consider new organizations of data, novel patterns, unique plans of actions, and a desire to search for possibilities heretofore unconsidered. It requires the raising of questions.

Metaphoric Thinking

Metaphors, which we all use but about which we rarely think, are figures of speech utilized to denote a relationship of likeness in one object or idea by employing another object or idea. "School is drama" is a metaphor explaining school essentially by comparing it to drama. Of course, to use metaphors requires that the person understand both objects or ideas to some degree. To grasp "School is drama," one requires at least awareness about school and also drama. Lacking this, the metaphor lacks sense.

A major part of our language involves the use of metaphors. "Life is a ball" is a familiar one. So is "Life's a game." We really cannot converse without this figure of speech. Likewise, we cannot really contemplate reality without metaphors. Employing metaphors in our reflecting is metaphoric thinking—creative thinking, using these terms. The types of metaphors we employ help us to structure or restructure our perception. Through metaphors we relate the world and its peoples. The composition of our everyday realities and our processing of these realities are impacted by our metaphors.

Creative thinking elaborates on moments of insight or imagery.[50] Through our metaphors we extend the boundaries of our thinking; we conceptualize our thinking in particular ways to systematize our reality. We highlight various aspects of concepts being addressed and hide others. If we say "Life is war," we highlight the struggles and pain of life, downplaying or hiding its joys. Considering life a party, we spotlight its joys and fun, downplaying its struggles. The more metaphors employed, the richer, the more creative is our understanding.

Metaphoric thinking can be taught; however, our teaching of such thinking needs to be creative so that the richness of the process is made apparent. The more metaphors, the more structures; the more diversity, the richer our understandings.[51]

There is a vast literature on metaphors. For our purposes, it is important to realize that these tools of language are not just reserved for poets; they are tools for the masses. We need to reflect and raise questions about our metaphors and perhaps how we can use such devices to generate more creative thinking and productive use of questions.

REFLECTION

Thinking About Thinking

Thinking about thinking: we all need to do it. Reflect on the types of thinking you engage in most often. Come up with some reasons why you seem to enjoy certain types of thinking rather than others. If you enjoy all, suggest to yourself why you do.

In your classrooms, do you emphasize only those types of thinking you feel comfortable with? How do you measure the types of thinking that are occurring among your students?

Ideally, you should make students aware of their types of thinking. What specifically do you do in your classrooms to foster such student awareness?

TRY IT

Select a topic and process it using at least two major approaches to thinking—problem solving, decision making, conceptualization. What questions are you asking as you go through the steps? How do you modify the steps when you use these various types of thinking?

Was it easier to process a particular topic with one type of thinking than another? Why do you think it was or was not?

In dealing with these questions, you are developing your own awareness of yourself as a thinker, a questioner; you are engaging in meta-cognition.

Share the results of your efforts with a colleague.

Getting Students to Think—To Question

Morton Hunt, in discussing recent activities within the field of cognitive science, mentions that "research suggests that our minds come equipped with highly efficient neural arrangements built into us by evolution; these predispose us to make certain kinds of sense of our experiences and to use them in that distinctly human activity we call thinking."[52] Despite humans possessing the biological equipment and the ability and general disposition to think, the specific ways in which one does think and interpret the world are to be learned. Left to ourselves we will not usually become skilled thinkers. Just left alone and told to think, our students will not gain the skill. We may be wired for thinking action, but we require instruction in how to employ our circuitry in particular ways to make meaning. David Perkins has argued this point, indicating that while "everyday thinking, like ordinary walking, is a natural performance mastered by all, good thinking, like running the 100 yard dash is a technical performance, full of artifice."[53] Therefore, good thinking, and effective questioning require deliberate conscious effort, require practice, modification of action, and reflection on action.

Students must be taught ways of thinking through direct and indirect means. They have to be acquainted with the general concept of thinking and the particular ways of thinking. Students must be taught the specifics of particular thinking strategies—shown the steps by which information can be processed so as to make meaning. Likewise, students require direct teaching of the nature of the question and its place within thinking. Types of questions to be raised at particular steps in thinking strategies should be good fare for the student. Of course, in our zeal to get students to think we should not overwhelm them with the myriad intricacies of the various means of thinking and questioning.

To foster our students' thinking, first we need to structure the classroom so that they begin to recognize the general ways to structure knowledge and feel comfortable and desirous of asking questions about their world. Classrooms must be interesting. They should be places that allow students to gradually use their innate abilities to process information and that guide them in reflecting on their actions so as to practice and perfect them. For students to think, they need time to raise questions about what they encounter and then to query their questions so they recognize the question's centrality to thinking, to making meaning.

In getting students to think, we are striving to empower them to perfect themselves as active learners. Young children arrive in school as novice active learners. Schooling should mold them into expert active learners.

The Good Thinker (The Good Questioner)

The good thinker, possessing attributes enabling him or her to create and use meaning—to add to knowledge and culture, possesses a spirit of inquiry, a desire to pose questions central to the world. The good thinker ponders the world, actual and desired, querying things valued and desired.

This thinker delights not in attaining certainty but in dancing in the dynamism of uncertainty. This person, while accepting that problems require solutions, relishes raising questions that identify problems. Glatthorn and Baron note that in classrooms, striving for the development of good thinkers, good questioners, the students are urged to engage in speculation, to discover problems, to reflect on the power of thought and to take time to appreciate awe and wonder.[54]

Good thinkers are good questioners, taking enjoyment in being doubtful and suspicious of their world, in a positive sense. They take advantage of uncertainty. Why is the world so? Why must it be so? Are other views possible? What other answers might be plausible? Good thinkers utilize questions in particular ways to get at deep rather than surface meanings. Good thinkers engage in "active, persistent, and careful consideration of any belief or sup-posed form of knowledge in light of the grounds that support it...."[55] Such thinkers realize that all meaning making commences with the acceptance that there is uncertainty, a gap in one's view of the world and one's place within it. Deny uncertainty, and thinking is stillborn.[56]

Good thinkers posit questions to determine when an uncertain situation is problematic and to produce possible approaches to the situation. Such students question the situation, search for evidence relevant to the situation, make revisions in findings in light of the particular situation, and determine, primarily through questioning, when the uncertain situation has been an-swered.

These individuals realize that productive inquiry essentially starts with the articulation of personal concerns or questions. In many ways, this is a major shift for students have been taught to wait for the authority, usually the teacher or textbook author, to furnish the problem, define the questions, and suggest the solutions. Indeed, in many schools, students are not challenged to make meaning; rather, they are asked to remember the meaning of others. The good thinker realizes that while some information originated with qualified others, much information and meaning is self-generated.

Good thinkers function independently, welcoming the challenge of func-tioning on their own. They embrace the problematic, confident that they have the requisite understanding of the nature of meaning and skill in the various means of processing information so that particular goals are attained.

The hallmark of the good thinker, the good questioner, is the inquiring mind. An individual so characterized is always doubting, always realizing the ambiguity of reality, always accepting the invitation to investigate further. This person realizes the potential relationships between oneself and his or her world. The thinking person realizes that learning is not the amassing of things but the creation and utilization of the relationships among things. The con-templative person fosters within himself or herself a creative encounter with life, a joy and openness to the unknown, a realization that the findings of any inquiry can never reveal the whole truth—there is always more for further questioning.[57]

THE PLACE OF THE QUESTION IN LIGHT OF THINKING

Educative Questions

Everyone asks questions, at least some of the time. In everyday encounters we do not usually reflect on our questions. Questions within the school con-text however, are not just everyday questions. These questions, whether raised by teacher or student, are educative questions—questions phased for pedagogical purposes, for classroom processes, to address educational ends.[58] With these questions students are to function in particular ways, view situations from special vantage points; students are to think.

The difference between everyday questions and educative questions, Dillon posits, are not readily apparent. Rather than the difference lying in the actual wording of the questions, it lies "in the greatness of care required to make a question an educative one."[59a] Everyday questions just happen; they pop into our minds with little or no forethought when we confront particular situations.

In contrast, educative questions require conscious preparation. We must work to formulate them, to give them form; we must reflect on the manner, timing, and place of their delivery. We must consider them in light of the educational goals set for the lesson within which the questions are a part. As Dillon stated, "To conceive an educative question requires thought; to formulate it requires labor; and to pose it, tact."[59b] Students need to realize that formulating such questions and employing them to make meaning, requires conscious effort.

Questions and Students' Thought

To know something, to think about something requires that an individual understand it with regard to some terms, some grasp of concepts.[60] There can be no thought without first recognizing and understanding certain words. Thought about mountains first requires some idea of the concept mountain. One cannot truly know mountains—think about them deeply and use the results of such thinking—without realizing that there are educative questions to be raised about mountains. Questions and thought coexist.

The level of students' thought is influenced by their questions. If questions deal only at a factual level, students will tend to think about, certainly recall, specific facts. If questions direct students to analyze information, perhaps looking for likely antecedents to some event, students will contemplate relationships and think critically. Certainly, questions at higher cognitive levels enable students to process information, to think about information, with greater depth. Even recall is increased when students process questions. Turnure has theorized that by engaging in questioning, students increase the semantic depth at which they process information.[61]

Having just argued that questions influence the level of student thought, it should be pointed out that the precise relationship between questions and thought is far from being perfectly clear. In part, this is due to our uncertainty as to what thought is—its actual "mechanics" of functioning. Also, the research on using questions to stimulate increased learning and thought has left us with more questions than answers. This is not too surprising since analyzing questions and their effects upon children is impacted by complex interactions of the children's developmental variables, curriculum variables,

---

REFLECTION

Educative Questions

Research indicates that the teacher is the major questioner. But what kinds of questions do we as teachers raise, incidental questions or educative ones? Think of your questions: How much planning goes into them? Do you write out the major ones for your lesson? Do you use a definite strategy for your questions?

Our tendency is to say we do use educative questions. Chat with a colleague and ask him or her to watch you in class with the goal of determining the educativeness of your questions. Schedule a debriefing time.

Now reflect. What change might you make?

---

environmental variables, cultural variables, and instructional variables.[62] Often research studies on questions have focused on only one or two variables and then only for a short time period. Furthermore, many studies have only dealt with single-age children. All this has prevented us from drawing unequivocal conclusions.

Despite this uncertainty, we do have sufficient information to be more precise in our questioning and in ways to facilitate our students becoming skilled questioners and thinkers. Research has shown that questioning procedures have increased children's learning and positively affected their thinking. While the effects of questioning frequently may not be dramatic, they will be consistent.[63] Using questions on Monday will not result in dramatic analytical skills by Friday. Recognizing this, we need to be sensitive to these small gains, for such gains do cause accumulation of material. Raising questions that ask children to think may only result in a slight raise in achievement on a particular unit compared to asking lower order questions, but children may experience joy at being able to derive more from their reading, from their studying. This adding to their positive feelings toward the material may continue day by day. At the end of the year, the result from such incremental pluses may indeed be more significant.

Questions not only contribute eventually to increased achievement, heightened knowing, and in many cases more positive affect; they also foster in students awareness of and skill in procedural knowledge. Students, skilled in questions, can generate inquiries that enrich their awareness of the cognitive processes they can and do employ. This use of questions relates to what has become a buzzword—metacognition. While metacognition was discussed earlier as a part of thinking, here it is discussed in relation to questions.

Questions and Metacognition

"Metacognition refers to one's knowledge of one's cognitive processes and products or anything related to them."[64] It concerns procedural knowledge and the means by which such knowledge is activated. Students should realize that the questions they raise influence the procedures, the cognitive strategies, by which they process information. Indeed, the question may cause the cognitive processes to be organized in particular ways.[65] Information is processed by the enactment of intentional plans or actions designed to attain particular goals.

Pressley argues that one can acquire knowledge about various cognitive strategies, a type of metacognition, by employing particular techniques designed specifically to produce such knowledge. He discussed metacognitive acquisition procedures (MAPs) as a means for attaining such awareness.[66] In one of these strategies, self-questioning, students raise the central questions: "Is the strategy I am employing really enabling me to learn? How valuable is this strategy?"

Hunkins over a decade ago suggested activities to get students to assess the effectiveness of their questions. These many strategies, some which will be discussed in later chapters, all relate to fostering metacognitive awareness of one's questions and questioning strategies. Students, taking a critical stance on the actual questions they are employing, generate a powerful knowledge base regarding types of questions and questioning strategies.

Metacognition, the consciousness of knowing how one goes about learning, means realizing where questions fit into approaches to learning. This is powerful knowledge. "Once you have learned how to ask questions, relevant and appropriate and substantial questions, you have learned how to learn and no one can keep you from learning whatever you want or need to know."[67] Learning how to ask questions and being able to deal with those phrased is the essence of metacognitive activity. It is the highest goal for it enables students to be autonomous learners, empowering them to control their learning. There will be times, and perhaps these times will be the most frequent in the early schooling years, when the metacognitive control may be exercised by another person, usually the teacher. The teacher guides the student through processing information by raising questions that direct students to attend to particular aspects of the information. In both of these stages, metacognitive activity is done at a conscious level.[68]

Question asking is a natural human behavior. The inquisitive posture of young children evidences itself with their constant asking of "Why?" and "How come?" This incidental questioning, however, results from the everyday interactions that children have and not as a consequence of careful thought. Young children often ask their original questions because someone has made a puzzling statement or raised a question. Children in dealing with these questions are unaware of the cognitive processes undergirding them.

Questions comprise procedural knowledge—knowledge acquired in direct consequence of teachers presenting such knowledge or putting children into situations requiring such knowledge and then asking children questions about how they did or might go about using process. Procedural knowledge depends in part upon declarative knowledge—knowledge that makes statements. While we in discussion can separate such knowledges, in actual fact they are inseparable. We acquire knowledge of procedure—knowledge of the how—in light of some particular content or declarative knowledge, knowledge of the what, and our attaining of one is not isolated from the attaining of the other.[69]

The teacher serves as an essential guide in making children increasingly aware of their questions and questioning, of making children capable of observing such linguistic processing. The teacher accomplishes this by stopping the children at definite points in their learning to request their explanations of their actions or pointing out to children their apparent behavior. If children are employing various types of information, the teacher through questioning can draw children's attention to numerous types of information available and the means by which questions can process the information to attain particular outcomes. In class discussions, teachers bring into children's consciousness the relationships extant between the raising of particular types of questions and the attainment of specific types of conclusions. This linkage is made more specific as children gain more formal experience in raising questions and thinking.

While making these linkages between means and ends specific, teachers point out to children that processing information is more than raising a question, getting an answer, and following with another question. Thinking with questions, while frequently linear, can assume other patterns. We can question in a circular fashion, continually returning to the beginning of the inquiry. We can also employ questions in a series of alternative directions, each direction coming back altered somewhat to a beginning point. Creative and metaphoric thinking patterns frequently assume a flow other than linear. Also, thinking and questioning may be going on at various planes simultaneously.

Informing children of these alternative ways, varied schema, is not to add confusion to their awareness of cognitive process but to make them realize from the outset that thinking and questioning are complex and much is not understood. The fun of learning goes beyond the declarative "whats" of information; it entails reflecting with a sense of wonder how marvelous it is that we can think and inquire.

Children will not completely grasp this complexity at first, or even at the end of their formal schooling. Truthful adults who have studied the meaning of mind readily admit that they do not comprehend completely this complexity; that is the excitement of the search. Children should strive for a fuller understanding of this process of cognition. As children and older youth gain awareness of the nature and complexity of questions and thinking, they

Pattern I

Ques. 1 ⟶ Ques. 2 ⟶ Ques. 3 ⟶ Ques. 4

Pattern II

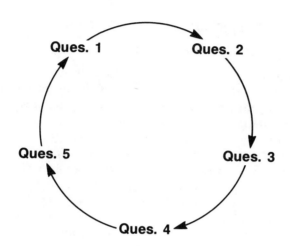

Pattern III

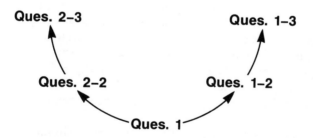

Pattern IV

Planes or levels of questions	(level 1)	Ques. 1 ⟶ Ques. 2 ⟶ Ques. 3
	(level 2)	Ques. 1 ⟶ Ques. 2 ⟶ Ques. 3

Figure 1–2
Patterns of Questioning

acquire power and wisdom—power in being able to actually employ various types of questions to foster numerous types of thinking; wisdom in realizing that particular types of questions and myriad modes of thinking can be employed to optimize learning.[70]

QUESTIONS WITHIN THE EDUCATIONAL ENVIRONMENT

School experiences generate many puzzlements that cause children to question. School encounters are punctuated with numerous situations in which questions are integral parts, where questions are presented formally. Children react to questions within text. Much work has been done to determine the impact of various types and placement of questions in text on students' understanding and processing of information.[71] Some of what we know about question placement in text will be addressed in later chapters.

Besides the ubiquitous questions in school text material, children process teachers' questions, a dominant aspect of teacher talk. Teachers' questions have been recognized since classical Greek times as powerful devices in promoting learning.[72] From recent research, we can conclude that student achievement is increased by teachers asking questions.[73]

Students also experience the questions of other adults within the school environment. The frequency of such questions depends greatly upon how open the teacher is to having resource persons in the classroom. The questions of significant others may increase in the future as schools establish more formal arrangements with other educational institutions within the community—museums, clubs, community organizations, and churches.

Other questions enter the classroom by way of electronic media. Television programming, film and audio disks, and computer programs also generate questions that impact the learner and cause responses either in the form of answers or additional questions. Aware of questions, students will see they are ubiquitious.

The final source of questions in the classroom environment is the children themselves. Children ask questions and respond to them; children react to questions phrased by their classroom or school peers. While currently children do not ask the majority of questions, this situation may change as we teachers realize that children do have this power.

THE FUTURE EDUCATIONAL ARENA

The current scene previews glimpses of the future as it is likely to evolve or as some would wish it to evolve. While the particulars of various educational futures remain fuzzy, there are some apparent constants: teachers, students, schools, books, curricula. Most of us in education desire that our students now and in the future be empowered to be in control of their learning—capable of creating questions and of generating particular and perhaps idiosyncratic thinking strategies in order to develop both personalized and public knowledge.

Students in control of their learning and self-motivated to use their cognitive powers will come not as a result of accident or guesswork. Committed and competent students will be those who have been given opportunities to and assistance in working hard to develop thinking and questioning, and working systematically. As Rothkopf indicated many years ago, "in most instructional situations, what is learned depends largely on the activities of the student."[74] In the future school, students will have increased control over their own activities and thus their own learning. Teachers will be facilitators and consultants to students, but students may indeed be their own best teachers. Future students will have a major role in determining the nature and direction of their learning, at least with regard to the particulars.

The future educational arena will see the teachers intent on creating an atmosphere of empathetic communication that fosters students' self-direction and control. Reflection time will be scheduled for students, time when they can introspect and react to teachers' comments in order to gain a greater consciousness of their own understandings, perceptions, feelings, and values.

Future teachers will serve as a collaborator co-inquirer with the student engaged in raising questions. Teachers and student teams will be essentially expert and novice cooperatively involved in raising significant questions and employing such questions in modes of thinking appropriate for a particular study focus. Teachers will guide students in raising questions directed to their feelings, to creating linkages leading to insights and further questions, and to questions regarding approaches to information or some observed reality. In the ideal future educational arena, the student will experience the excitement of the learning moment, the joy of discovery, the sense of accomplishment. The future can be now; for some of us it already is.

CONCLUSION

This chapter has centered on questions and their place within the educational arena, especially within the realm of thinking. Much current dialogue addresses ways to get students involved with and in control of their thinking and learning—to develop in students critical awareness.

Our task is challenging for there is still diversity of opinion as to specifically what questions are and what thinking and learning are. Several definitions of questions and thinking were presented for consideration.

While we all ask questions, we do not always ask educative questions. This is also true of students and their questions. As Dillon noted, such questions require conscious thought, labor, and even tact. If questions are to be integral parts of students' procedural knowledge, students must gain requisite skills in and understandings of questions. Attaining such information and competencies should empower students to be active students, good thinkers, good questioners. Both we as teachers and our students have major roles to play in reaching this goal.

NOTES

1. James R. Gavelek and Taffy E. Raphael, "Metacognition, Instruction, and the Role of Questioning Activities," in D. L. Forrest-Pressley, G. E. MacKinnon, and T. Gary Waller, eds., *Metacognition, Cognition, and Human Performance*, Vol. 2 (Orlando, Fla.: Academic Press, Inc., 1985), 103–36.

2. M. Hunt, *The Universe Within: A New Science Explores the Human Mind* (New York: Simon & Schuster, 1982).

3. John Naisbitt, *Megatrends* (New York: Warner Books, 1982).

4. Alvin Toffler, *The Third Wave* (New York: Bantam Books, 1981).

5. Alvin Toffler, *The Third Wave*, p. 168.

6. Alvin Toffler, *The Third Wave*.

7. Alvin Toffler, *The Third Wave*, p. 174.

8. *Educating Americans for the 21st Century* (Washington, D.C.: The National Science Board Commission on Pre-College Education in Mathematics, Science, and Technology, 1983). Quote cited in Jay McTighe and Jan Schollenberger, "Why Teach Thinking: A Statement of Rationale" in Arthur L. Costa ed., *Developing Minds, A Resource Book for Teaching Thinking* (Alexandria, VA: Association for Supervision and Curriculum Development, 1985), pp. 3–6.

9. *Essentials of English* (Urbana, Ill: The National Council of Teachers of English, 1982). Quote cited in Jay McTighe and Jan Schollenberger, "Why Teach Thinking: Statement of Rationale."

10. John I. Goodlad, *A Place Called School* (New York: McGraw Hill, 1984).

11. Harold G. Shane and June Grant Shane, "Educating the Young for Tomorrow," in Alvin Toffler, ed., *Learning for Tomorrow, the Role of the Future in Education* (New York: Vintage Books, 1974), p. 185.

12. Zelda F. Gamson and Associates, *Liberating Education* (San Francisco: Jossey-Bass, 1984).

13. Chet Meyers, *Teaching Students to Think Critically* (San Francisco: Jossey-Bass, 1986).

14. Hugh G. Petrie, *The Dilemma of Enquiry and Learning* (Chicago: The University of Chicago Press, 1981).

15. Jane Roland Martin, *Explaining, Understanding and Teaching* (New York: McGraw-Hill, 1970).

16. Zelda F. Gamson and Associates, *Liberating Education.*

17. Hugh G. Petrie, *The Dilemma of Enquiry and Learning.*

18. Zelda F. Gamson and Associates, *Liberating Education.*

19. Paulo Freire, *Pedagogy of the Oppressed* (New York: Herder and Herder, 1970).

20. Barry K. Beyer, *Practical Strategies for the Teaching of Thinking* (Boston: Allyn and Bacon, 1987).

21. Timothy J. Teyler, "The Brain Sciences: An Introduction," in Jeanne S. Chall and Allan F. Mirsky, eds., *Education and the Brain*, The Seventy-seventh Yearbook of the National

Society for the Study of Education, Part II (Chicago: University of Chicago Press, 1978), p. 21.

22. Timothy J. Teyler, "The Brain Sciences: An Introduction," pp. 1–32.

23. W. Edgar Vinacke, *The Psychology of Thinking* (New York: McGraw-Hill, 1952), p. 57.

24. Lyle E. Bourne, Jr., Brace R. Ekstrand, and Roger L. Dominowski, *The Psychology of Thinking* (Englewood Cliffs, N.J.: Prentice-Hall, 1971).

25. Cited in Bourne, Ekstrand, and Dominowski, *The Psychology of Thinking.*

26. Bourne, Ekstrand, and Dominowski, *The Psychology of Thinking.*

27. Barry K. Beyer, *Practical Strategies for the Teaching of Thinking,* p. 23.

28. Barry K. Beyer, *Practical Strategies for the Teaching of Thinking.*

29. James H. Flavell, "Metacognitive Aspects of Problem Solving," in L. B. Resnick, ed., *The Nature of Intelligence* (Hillsdale, N.J.: Erlbaum, 1976), p. 232.

30. P. J. Babbs and A. J. Moe, "Metacognition: A Key for Independent Learning from Text," *The Reading Teacher* 36 (1983): 422–26.

31. Barry K. Beyer, *Practical Strategies for the Teaching of Thinking.*

32. Lyle E. Bourne, Jr., Brace R. Ekstrand, and Roger L. Dominowski, *The Psychology of Thinking,* p. 9.

33. Barry K. Beyer, *Practical Strategies for the Teaching of Thinking.*

34. Irwin D. J. Bross, *Design for Decision* (New York: The Free Press, 1953).

35. Barry K. Beyer, *Practical Strategies for the Teaching of Thinking.*

36. Lyle E. Bourne, Jr., Brace R. Ekstrand, and Roger L. Dominowski, *The Psychology of Thinking.*

37. Barry K. Beyer, *Practical Strategies for the Teaching of Thinking.*

38. Barry K. Beyer, *Practical Strategies for the Teaching of Thinking.*

39. Paul L. Dressel and Lewis B. Mayhew, *Critical Thinking in Social Science* (Dubuque, Iowa: William C. Brown, 1954).

40. David H. Russel, *Children's Thinking* (Boston: Ginn and Co., 1956).

41. Robert H. Ennis, "A Concept of Critical Thinking," *Harvard Educational Review* 32 (Winter, 1962): 81–109.

42. Robert H. Ennis, Jason Millman, and Thomas N. Tomoko, *Manual for Cornell Critical Thinking Tests Level X and Level Z* (Champaign, Ill.: Thinking Project, 1982), p. 1.

43. Donald A. Sanders and Judith A. Sanders, *Teaching Creativity Through Metaphor* (New York: Longman, 1983).

44. Alan J. McCormack, "Teaching Inventiveness," *Childhood Education* (March/April 1984): 249–55; David Perkins, "Learning by Design," *Educational Leadership* 42:1 (September 1984): 18–25.

45. David N. Perkins, "What Creative Thinking Is," in Arthur L. Costa, ed., *Developing Minds, A Resource Book for Teaching Thinking* (Alexandria, Va.: Association for Supervision and Curriculum Development, 1985), pp. 58–61.

46. David N. Perkins, "What Creative Thinking Is," in Costa, *Developing Minds.*

47. David N. Perkins, "What Creative Thinking Is," in Costa, *Developing Minds.*

48. J. P. Guilford, *The Nature of Human Intelligence* (New York: McGraw-Hill, 1967).

49. George Prince, *The Practice of Creativity* (New York: Macmillan, 1970), p. 24.

50. Donald A. Sanders and Judith A. Sanders, *Teaching Creativity Through Metaphor.*

51. Donald A. Sanders and Judith A. Sanders, *Teaching Creativity Through Metaphor.*

52. Morton Hunt, *The Universe Within: A New Science Explores the Human Mind* (New York: Simon & Schuster, 1982), p. 13.

53. David N. Perkins, "What Creative Thinking Is," in Costa, *Developing Minds.* Also given in speech at I/D/E/A conference, Seattle, Wash., 1985.

54. Allan A. Glatthorn and Jonathon Baron, "The Good Thinker," in Costa *Developing Minds*, pp. 49–53.

55. John Dewey, *How We Think* (Lexington, Mass.: Heath, 1982, originally published 1910), p. 74.

56. John Dewey, *How We Think.*

57. John P. Miller, *The Educational Spectrum: Orientations to Curriculum* (New York: Longman, 1983).

58. J. T. Dillon, *Teaching and the Art of Questioning* (Bloomington, Ind.: Phi Delta Kappa Educational Foundation, 1983), p. x.

59a,b. J. T. Dillon, *Teaching and the Art of Questioning,* p. 8.

60. Hugh G. Petrie, *The Dilemma of Enquiry and Learning.*

61. H. E. Turnure, N. Buium, and M. Thurlow, "The Effectiveness of Interrogatives for Prompting Verbal Elaboration Productivity in Young Children," 47 *Child Development* (1976): 851–55.

62. Michael Pressley and Donna Forest-Pressley, "Questions and Children's Cognitive Processing," in Arthur C. Graesser and John B. Black, eds., *The Psychology of Questions* (Hillsdale, N.J.: Erlbaum, 1985), pp. 277–96.

63. Michael Pressley and S. L. Bryant, "Does Answering Questions Really Promote Associate Learning?" *Child Development* 53 (1982): 1258–67; D. L. Redfield, and E. W. Rousseau, "Meta-analysis of Experimental Research on Teacher Questioning Behavior," 51 *Review of Educational Research* (1981): 237–45.

64. J. H. Flavell, "Metacognitive Aspects of Problem Solving," in L. B. Resnick, ed., *The Nature of Intelligence* (Hillsdale, N.J.: Erlbaum), p. 232.

65. J. G. Borkowski and F. P. Buchel, "Learning and Memory Strategies in the Mentally Retarded," in Michael Pressley and J. R. Levin, eds., *Cognitive Strategy Research: Psychological Foundations* (New York: Springer-Verlag, 1983).

66. Michael Pressley and Donna Forest-Pressley, *Questions and Children's Cognitive Processing.*

67. Neil Postman and C. Weingartner, *Teaching as a Subversive Activity* (New York: Delacorte Press, 1969), p. 23.

68. James R. Gavelek and Taffy E. Raphael, "Metacognition, Instruction, and The Role of Questioning Activities," in Donna L. Forest-Pressley, G. E. Mackinnon, and T. Gary Waller, eds., *Metacognition, Cognition, and Human Performance.*

69. B. Rogoff, "Integrating Context and Cognitive Development," in M. E. Lamp and A. L. Brown, eds., *Advances in Developmental Psychology,* Vol. 2 (Hillsdale, N.J.: Erlbaum, 1982).

70. James R. Gavelek and Taffy E. Raphael, "Metacognition, Instruction, and the Role of Questioning Activities."

71. Ernst Z. Rothkopf, "Learning From Written Instructive Material: An Exploration of the Control of Inspection Behavior, Test-like events," 3 *American Educational Research Journal* (1966): 241–49.

72. J. T. Dillon, "The Multidisciplinary Study of Questioning," *Journal of Educational Psychology* 74 (1982): 147–65.

73. Meredith D. Gall and others, "Effects of Questioning Techniques and Recitation on Student Listening," *American Educational Research Journal* 15 (1978): 175–99; Richard Merritt Wyman, Jr., *The Effects of Question Training and Generation of Adjunct Postquestions on Sixth Graders' Com-*

prehension and Retention of Social Studies Text. (Seattle: Univ. of Washington, 1984).

74. Ernst Rothkoph, "The Concept of Mathemagenic Activities," *Review of Educational Research* 40 (1970): 325–36.

2

The Nature

of Questions

and Questioning

Questions: we all use them, recognize them upon hearing or seeing them in print, and respond to them in various ways. We employ them when we desire response from ourselves or others or express puzzlement regarding some situation. We recognize them by people's intonation or upon seeing a reversal of predicate and subject and the stylized question mark. Yet these features of the question—a special type of sentence—are not always sufficient to classify a statement as a question.[1]

THE QUESTION

Questions usually have a rising intonation—"What did you *do*?"—but instances exist where this is not the case. The stress could be on the first word—"*What* did you do?" However, while still a question, the meaning has been altered. Other sentence forms can accentuate some other word. For example, "This is the best?" could have the stress on the next to last word— "This is *the* best?" While important, intonation is not the sole criterion for a question. Both students and teachers can play with this characteristic showing that not all statements that rise at the end are questions and that by varying the emphasis of words in the same question, they actually create other questions. "*What* did you do?", "What *did* you do?" and "What did you *do?*" all are different inquiries.

The placement of subject and predicate also is not always a reliable check for ways detecting a question. "Finished yet, George?" is a common reversal of the predicate "finished" and subject "George." But, the question could be phrased, "George, finished?" We have the regular sentence phrasing of subject first and predicate second. We acknowledge the statement as question by its intonation, emphasizing the last word, "*finished?*" Even so, there might be times when we say, "*George,* finished?", still maintaining a question.

The usual marker for a question is the presence of the question mark. This helps in recognizing the question in print, but sometimes students may not realize that they need such a punctuation mark. Also, there are some instances where a statement is a command that really makes a request. "Turn off the lights." This imperative sentence is technically asking the person to perform an action. Despite all, we are naturals in recognizing and raising questions. Our identification of questions is due to an almost unconscious reading of the cues obtained from the context of the situation, peoples' speech patterns, peoples' gestures, and from our understanding of grammar, however intuitive.[2]

But, *what* is a question? Wilen defines a question as a specialized sentence possessing either an interrogative form or function. When raised by teachers, questions are instructional cues suggesting to students content elements to be learned and ways of learning or experiencing said content.[3] When employed by students, questions serve as guides to particular actions, as sentences that cause thinking and behaving along particular lines.[4]

Aqvist classifies questions as special types of commands, commands that the questioner's desire for knowledge be met. People ask questions so that they can obtain information, satisfy their desire for knowledge.[5] Implicit in questions as commands is the acceptance of the belief that what is questioned is known or is possible to be known. It would be folly to raise a question realizing that the probable response was not known or possible. Chaudhari over a decade ago expressed a similar view of questions, noting specifically that "Student questions are "curiosity in action" . . . their "mind hunger."[6]

Kubinski presents the question as a linguistic expression possessing a strictly defined shape. However, as already noted, the placement of words is not a foolproof indicator of a question. But Kubinski posits that questions always begin with an *interrogative operator,* some clustering of words that set the stage for the person hearing or answering the question to make a response. It is the diversity of interrogative operators, he argues, that gives the basis for different classifications of questions.[7]

"Which candidate for president favors lower taxes?" starts with a numerical operator—that is "which" is asking for a listing that requires a quantification of some variable. Another question having a numerical operator is "What are the five football teams vying for first place?" The question requests a listing, an indication of quantity—three teams, four teams, two teams. The respondent is to note the number of teams.

While Kubinski elaborates interrogative operators giving each a complex code, the central point is that operators serve different functions. A question such as the following, "How would you fix the traffic problem?" is begun with a "means" interrogative operator—the question essentially asking for a consideration and identification of a means for solving a problem. Some interrogative operators ask the respondent to make a placement or notation of something. "Which state had the first public high school?" has a placement operator. "Who was the oldest person at the signing of the Declaration of Independence?" while starting with a different word still is asking for a notation of something—in this instance, noting who the person was. Essentially, interrogative operators comprise part of the syntax of the question.

A more simple definition of a question is an expressed desire for information.[8] However, questions and their nature really cannot be grasped by just looking at their forms. Kubinski, noting that questions are special kinds of declarative sentences, argues that they can be identified by taking into consideration their potential answers.

Dillon tackles questions from this posture, pointing out that in considering questions one must also consider that which is entailed within them, their presuppositions and their potential answers.[9] Such thinking about questions is enunciated in the expression "In a question well phrased, we have two thirds of the answer." Dillon identifies presuppositions as sentences that precede the question sentence, and answers as sentences that follow the question sentence. It is a bit more complicated than that, but we need not get too deeply into the underlying logic. What we need to remember is that it is from the presupposition that the question is generated. It is from our notions that we first contemplate our question. Presuppositions are the stuff of questions. Answers are devices employed to complement our questions.

A presupposition is a proposition or statement of implications assumed true. If no truth is recognized in the statement, then a question is impossible to answer. It makes little sense to ask when did Lindbergh fly his Atlantic solo if it was not assumed to be fact that the flight had taken place. Neither would we ask what the nature of the human living cell is if we did not accept as true that humans were comprised of cells. Our answer to the question also augments the validity or truthfulness of the proposition. That we answer the question about the nature of cells explaining their nature supports the truthfulness that such cells exist. For educators, knowing about the presupposition of questions allows a reading of the student's level of knowledge and understanding.[10] For students to know this allows them to assess their present state of information and denote possible future directions for their inquiry.

Upon receiving answers to their questions, students obtain information that enables them either to keep and enrich their propositions or to revise or discard them. Teachers in responding to students' questions serve to validate students' knowledge and to encourage them to continue questioning. Of course, the answer to questions may not come from the teacher but rather from the material students are processing.

It would be simple indeed if each question phased had only one proposition. However, questions often are consequences of a series of propositions frequently linked as major and minor ones. Just asking about when Lindbergh flew the Atlantic assumes, one, that he did; two, that we had a level of technology to permit the feat; three, that we had the means to record such an event; and four, that some record of the event was made so that we can obtain an answer to our inquiry. Essentially, a particular question arises from the complex interconnections of the total complex of knowledge. This fact or happening relates to that one, and that happening relates to that other one, and that relates to another one.

Realizing this, students and educators begin to appreciate the complexity of knowledge and that a simple question really is not simple and that the resultant answer may have many variations. A one-word answer depends in part upon which particular presupposition is considered primary. In the Lindbergh example, perhaps students only need to reflect on the proposition that the event occurred, neglecting at least for this question, the presuppositions about the requisite level of technology.

All question sentences suggest an answer sentence, some statement that completes the question. Actually, and more often the case, there can be several answer sentences. If the answer, once given, is obvious, then it can be considered a direct answer. Kubinski defines such answers as answers that are very simply and closely related to a particular question. These answers are obvious to anyone who understands the question and has some knowledge of the field to which the question refers.[11] In contrast, there can be indirect answers to questions, answers that are not related to a particular question but can apply given certain situations. The answer, "a patriotic American," can be an answer to "Who was George Washington?", but it is an indirect answer. It could also answer the question, "Who was Abraham Lincoln?" However, there is no doubt that the answer "the first President of the United States" is in fact a direct answer to the question, "Who was George Washington?" Realizing the distinction between direct and indirect answers allows teachers and also students to gain skill in judging the acceptability of answers.

Dillon indicates that most questions can trigger a diversity of answers, their range, nature and specific content determined by the particular question framed.[12] While the question does influence answers, the range of answers to questions may in fact lie more with the individual hearing the question than with the question. An individual, student in our case, with a broad experience in some realm of knowledge may actually see more answers in a question than a student new to the content area. Additionally, a student already somewhat expert in the content field may, besides generating a greater network of potential answers to a particular question, map out an interaction of questions related to the initial question.

For every question that is valid, there is at least one direct answer. There is also at least one indirect answer possible.[13] A sentence assumes the character of answer only in relation to some other sentence that assumes the character of question.[14] Always at issue is "To *which* question does this sentence represent an answer?" Teachers need to realize that the meaning a student derives from processing information exists in the relation between question and answer. Thinking about information and processing information are acts in which the student plays the linguistic game of questions and answers, answers and questions. As students realize the dynamics of this game, they come to understand that an effective question will not only lead to new answers, but to new questions. Likewise, an effective answer will lead to new answers to the original question. Students begin to perceive that knowledge, rather than being comprised of isolated events, is an integrated and interacting complex.

QUESTIONING, ITS NATURE

Question asking and answering comprise two aspects of a game. A question does not stand alone; we must do something with it, accept it, reject it, process it, disregard it, rework it, and then we must respond to the answers it generates. Our play with questions may at times be random, but often it follows a sequence, albeit at times a loose one. We bring various assumptions to our question playing; these assumptions will be discussed later in this chapter. For now, let us just focus on the game.

Many can play the questioning game. Certainly, the teacher can be a major player. Ideally, the student is a major participant. The procedure or procedures employed in questioning do not essentially differ for the teacher or student; however, the purpose of the questioning may. Usually, teachers raise questions attempting to get students to engage in some process, supply some response, or both. Teachers' questions have an evaluative aspect. What do students know? In contrast, when students employ questioning, they are primarily concerned with learning, trying to obtain a better handle on information before them.

While the questioning game is frequently socially mediated, it is distinguished from other speech games in that its ultimate purpose is to gain control of knowledge. The game has various rules (many will be made clear when general and specific questioning strategies are discussed in chapter six). There are steps, arranged in sequences, either prearranged or spontaneously generated in response to a particular context. Many of these sequences are influenced by the stages apparent in various modes of thinking.

Gavelek and Raphael denote several features of this questioning game. First, the strategy engages students in actively raising and answering the

Activity

CLASSROOM GAME

Inform your students that while the general way of indentifying questions is through a rising intonation, we can emphasize other words in the question sentence. Have children take one question and play with it by putting the emphasis on different words. Have the children discuss how the question meaning changes?

Start the class with a simple sentence:

What is the answer to the *question*?

Ask children if they engage in actually playing with the word emphasis in their questions.

Point out that not only does one often get a different question when changing word emphasis, but the reason for the question changes. Give the example "*Yes*?" in which a teacher asks the question, not expecting an answer at all, but utters it to call the class to attention.

Sometimes, children answer "Yes" in a tone that says, I will do it, but I really do not like it. Have children verbally experiment with their voices.

This activity might well be placed in a speech section of a language arts lesson.

---

questions. Students may devise questions in reaction to material read or from listening to the teacher or peers. Second, the steps engaged are most likely to be recursive—students will go through a series of particular questions and particular answers before accepting their conclusion or answer as adequate or warranted. Third, the process can be under student control. Fourth, the process is amenable to social mediation. Another person, either fellow student or teacher, may coach the student through the process by asking questions, suggesting procedures for processing the question, suggesting criteria for assessing answers, recommending sources for answers, and raising questions regarding procedures to consider.[15]

In learning the game of questioning, students gain procedural declarative knowledge; they learn process, the assumptions behind process, and the specifics of process. Students discover that questions follow particular strategy sequences designed to achieve a given goal.[16]

"In the milieux circumscribed by the questioning act there are subject-matters, phenomena and events, and people such as fellow students and the teacher or other pedagogical actors or educative agents. In performing the questioning act, the student does not merely exhibit qualities that describe self but also appeals to others to share in the presumptions (regarding the questioning act) and to join in the act and its sequel."[17]

REFLECTION

Jot down your initial thoughts about the material you have just read. What has been your level of understanding regarding questions? What presuppositions do you bring to your own questions and questioning?

How do you employ questions in your classroom? For what reasons do you encourage students to question?

Share your thoughts with a colleague, especially one who has read the same chapter.

DIMENSIONS OF QUESTIONS

Questions are linguistic devices possessing more than particular form and specific function. Questions have several dimensions: function level, focus level, dynamic level, difficulty level, interest level, and feasibility level.

Function Level

Function level refers to the cognitive or affective level that all questions possess regardless of how we might classify them. In Chapter 3 the cognitive and affective types of questions are discussed employing the familiar classification schemes developed by Bloom and Krathwohl. Other classifications, however, exist.

At this juncture, all we need to realize is that questions, while demanding that an information goal be satisfied, make requests of the questioner to process data encountered in particular ways with particular feelings. A question having the cognitive function of comprehension requests that students react to information read or encountered in particular ways—to put the information or situation together so as to understand it. A question having a synthesis cognitive level requests that the actor join information in novel ways. Questions at the analysis level serve an opposite function demanding students break down information to identify key components of information or situations encountered. All questions demand a general or particular intellectual cognitive response, some type of thinking. Teachers realizing this select or create questions to elicit from students certain ways of thinking about and with the material. Students, coming to understand this dimension of questions, come to gain executive control over their use of questions.

In addition to questions implicitly and explicitly requesting a cognitive response, they also request the respondent to act on the information with a particular emotional or affective mind set. The affective level of a question relates to the question's focus on feelings, interests, emotions, appreciations, values, and attitudes. Both teachers and students gain a greater understanding of a question by attending to these affective aspects. Teachers wishing students to respond in particular emotional ways to information, raise questions directing students to consider their values, their interests, their feelings about the information encountered. Realizing this dimension of questions, students also develop greater insight into why they are reacting to information in particular ways. Armed with recognition of the affective level of questions, students better grasp their own identity and why they hold particular dispositions toward knowledge, situations, and even people.

While we can write about the cognitive and affective levels of questions separately, in actuality they are inseparable: essentially different aspects of thinking, learning, behaving. Affect or feeling is central to all learning. It begins with the threshold of consciousness; it influences the manner in which we all attend to the world around us. It is the basis for our behavior, molding our personality. Thus, teachers should consider this dimension of questions when planning learning encounters. Likewise, students should realize that affect parallels and interacts with cognition.

Focus Level

The focus of a question refers to its power to direct the respondent to either center or expand his or her attention regarding a particular topic or situation. The focus also clues the person to the level of detail appropriate for dealing with the question. A person dealing with the question serving a centering function is to engage in convergent cognitive behavior relative to a topic or aspect of a topic. Often questions have this focus when teachers are introducing a lesson. Such questions are employed to direct students to deal with a particular aspect of information gathered. In a lesson dealing with ways in which to clean up the environment, several might have been suggested. Now questions are required that encourage students to think of one or just a few means most appropriate for addressing environmental pollution. Centering questions channel the students' consideration of many ideas or situations into a few major ideas or significant situations. In much of the writing on questions, centering has been treated indirectly when addressing convergent thinking.[18]

There are times when questions focus on having students look more broadly at the topic under consideration—to engage in expanding their thinking or the range of their attention. Questions can exist at the same cognitive level—in which case breadth is stressed—or at increasing cognitive levels—in which case depth is emphasized.

Questions having the expansion focus stress divergent thinking. If working at the comprehension level, students can deal with questions that require them to extrapolate information—to go beyond the information—to expand their thinking. Students dealing with questions with the expansion focus make more precise their thinking, their processing of information. As a consequence, students become more involved in their investigating.

A teacher interested in getting students to consider information from varying stances to keep them from arriving at unwarranted conclusions might select or encourage students to choose or phrase questions that ask for options, other views, additional relationships. Perhaps the focus of the lesson is on international trade. In the lesson, analysis level questions are raised to get students to think divergently about ways of dealing with the lesson focus. Questions ask students to contemplate a variety of materials useful for the lesson. The teacher requests that students list those major goods traded on the international market. This request is followed by questions asking for a listing of the reasons that these goods have a market. Other questions, with an expansion focus, direct students' attention to other factors that might influence marketplace demands.

Frequently questions having an expansion or centering focus are placed in a series comprising the questioning act. This questioning act itself will have either a centering or an expansion focus, the focus of the majority of the questions in the act.

Dynamic Level

The dynamic level refers to the ability of the question to stimulate additional questions or answers. All questions have it to varying degrees, from great to little. In part, dynamism lies with the linguistic structure of the question. A question contains one or more propositions; the greater the number of propositions, the more dynamism. For instance, the question "Who was Christopher Columbus?" has imbedded within it the proposition in the form of a presupposition that such a man existed. It also can be assumed that there is only one man who will fit this linguistic inquiry. This question has limited dynamism suggesting primarily only one answer and no further questions. In the question "What were some of the reasons that led Christopher Columbus to discover America?" there is a series of implicit propositions: first, that a person named Columbus discovered America; second, that there was such a place as America; third, that this place was not known before Columbus discovered it; and fourth, that there are several reasons for his action. The student reading the question may not realize all of the propositions but should realize that the question suggests more than one answer and other possible questions regarding these answers. For instance, the pupil could respond that Columbus discovered America for fame, for fortune, for patriotic reasons, to advance knowledge, to extend the political influence of the king. Each answer suggests other questions. "What information would lead you to believe that Columbus wanted fame? Why is fame important? What actions did Columbus take that would make one believe that he was interested in uncovering new knowledge?"

A question possessing dynamic quality contains within its structure an intentionality; the question intends the student to deal with the interrogative statement in particular ways.[19] A question with limited type dynamism strives to get from the respondent a limited response. The clearness of the intention rests with the words selected for the question. It was very clear, or should be, with the question asking for the reasons that lead Columbus to act that the question asks for several reasons. Likewise, the question "Who was Christopher Columbus?" is clear in that its words intend students to respond with a one-word or rather narrow and perhaps precise response.

Dynamism relates to the openness or closedness of the question. An open question suggests alternatives; however, these alternatives need not be identified, the question respondee is free to proceed in any direction. "Why do you suppose the discovery of the New World caught the attention of Europeans?" is an open dynamic question. Its openness is evident in that no precise answer is demanded. Such openness allows, perhaps even suggests to the skilled student, several avenues of response, about which additional questions can be generated; open questions call for divergent production.

In contrast, a closed question is convergent, requesting of the respondent a centering of thought. Often, the person, from analyzing the wording of the question, knows precisely what the answer should be. The closed question "Did the President visit Seattle this year?" can be answered with either a "Yes" or a "No." It has limited dynamics; after the response, no other question is necessary.

Difficulty Level

All questions have a level of difficulty. While seemingly obvious, there is some challenge in determining its difficulty for such a quality rests only partly with the complexity of the question and the sophistication of the information to which the question refers. A question's difficulty is contextual, determined by students' level of skill in and understanding of the subject about which the question is raised.

The syntactical structure of a question affects difficulty. A simple question may have only one primary interrogative word in it, such as *What* in "What is the name of the most active volcano in Washington State?" A difficult question might have several interrogative words; for instance, "What did the speaker say, and how did he express it?"

Questions written as simple sentences may or may not be easy. Questions worded in complex sentences most often are difficult. However, exceptions exist. A simple interrogative sentence, while having only one interrogative word, may be formidable because of the information requested. For example, "Explain the continental drift theory?" is rather simple syntactically, but to a student just learning about this theory, the question may be very challenging. Conversely, the question, "How many miles of interstate highway do we have, and what are the names of the major east-west highways?" is rather easy despite its compound syntax and two interrogatives, *how* and *what.*

Question difficulty is also determined by whether the question asks the person to provide an informational bit of knowledge or to engage in some process. To furnish an answer drawn from memory is easier than to furnish an answer as a consequence of some experiment. However, difficulty still is relative in that while an investigation comsumes time, it still might be rather easy for a student already expert in the processes required.

For these reasons, it is easy to report that a question has a difficulty level but problematic to say with certainty that "This particular question is difficult and this one is easy." It all depends—upon the phrasing of the sentence, the subject matter itself, the level at which the student is with regard to the content, the background the student brings to the question, the student's innate abilities, and the resources available for processing the question.

Difficulty of the question, besides being related to the number of interrogative words, is also determined by the number of syntactical presuppositions of the question—those statements assumed true in order to process the question.[20] The number of presuppositions imbedded in the question relates the difficulty dimension with the dynamism of the question. Dynamic questions have more presuppositions, often making such questions hard. Consider the question, "Explain the reaction in which energy is released from the splitting of an atom?" This question assumes, presupposes, that there is something called energy, that energy is released when an atom is split, that there is such a thing as an atom, that this atom can be split with the current level of technological skill. In responding to the question, the student either accepts these presuppositions or challenges each before addressing the central thrust of the question—to explain the reaction. Because of the syntactical complexity of the question, the student must possess a greater awareness and most likely understanding of many variables. He or she cannot just utter a one-word answer. Also, each aspect of the explanation must be considered in light of each presupposition implied in the question; just thinking about these various interrogatives tends to make the question more difficult. Put another way, the student must ask himself or herself if the particular syntactic presuppositions of a question would be logical consequences of all the possible direct answers to this particular question.[21] All questions, regardless of type or purpose, require such consideration. In other words, for every interrogative sentence, there must be a declarative sentence. "Someone painted the Sistine Chapel" is a logical declarative consequence of the interrogative sentence, "Who painted the Sistine Chapel?"

Interest Level

Interest is a feeling of intentness, concern, or curiosity about something or something causing this feeling.[22] Questions possess interest potential, the power to elicit from students the above defined feelings. All educators want their questions to be interesting, and all students posing their own questions are hopefully addressing their intentness or curiosity. Notwithstanding this, it is somewhat problematic to decide the interest aspect of questions, mainly due to the uniqueness of students' abilities, backgrounds, and prior and current experiences in school and out.

Ideally, an interesting question contains challenge to the responder, whether the responder is the same person who has asked the question (the case with a student raising his or her own question) or whether the responder is a different person (the case when the teacher asks the question of a pupil). The challenge is tied to the "Socratic notion that a growth in personal knowledge comes through a realization of the ignorance at the heart of what we 'formerly imagined we knew.' "[23]

An interesting question makes the person receiving the query realize that his or her current state of understanding is incomplete and that he or she really should strive to work toward completeness. Of course, teachers and pupils should realize this as an ongoing challenge; one's knowledge will never be complete. With further questioning, however, students and teachers distinguish with greater clarity between what they already know and what they do not know. Knowledge is challenged by the realization of incomplete knowing, by recognizing the need for further questioning; the question demands our interest, our concern. We question in order to know; we reflect on our knowledge and make boundaries around what we do not know, our ignorance.[24]

A question of high interest has implicit within it the proclamations "You can know this information" and "You should know this information." Such questions within the classroom say to students you can do this, you should do this. Sometimes the fascination of the question is determined by a force external to the question asker. For instance, the interest of a question posed to a student is determined by the teacher just asking the question. The implication is that you the student should attend to this question for its very asking identifies it as one of concern.

Questions can be intriguing just by the nature of the content to which they refer. Sports-related questions usually engage most students. This is also true of many aspects of science that might be classified as "strange but true." Children like questions relating to dinosaurs.

Teachers skilled in selecting questions of interest to students realize that students' backgrounds must be considered. Also, the cognitive development of students figures into the interest equation. At certain ages children have particular fascinations. Young children always seem to be intrigued with things relating to themselves. "Me-ism" is a major part of young children's perceptions of what is important. If it is about me or about children like me, then I am curious; I am intent in learning about these people. This dimension of questions also relates to children's learning styles. Questions worded so that a process is suggested for dealing with the question or raising additional questions in a manner that resembles the way a child likes to process information will draw that child into response. If a question requires a student who likes to arrange ideas in a concrete sequence to arrange ideas systematically in a particular fashion, then that question might get the student's attention. To a random thinker, such a question might not catch his or her fancy.

The interest potential of a question depends upon the student's perception of that question with regard to his or her purpose for learning or even general view of life. To a student fascinated with things scientific, almost any question dealing with science will kindle attention. To the lover of literature, a question focusing on some aspect of a particular writer's life will most likely be engaging.

Pupils, responding to questions about content that interests them, are voicing "I want to know more about this"; "I can know more through these questions."[25] Teachers, realizing that some students are unwilling to attend to a particular content area, have the challenge of pointing out by statements and questions that such information is important and/or enjoyable to possess. Effective teachers tie the interest potential of new questions to areas where students have already expressed interest. Suppose that a student dislikes language but enjoys mathematics. Suppose further that the teacher wishes the student to learn more about how the structure of sentences can be played with to create certain meanings. The teacher can engage her student in responding to questions about sentences by putting into her questions references to mathematics. Perhaps the following question sentence can start off the inquiry, "If we think of a sentence in our everyday language as similar to an equation in mathematics, what new insights can we get regarding the nature of sentences and their use?" Not only can linking two subject areas together by means of a question serve to generate student interest in the area originally found unchallenging, it can also lead students to begin generating questions that focus on relating these two areas in further ways. The student may begin to reflect on the relationships of known knowledge to what first appears unrelated information.

Ideally, teachers should get their students to ask themselves if questions are of interest to them and if so, why so, and if not, why not? Doing this is part of allowing students to gain executive control of their own learning (meta-attention) to become cognizant of their ways of processing and thinking about information.

Feasibility Level

Feasibility relates to whether the question can be processed given the student's ability, interest, background, resources available, time schedule, and community mores. A rule of thumb is that if a question cannot be processed, it should not be asked. Of course, if a question should be asked but cannot be because of some limitation of student's background or insufficient time, then the teacher may ask himself or herself what can be done to make it feasible.

All children possess the ability to process any question asked at some level of sophistication. Sophistication will vary with regard to their innate abilities and developmental stage. However, there are some questions that just do not make sense to children because of their backgrounds. The teacher can either decide not to use the question—consider it irrelevant—or strive to adjust the students' backgrounds so that the question gains meaning. If a teacher asks students who have no backgrounds regarding primitive cultures, deserts, or even Africa, "In what ways have the bush people of the Kalahari desert in Africa culturally interpreted their resources?" the teacher has a question with low feasibility. Despite this, the teacher may realize that the community expects the children to know some responses to this question. If this is the case, the teacher has to get the appropriate resources and schedule sufficient time to enrich pupils' backgrounds requisite for dealing with the question.

Another teacher wanting to ask the same question may realize that while the question might relate well to a unit on various cultures, there is really little likelihood that the necessary resources will be forthcoming. In this instance, the question is not feasible. Some teachers will discover that in particular communities certain questions are taboo, community mores preventing specific avenues of inquiry.

For questions that require extensive inquiry, there must be time available. Frequently, teachers just do not have enough hours in the day to enable a serious avenue of inquiry. Rather than get children interested about investigating a particular topic only to have them rush to conclusions, it is better that the teacher not raise the question initially. Raising valid and powerful questions and then not scheduling sufficient time to process them produces frustration in students and diminishes their enthusiasm for inquiry.

Ideally, both teacher and student when contemplating questions consider all the dimensions of questions. Those questions employed should be marked with a plus regarding all of these dimensions. Effective questions have a definite cognitive and affective focus, are at the appropriate difficulty level, have a dynamic quality, address or create students' interests, and are feasible given present and anticipated situations.

ASSUMPTIONS OF QUESTIONING

Questions rarely exist in isolation. For the greatest impact questions are usually combined in a type of sequence in which the combination of the individual questions into a cohesive whole provides impact to the entire process.[26] As students see their questions arranged in sequence, other questions surface and new ways to look at questions appear.

Activity

TRY IT

Your questions contain those dimensions just discussed to some degree. We all want our questions to score high. Tape a fifteen minute segment of your own class talk and make a list of the questions you ask. Mark each of your questions as to how well it does regarding the various dimensions.

Dimensions

My Questions	Function	Focus	Dyna-mism	Diffi-culty	In-terest	Feas-ibility
⎯	⎯	⎯	⎯	⎯	⎯	⎯
⎯	⎯	⎯	⎯	⎯	⎯	⎯
⎯	⎯	⎯	⎯	⎯	⎯	⎯
⎯	⎯	⎯	⎯	⎯	⎯	⎯
⎯	⎯	⎯	⎯	⎯	⎯	⎯

Under function, list the cognitive or affective level (C or A).
Under focus note whether it centers or expands.
Dynamism—note a + if dynamic or − if not.
Difficulty—note D if difficult or E if easy.
Interest—indicate a Yes or No.
Feasibility—indicate a yes or no.

When you have finished you will have a profile of the dimensions of your questions. Hopefully, they will have the proper functioning, diversity of focus, be dynamic, appropriately difficult, be interesting and feasible. Share your questions with a colleague; see if he or she classifies your questions in a similar manner. (Students can do the same regarding their questions).

As mentioned earlier, questioning can be seen as a recursive sequence of organized problem-solving processes designed for specific purposes.[27] The scheme can either be planned or assumed. When planned, students are aware of the scheme and the reasons for its particular organization. The various schema suggested for types of thinking strategies (noted in Chapter 1) are essentially planned questioning sequences. Later in this book, attention is given to particular general and specific strategies that teachers and students can employ. At this juncture, it is important to consider the assumptions that exist with regard to the act of questioning, regardless of the specific type of strategy used.

Assumptions

When teachers and students raise questions, they frequently ignore the assumptions regarding the act of questioning. However, if teachers and students become aware of the presumptions brought to questioning, they will become more powerful questioners.

Lack of Knowledge

Perhaps the primary assumption deals with lack of knowledge or what Dillon calls ignorance—the state and realization of not knowing.[28] Anyone raising a question must assume that he lacks the information about which he is inquiring. Of course, to be cognizant of this, one must possess sufficient information to realize what is not known.[29] Awareness of not knowing, and not knowing in sufficient degree to raise a question, is part of the dilemma of inquiry and learning.[30] But, knowing our areas of ignorance is essential to trigger learning. Before the learner will ask a question, he or she must admit that he or she does not know the information.

This assumption does not reveal the precise nature of the questioner's lack of knowledge; rather, it provides a focus to his ignorance. The questioner is not asking questions about all knowledge and reality. The questioner is raising particular questions and putting them into particular sequences to define the area of his investigation. By his or her questions, the questioner also is making known the types of answers appropriate to the inquiry.

At a time when it seems that certainty and precise answers are the favored norm of classrooms, it may be somewhat unsettling to suggest that students should place recognition of ignorance as a goal of learning. However, implicit in all question asking is the statement that "I do not know this; I am ignorant of this." There is no shame in admitting it; indeed, admitting it is the key prerequisite to learning. It certainly makes little sense to ask questions if one does know the answer. Those students who in the classroom identify areas about which they possess ignorance are well on their ways to learning and thinking.

The Question's Presupposition(s)

It is the presupposition that gives rise to the question.[31] The presupposition is the proposition, the statement implied by the particular question. Kubinski discusses the various presuppositions that questions can contain in discussing a logical theory of questions.[32] Linguists also attend to the nature of presuppositions as an integral part of questions.[33]

The presuppositions of a question refer to all those things that the questioner accepts without challenge. If I ask a student what is the atomic weight of the element lead, the student before even attempting an answer must first accept as true that there is an element, its name is lead, and there is such a thing as atomic weight. If the student challenges any of these presuppositions, then the question is unanswerable.

There may be times when students fail to realize that an implied presupposition of a question is indeed false. He or she may ask the question, "How much carbon dioxide does a bean plant give off?", not realizing that plants give off oxygen during the day. The teacher should point this out to the student rather than taking time for the student to investigate it. However, if the student asks the question, "What gas does a plant give off?" then the teacher should allow the inquiry. The question presupposes that plants do give off gases, which is true.[34]

The Question's Answer

A logical link exists between a question's presupposition and answer. As Dillon notes, any answer will reaffirm the validity of the proposition that a question has presupposed.[35] Just as the questioner must believe the truthfulness of the presuppositions implied by the question, so also must he or she admit that there is indeed an answer to the question. He or she may even have an idea as to what the answer is. This does not mean an answer to be had with ease but rather one that with appropriate effort can be framed to satisfy the question. This assumption reflects that questions stand because of answers and answers occur because of questions.[36]

The mutual dependency of answers and questions is revealed in the statement, "If a question is framed, one has already at least two-thirds of the answer." Accepting this, wise educators look at the answers they accept from their students to determine if they are processing questions of value. This close link enables students to judge the value of the answer.

The Questioner's Desire

A simple absence of knowledge does not bloom into a framed question.[37] Likewise, recognizing a gap in one's information does not automatically elicit answer seeking. A desire to know, a felt need to travel from no knowledge to knowledge, must exist. Dillon refers to this as the person's aspiration to know.[38]

Why some students fancy to know some things and not others is tied up with their backgrounds, their abilities, their aspirations, and their current successes in raising questions. Teachers are challenged to select questions to which most students most of the time desire answers. Effective questions create in students what has been called a cognitive conflict or epistemic interest,[39] triggering in students curiosity, an unwillingness to allow a recognized ignorance to remain. To the ideal question students respond, "I must know the answer or answers to that." Students' desire should go beyond one answer. In some instances, students reacting to a particular question may strive to know everything.

Related to the questioner's desire is a commitment to seeking "truth."[40] In fact, a desire to know implies an acceptance of the need to uncover truth. It also reveals that the questioner has a faith, a confidence that that which is not known can be known. A student not feeling that something can be known or that something is impossible will resist seeking answers. Our challenge as educators is to point out to students that what at first might seem impossible or not feasible may indeed be possible through skilled questioning.

Dillon notes that students who desire an answer must have courage—boldness to take the time to confront the mysteries, the unknown, their not knowing—to face thoughts that will challenge old views, comfortable feelings, to invite variations in perceptions, in actions. Such valor must be nurtured; students must realize that they must demonstrate bravery so as to raise significant questions, for it is in the raising of questions that knowledge is attained.

It takes courage to confront oneself, to encounter our "weaknesses, our own ignorance." Clark notes that "I question in order to know."[41] But in our questioning, we become surer of our ignorance, just how little we do know. This generates in us insecurity, feelings of inadequacy. Students need daring to face their shortcomings. The reward of questioning does not diminish the desire for answers.

The Questioner's Skill

An effective questioner, besides possessing knowledge of questions and skill in formulating questions that uncover desired answers, can assess whether the response to the question, whether given orally or in print, constitutes a reply or an answer. The questioner already has some idea as to possible answers. He or she realizes the distinction between a response that does not address the question, a mere reply, and a response that does, an answer.

Questions are raised for a purpose, thus students should clearly realize why they asked the question. If the questioner is the teacher, he or she should recognize why the question was asked and what are acceptable answers. Determining if the question has been answered and the quality of the response requires applying evaluative criteria. Several such criteria exist.

One criterion is information match. If I ask the question, "How many oceans are there in the world?" and the response is, "Sea water has many minerals dissolved in it," then I should recognize that this is not an answer to my question.

Another criterion is information yield.[42] Just how much information do I get from the explanation to my question? Just how much information does my question suggest? The question about the numbers of oceans should generate an answer containing a number. I now have to determine if the number obtained is reasonable. "There are twenty-five oceans" should trigger suspicion. If I hear five, I judge it at least reasonable.

In some instances, the pupil lacks the necessary information to judge the question but must rely on the integrity of the person responding or the source containing the answer. In this case, the student's skill is in selecting the authority or the authoritative written source. If one seeks from a geographer or a geography textbook the answer to the question, "How many oceans are there?", one should be fairly certain that the answer given will be accurate. Here the student is engaged in critical thinking.

The Necessary First Step

Central to questioning is the inquirer's realization that if the question is not posed, no information will be given or obtained. Accepting that I question in order to know requires believing the corollary if I do not question, I will not know. The student realizes that the responsibility of attaining an answer or answers rests with the person making the first step—asking the question. People need to bid for desired information.[43]

Belief in the Respondent and/or Information Source

A questioner assumes that the source to which the question is directed contains the answer and that, if the source is a person, a willingness to disclose the answer. Certainly, verbal questions are designed to elicit some response; written questions are structures created to uncover an answer response.

It makes little sense to request information if one believes the person does not have the answer or the ability to obtain one. Likewise, it is foolishness to go to written sources that one knows will not contain answers to one's queries. While this is obvious, it is not always evident which person or persons is or are authorities in the field. Often, one must engage in a major search of written material before finding appropriate sources. Finding the right sources, whether people or material, is an essential skill of questioning.

Teachers who are effective questioners possess awareness and understanding of these assumptions. Students who also strive to be effective questioners, and thinkers, need to be knowledgeable of the assumptions. Knowing the assumptions makes the person, whether teacher or student, realize "All I know or think or say is a reply to questions I at least implicitly pose and for which I am responsible as my way of perceiving and of articulating experience. I find myself in the world but as a subject able to make sense of it in various ways as my world ... Any view of the world is some particular realization of the possibilities of being a knower."[44]

Realizing the nature and power of questions students can take joy in the notion that they are capable of being knowers. Students come to accept what Clark has called the "I can" of a questioner. To give our students belief in "I can" is one of the greatest "gifts" we can present these youth.

CONCLUSION

Those who understand that asking questions is more than phrasing "What?" realize that questioning is a valuable skill that will require time and effort to develop within the confines of the classroom. The nature of the question is complex, influencing the dynamics of classroom dialogue.

It was pointed out that in a very real sense we are all natural questioners, but in the classroom, we wish to posit educative questions. This takes knowledge; it takes time and effort. But the time and effort is well spent, for in the effective use of questions, students can get at more than surface knowledge; they can approach understanding the deep structure of information—the presuppositions behind the information, the implicit answers, the myriad directions of potential inquiry.

To accomplish this, teachers and students must have in-depth understanding of the dimensions of questions and how to draw on these dimensions when furnishing or creating questions in the school arena.

The reader may challenge this position that we must be very knowledgeable about questions; we are natural questioners, we do not need more depth of knowledge than that. Hopefully, the discussion dealing with the assumptions of questions gives the reader "food for thought" that the question is indeed important and we need to reflect on the various assumptions relating to questions when planning questions. The good questioner realizes and relishes the possibilities of being a knower.

NOTES

1. H. van der Meij, *Questioning* (The Hague, The Netherlands: Foundation for Educational Research in the Netherlands, SVO, 1986).

2. H. van der Meij, *Questioning.*

3. William W. Wilen, *Questioning Skills for Teachers* (Washington, D.C.: National Education Association, 1982).

4. Ronald T. Hyman, *Strategic Questioning* (Englewood Cliffs, N.J.: Prentice-Hall, Inc., 1979).

5. Aqvist cited in Tadeusz Kubinski, *An Outline of the Logical Theory of Questions* (Berline: Akademie-Verlag, 1980).

6. U. S. Chaudhari, "Questioning and Creative Thinking: A Research Perspective," *The Journal of Creative Behavior,* Vol 9, no. 1 (First Quarter, 1975), 31.

7. Tadeusz Kubinski, *An Outline of the Logical Theory of Questions.*

8. Tadeusz Kubinski, *An Outline of the Logical Theory of Questions.*

9. J. T. Dillon, *Student Questions and Individual Learning* (Paper presented at Conference on Individual Differences and Individualized Education, Minister of Education, Plovdiv, Bulgaria, October 1985), 1–24; *Educational Theory* in Press.

10. J. T. Dillon, *Student Questions and Individual Learning.*

11. Tadeusz Kubinski, *An Outline of the Logical Theory of Questions.*

12. J. T. Dillon, *Student Questions and Individual Learning.*

13. Tadeusz Kubinski, *An Outline of the Logical Theory of Questions.*

14. J. T. Dillon, *Student Questions and Individual Learning.*

15. James R. Gavelek and Taffy E. Raphael, "Metacognition, Instruction, and the Role of Questioning Activities, in D. L. Forest-Pressley, G. E. Mackinnon, and T. Gary Waller, eds. *Metacognition, Cognition, and Human Performance* (Orlando, FL: Academic Press, Inc., 1985), 103–136.

16. Ronald T. Hyman, *Strategic Questioning,* p. xii.

17. J. T. Dillon, *Student Questions and Individual Learning,* 10–11.

18. Ronald T. Hyman, *Strategic Questioning.*

19. Robert C. Stalnaker, *Inquiry* (Cambridge, MA: MIT Press, A Bradford Book, 1984).

20. Tadeusz Kubinski, *An Outline of the Logical Theory of Questions.*

21. Tadeusz Kubinski, *An Outline of the Logical Theory of Questions.*

22. *Webster's New World Dictionary* (College Division, Cleveland: The World Publishing Company, 1964).

23. Malcolm Clark, *Perplexity and Knowledge* (The Hague: Martinus Jijhoff, 1972), 182.

24. Malcolm Clark, *Perplexity and Knowledge.*

25. Malcolm Clark, *Perplexity and Knowledge,* 185.

26. Ronald T. Hyman, *Strategic Questioning.*

27. James R. Gavelek and Taffy E. Raphael, "Metacognition, Instruction, and the Role of Questioning Activities."

28. J. T. Dillon, *Student Questions and Individual Learning.* H. van der Meij in his book *Questioning* (The Hague, The Netherlands: Foundation for Educational Research in the Netherlands, SVO, 1986) introduced the initial listing of assumptions of questions to the field.

29. M. Miyake and D. Norman, "To Ask a Question, One Must Know Enough to Know What is Not Known," *Journal of Verbal Learning and Verbal Behavior,* Vol. 18 (1979), 357–364.

30. Hugh G. Petrie, *The Dilemma of Enquiry and Learning* (Chicago: The University of Chicago Press, 1981).

31. J. T. Dillon, *Student Questions and Individual Learning.*

32. Tadeusz Kubinski, *An Outline of the Logical Theory of Questions.*

33. M. Meyer, *Meaning and Reading, A Philosophical Essay on Language and Literature.* (Amsterdam: John Benjamins, 1983).

34. H. van der Meij, *Questioning.*

35. J. T. Dillon, *Student Questions and Individual Learning.*

36. H. van der Meij, *Questioning.*

37. Malcolm Clark, *Perplexity and Knowledge.*

38. J. T. Dillon, *Student Questions and Individual Learning.*

39. H. van der Meij, *Questioning.*

40. J. T. Dillon, *Student Questions and Individual Learning.*

41. Malcolm Clark, *Perplexity and Knowledge,* p. 185.

42. H. van der Meij, *Questioning.*

43. H. van der Meij, *Questioning.*

44. Malcolm Clark, *Perplexity and Knowledge,* p. 225.

3

Question Types

as to Function

Teachers, students, even authors, ask questions for several reasons: to stimulate some type of mental activity or level of thinking, to trigger an affective response, or to elicit some psychomotor reaction. Some questions evoke all three. Researchers argue that indeed, every question has the potential to do all three. A person can raise a question that gets you to think about a question in particular ways, makes you conscious of your feelings regarding such thinking, and engages you in some specific action. Questions can engage persons in in depth processing. Reflecting on our thinking has us realize that we are engaging in not just one but several actions—forming mental pictures about the focus of our thinking; putting into words our thoughts; becoming aware of our emotional responses; and actually experiencing physical sensations.[1]

If I ask you, "What is your grandmother like?", you in responding may first form some mental pictures about your grandmother; you may picture some event or events in which your grandmother was a player. You then may search for words that will express what your grandmother was really like. Still reacting, you realize that you are feeling somewhat emotional as you think about your grandmother, actually experiencing a physical response, perhaps tears welling in your eyes.

Questions get total response from us. However, in schools, we have primarily been concerned with the cognitive and the affective dimensions of information processing. These two dimensions really engage the three aspects of in depth processing: (1) mental pictures (cognitive), (2) linguistic information (cognitive), and (3) emotions (affective).[2] The physical sensations might be classified under the psychomotor domain. While we may want students to realize their physical sensations in response to thinking, we are still more concerned with cognitive awareness of such sensations rather than having students engage in particular physical actions. For this reason physical sensations can be considered part of the cognitive and affective dimensions.

COGNITIVE DOMAIN QUESTIONS

Questions, as a specialized class of expressions, are concerned with information seeking.[4] Questions reflect a cognitive state of information need suggesting a particular level at which the information should be processed.[5] For instance, the question, "What is the highest mountain in the United States?" suggests that students need specific knowledge processed primarily from memory. In contrast, the question "Does the author have any basis for making such a statement?" suggests a cognitive need for analyzing the relationships among statements and for engaging in analytical thought.

Knowing that questions are concerned with information seeking and processing said information allows us to classify questions on the basis of their informational intent and implicit cognitive operation. There have been numerous attempts to classify questions according to taxonomies that would not only give us a greater understanding of question types but allow us to formulate specific questions to elicit from our students particular cognitive operations.

Benjamin Bloom's Taxonomy is a well-known guide for classifying the cognitive types of questions.[6] While this taxonomy has and continues to serve us well, it is important to note that the taxonomy presents question types apart from context.[7] This is crucial for the reader to bear in mind, for the context in which the question is phrased as well as the background knowledge of the respondent influences the actual cognitive level of the response. For instance, if I ask a student to prove that the answer to a mathematical problem is correct, it may be an analysis question if the experience is new to the student. However, if the student has had extensive work with such problems, the same question might only elicit from the student comprehension. For this reason, we teachers must classify the question and its goodness relative to the question's context. The reader may think that given this, no precise classification of questions as to cognitive type exists. However, he or she should realize that in dealing with particular students, one usually does have a fairly good reading of the context in which questions are phrased as well as students' experiental background. And if the questions are being raised by the students, they have a fairly good reading of their informational backgrounds.

Teachers can classify questions as to cognitive level by looking at the wording of the questions. Figure 3–2 shows the key words that can be used at the various cognitive levels.

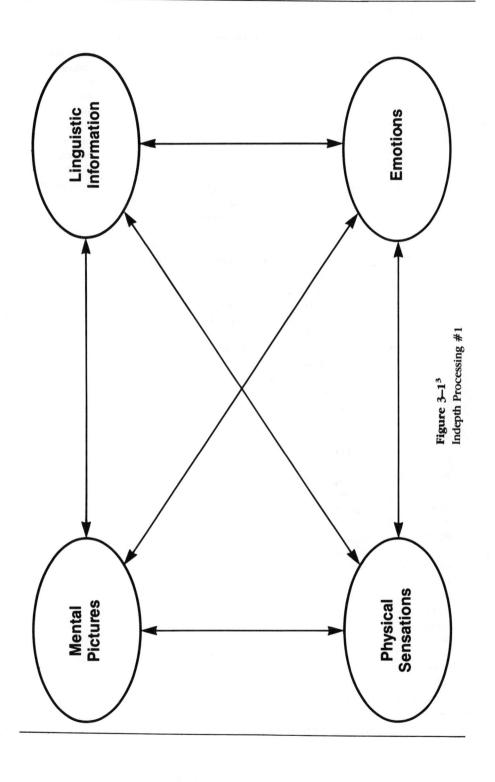

Figure 3–1[3]
Indepth Processing #1

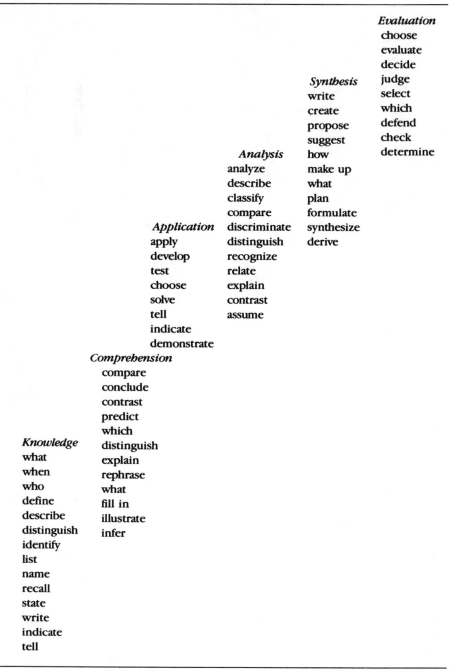

Knowledge	Comprehension	Application	Analysis	Synthesis	Evaluation
what	compare	apply	analyze	write	choose
when	conclude	develop	describe	create	evaluate
who	contrast	test	classify	propose	decide
define	predict	choose	compare	suggest	judge
describe	which	solve	discriminate	how	select
distinguish	distinguish	tell	distinguish	make up	which
identify	explain	indicate	recognize	what	defend
list	rephrase	demonstrate	relate	plan	check
name	what		explain	formulate	determine
recall	fill in		contrast	synthesize	
state	illustrate		assume	derive	
write	infer				
indicate					
tell					

Figure 3–2
Key Words for Cognitive Questions

These words not only furnish useful guides to teachers but also enable students to formulate their own questions in ways consistent with their goals. Knowing such words allows students to obtain a strategic awareness not only of question types but also of ways to sequence the questions. Teachers and students need to realize that the taxonomy suggests both cumulative and sequential processing of information by means of specific question types. Furthermore, the taxonomy provides a heuristic for processing information both inductively and deductively. Figure 3–3 shows that starting at the knowledge level and raising questions at increasingly higher levels enables one to process the information inductively, from specific to general. In processing information deductively, one reverses the questioning sequence, making judgments as to some conclusion or generalization presented.

Bloom's Taxonomy of Educational Objectives: Cognitive Domain

Following is an overview of Bloom's taxonomy of educational objectives in the cognitive domain, followed by examples of questions at these levels. Even after all these years, this taxonomy remains a useful framework for students and teachers alike in formulating their questioning and obtaining executive control over their information processing.

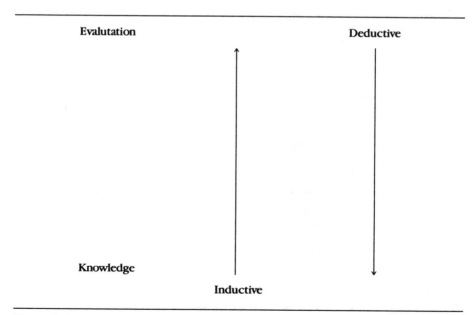

Figure 3–3
Inductive-Deductive Processing of Information

KNOWLEDGE. Knowledge involves the recall of specifics and universals, the recall of methods and processes, or the recall of a pattern, structure, or setting.

Knowledge of Specifics. Knowledge of specifics involves the recall of specific and isolable bits of information, knowledge of terminology, and knowledge of specific facts.

Knowledge of Ways and Means of Dealing with Specifics. This subdivision has the following categories:

> Knowledge of conventions
> Knowledge of trends and sequences
> Knowledge of classifications and categories
> Knowledge of criteria
> Knowledge of methodology.

Knowledge of the Universals and Abstractions in a Field. This subdivision has the following categories:

> Knowledge of principles and generalizations
> Knowledge of theories and structures.

Intellectual Abilities and Skills

COMPREHENSION. This cognitive level refers to a type of understanding or apprehension which implies that the individual knows what is being communicated and can make use of the material or idea being communicated without necessarily relating it to other material or seeing its fullest implications.

Translation. Comprehension as evidenced by the care and accuracy with which the communication is paraphrased or rendered from one language or communication to another.

Figure 3–4
Bloom's Taxonomy of Educational Objectives: Cognitive Domain[8]

Questions at Various Cognitive Levels

Knowledge Questions

The first type of question, according to Bloom's schema, is the knowledge question of which three subtypes exist. The first subtype is *knowledge of specifics,* which has two subcategories: knowledge of terminology and specific facts.

EXAMPLES:

Terminology

- What do we call the continual increase in the prices of goods?

Interpretation. The explanation or summarization of a communication.

Extrapolation. The extension of trends or tendencies beyond the given data to determine implications, consequences, corollaries, effects, etc., which are in accordance with the conditions described in the original communication.

APPLICATION. This is the use of abstractions in particular and concrete situations. The abstractions may be in the form of general ideas, rules of procedure, or generalized methods.

ANALYSIS. Analysis is the breakdown of a communication into its constituent elements or parts.

Analysis of Elements. Identification of the elements included in a communication.

Analysis of Relationships. The connections and interactions between elements and parts of a communication.

Analysis of Organizational Principles. The organization, systematic arrangement, and structure which hold the communication together.

SYNTHESIS. Synthesis is the putting together of elements and parts to form a whole.

Production of a Unique Communication. The development of a communication in which the writer or speaker attempts to convey ideas, feelings, and/or experiences to others.

Production of a Plan, or Proposed Set of Operations. The development of a plan or the proposal of a plan of operations.

Derivation of a Set of Abstract Relations. The development of a set of abstract relations either to classify or explain particular data or phenomena; or the deduction of propositions and relations from a set of basic propositions or symbolic representations.

EVALUATION. Evaluation calls for making judgments about the value of material and methods for given purposes.

Figure 3–4
Continued

1. interest
2. inflation
3. gross national product
4. depression

- What is a sonnet?
- Define the meaning of the term "element."

These questions only ask learners to repeat a definition or recognize one for a particular term. Students do not have to use their knowledge.

EXAMPLES:

Specific Facts

Match the name with the correct descriptive phrase.

1. John Adams	President during the Civil War
2. Abraham Lincoln	First president to come from the Frontier
3. Andrew Jackson	President who advocated membership in
4. Woodrow Wilson	League of Nations
	Established the American Navy

- The Monroe Doctrine was created

    1. to encourage the development of the New World

    2. to prevent foreign powers from obtaining a control in the New World

    3. to assure that the U.S. Navy would remain strong

    4. to prevent the outbreak of war

- The U.S. Constitution was born on

    1. September 17, 1787

    2. July 4, 1776

    3. August 3, 1783

    4. April 19, 1773

- Which state has the fastest growing population?

These questions center on facts, making no attempt to ascertain if learners really know the significance of the information, value such information, or truly understand the significance of the information. Memory is what is primarily being tapped.

The second major subtype of knowledge is *knowledge of ways and means of dealing with specifics.* This division has five subdivisions: knowledge of conventions, knowledge of trends and sequences, knowledge of classifications and categories, knowledge of criteria, and knowledge of methodology.

EXAMPLES:

Knowledge of Conventions

- How is the point system in tennis figured?
- When is it correct to say "whom" in a sentence?
- What is the symbol for greater than? Less than?
- Underline the proper word in the space provided:

My friend and (me, I) went swimming.

My teacher presented (me, I) with an attendance award.

These questions require cognizance of the ways one can react to and process information and reality. Still, students need not act with the information; they only need to recall it.

Knowledge of Trends and Sequences

- Which are the correct stages in the life of a silkworm?

    1. adult, egg, larva
    2. egg, adult, larva
    3. egg, larva, adult
    4. adult, larva, egg

- In the future, the economy will be primarily

    1. heavy manufacturing
    2. service and high tech
    3. service only
    4. high-tech only

Questions at this sublevel of knowledge ask individuals to indicate awareness of happenings with reference to time. Again, the questions are not designed to determine the students' understanding but only if they recognize the trend or sequence and recall it.

EXAMPLES:

Knowledge of Classifications and Categories

- Biology is part of

    1. the natural sciences
    2. the physical sciences
    3. the social sciences
    4. the psychological sciences

- Which of the following bone specialists work with bone ailments?

    1. plastic surgeon
    2. neurologist
    3. orthopedist
    4. radiologist

- How many types of mountains are there?

    _____

The above examples elicit students' remembering certain groupings of information. Students need not work with these classifications to group information. All that is required is pulling from memory necessary information.

EXAMPLES:
_____
Knowledge of Criteria

- What are ways in which we can determine if a question is an effective one?
- Andy Warhol stated that art is

    1. that which elicits great emotion
    2. anything that can be sold
    3. that which has elements of great composition
    4. that which pushes the boundaries of knowing

    _____

Thinking, especially critical thinking, requires making judgments as to the appropriateness or correctness of information or situations considered. However, judgments can only be made if students know appropriate criteria. Knowledge of criteria questions probe such awareness.

EXAMPLES:
_____
Knowledge of Methodology

- An effective problem starts by

    1. determining what authorities say about the situation
    2. making careful observations
    3. developing a plan of action
    4. considering alternatives

- When one has conflicting statements regarding an event, the process to follow is

  1. to disregard both statements

  2. to get yet another opinion

  3. to report both

  4. to rephrase the question

  _____

With much attention now on the active learner, some teachers think that just the raising of such questions is sufficient. Notwithstanding the importance of such questions, teachers need to realize that these questions only address students' awareness of various methods or processes, not their ability to utilize them in actual situations. Often, students can state a good response to such questions, still not realizing when such procedures are necessary or how to carry them off.

The third major division under knowledge is *knowledge of universals and abstractions in a field.* This major category deals with two major divisions: knowledge of principles and generalizations and knowledge of theories and structures. Again, the emphasis is only upon the student drawing this knowledge from memory. Questions at this level are asking only for awareness of diverse abstractions or universals. In responding to such questions, students only have to recall or put into writing principles, generalizations theories, or concepts. No attempt is made to determine if students comprehend their answers.

EXAMPLES:

Knowledge of Principles and Generalizations

- Which of the following explains the continued interest in the Middle East?

  1. The geographic location of a region determines its importance.

  2. The cultures of all peoples favor heightened conflict.

  3. The resources of a region always determine its value to the world community.

  4. The physical appearance of a region changes over time.

- For effective team work, there must be

  1. a favoring of one's individual talents

  2. a realization of the importance of cooperation

  3. a belief that winning must be striven for at any cost

_____

4. a belief in the importance of good salaries

_____

These questions just emphasize knowing the principle or generalization, not applying it.

<u>*EXAMPLES:*</u>
Knowledge of Theories and Structures

- What concept is central to the structure of geography?

    1. humans
    2. region
    3. globe
    4. time

- The understanding that life forms have gradually developed over time from simpler organisms to more complex organisms is the basis for the theory of

    1. evolution
    2. mutation
    3. relativity
    4. change

_____

Questions at this final level of knowledge ask students to demonstrate their position on theoretical statements and awareness of how all information ties together in an overarching relationship. Whereas questions at the knowledge of principles and generalization level ask students to recall the information as particular bits of information, ideally, questions at this final level of knowledge suggest that students not only know this information at the level of the particular but also voice how it is related to other information.

The knowledge division of the taxonomy has the most divisions. This richness of categories attests to the importance of knowledge in our culture and our belief that the gathering of much information is essential to learning. However, gathering knowledge is not the entire story. Effective teachers—committed to thinking students, active students, questioning students—realize that knowledge only furnishes the grist for intellectual action. Students must raise questions about what the knowledge means, how it can be used, and how it can further their intellectual growth.

Comprehension Questions

Comprehension deals with understanding information in contrast to the knowledge-level where information is only recalled. The importance of this level is revealed by the frequency of our asking, "Do you understand?" While comprehension is often expressed as a goal of education, Bloom uses the term in a somewhat specialized manner "to include those objectives, behaviors, or responses which represent an understanding of the literal message contained in a communication."[9] In this multimedia world, the communication is the conveyance of meaning by means of linguistic and nonlinguistic devices, the written and spoken word, and nonverbal communication.

Comprehension has three major divisions: translation, interpretation, and extrapolation.

EXAMPLES:

Translation

- A student is listing various events under either "Yes" or "No." Specifically, what is this student doing?

  1. engaging in critical thinking
  2. engaging in concept attainment
  3. engaging in creative thinking
  4. engaging in recall

- "Idle hands are the devil's workshop." Explain what this statement means.

- Explain in your own words the following figure:

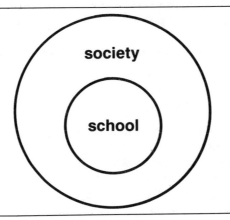

Figure 3–5

Activity

TRY IT

Research notes that we teachers are overly fond of knowledge questions. While this imbalance may need to be corrected, we cannot ignore such questions; indeed they are basic to any inquiry, any thinking we or our students will do. There are numerous types of knowledge questions that should be in our repertoire.

Make an audio tape of one or two classroom discussions. Record the types of knowledge questions you ask. Figure the percentages for these various types of knowledge questions.

The format for recording these questions can resemble the following:

Classroom discussion #_____

Questions Asked   **Knowledge type**

	Term	Spec. F	Con	Tr & Seq.	Clas.	Cri.	Meth. Pri Theories
____	__	__	__	__	__	__	____
____	__	__	__	__	__	__	____
____	__	__	__	__	__	__	____
____	__	__	__	__	__	__	____
____	__	__	__	__	__	__	____

Where do your questions cluster? What reasons can you offer for your question profile? Should you keep these questions in the same proportion? Should you change the proportion? Discuss the results of this self-analysis with a colleague.

Questions aimed at getting students to translate information are designed to serve as a type of bridge from merely possessing knowledge to employing knowledge. These questions ask students to translate or paraphrase a communication from one form to another. Students might repeat in their own words what an author means by his statements. There may be times when students in responding put a communication into more abstract terms.

Interpretation

- Using the above graph, which of the following statements is most likely true:

    1. There has been a greater rise in real income for women than for men.
    2. There has essentially been no change in the actual income of women compared with 1950.
    3. There has been a steady decline in the real income of women compared to men.
    4. There was an initial decline in the income of women until the mid '70's when an actual increase began.

- Compare the ideas presented in the *Nation at Risk* report and the ideas presented in the *Closing of the American Mind* by Alan Bloom.
- Consider the current demands for educational access made by major minorities in this country. Drawing upon the material we have read in class, what are possible conclusions?

Interpretation questions have the reader derive the essential meanings of a communication—to relate different elements of the communication. Basically, these questions direct the student to focus on the central meaning of the material being read or situations being encountered, to go beyond a part-for-part rendering of the communication. The teacher, and for that matter the student, realizes that a question has been successfully processed when the major ideas are identified and comprehended. The student has gone beyond mere repetition.[10]

Extrapolation

- From our discussion of superconductivity, what might be the future benefits of this discovery?
- Look at the data presented on the chart dealing with the expenditures of the State of Washington for basic services and check off those statements likely to be true in ten years.

    1. There will be less money spent on elementary education.
    2. There will be a need for additional monies spent on highways.
    3. There is likely to be a downturn in monies spent for health services.

4. The welfare costs of the state will be doubled.

■ From the maps showing the migration of people, which states should have the largest population in the year 2010?

1. California, Florida, Arizona

2. California, Georgia, Washington

3. California, Oregon, Washington

4. California, Florida, Texas

These extrapolation questions urge students to go beyond a recounting of the basic idea of the material read or situation encountered. Students must consider the consequences of a situation currently reported. Such questions challenge learners to formulate an inference or inferences; to proceed beyond the data presented; to report implications, effects likely to arise given the current situation or interpretations. Students engaged in responding to these questions are asked to think, but the thinking is closely connected to the information presented. It is an extension of material that is quite clear to the student; no need exists to determine what information is required for extension. While these questions elicit valid thinking on the part of students, the thought is still not very abstract.

Application Questions

Application questions raised either by teachers or students trigger utilizing some understanding or techniques to process a problem situation. Sometimes these questions only ask for identifying the principle without demanding that the data or situation actually be processed. These questions, built on a student's understanding, differ from the previous types in that they refer to a situation novel to the student. The question does not ask the student to apply a well known and obvious abstraction. Part of the challenge is for the student to think "What is the appropriate abstraction, rule, heuristic, algorithm, required to solve the problem?"

Application questions can focus on a wide variety of student activities—applying a generalization, a concept or a principle to a particular situation. The question may request student activation of a particular skilled behavior, perhaps engagement of a particular critical thinking skill such as detecting bias.

EXAMPLES:
Application

■ The school district is confronted with building a new school that will accommodate sufficient numbers of students for the next fifty years. Using the maps and the charts, indicate an ideal location for this school. (Need to have some understanding of location theory and the need to apply it. Need also to apply various generalizations about demographics).

- A school classroom has an aquarium that contains 20 gallons of water. Presently it has ten tropical fish in it. The children wish to add more fish.

  How many fish can be added if:

  The aquarium is just left alone as is with no plants?

  The aquarium has five additional plants added?

- Ms. Murphy wishes to paint a room that has four walls, each ten feet high and twelve feet long. How much paint will she need if one gallon will cover 300 square feet?

- Mr. Peterson has a boat. To protect his boat he hangs from its side fenders rubber tube-like structures filled with air. One winter day, in checking his boat he sees that the fenders are depressed in the middle. Explain why.

_____

Analysis Questions

Responding to analysis questions, students diagnose material, situations or environments, separating them into their component parts and focusing on the relationships between those parts and the total organization. These questions direct students to understand more fully the information or situation and to develop that level of understanding essential to thinking about the material more abstractly. Such questions are basic to the enactment of critical thinking skills.

Analysis questions, drawing on Bloom's classification schema, have three parts: analysis of elements, analysis of relationships, and analysis of organization principles.

EXAMPLES:

Analysis of Elements

- In our book, much attention is given to discussing acid rain. Which statements in our book are factual? Which are opinion?

- Arguments for national health insurance are based primarily on the belief that:

  1. such insurance would provide health care treatment
  2. present health care treatment is too expensive
  3. private health care leaves gaps in the coverage
  4. all of the above.

- Our newspaper editorial presents the writer's views on why certain minority students are not doing as well in school as other groups. Which assumption seems specific to this editorial?

    1. Minority students have less ability than mainstream children.
    2. The school is not adjusting its curriculum to address the particular needs of these students.
    3. The families of these students do not furnish the necessary support for school success.
    4. Teachers do not have an understanding of the cultures from which these students come.

_____

A communication—whether written, oral, or graphic—and a situation can be thought of as being comprised of a great many elements, some stated, some implied. The various elements possible in a communication are facts, hypotheses, assumptions, motives, conclusions. Questions dealing with the analysis of elements ask students to process information so that the constituent parts are not only identified but are thought about to uncover relationships.

Many of the critical thinking skills identified in Chapter 1 are drawn into play by analysis of elements questions: distinguishing between verifiable facts and value claims, identifying unstated assumptions, detecting bias, distinguishing relevant from irrelevant information.

EXAMPLES:
_____
Analysis of Relationships

- The above paragraph presents a view on the recycling of waste materials. Which of the following statements supports the general position stated in the paragraph?

    1. There is really no need to recycle.
    2. There is an immediate need to recycle.
    3. Only some things need to be recycled.
    4. Recycling is really not possible until the next century.

- Study the picture showing sheet erosion in the Midwest region. Which of the following was needed in order for this erosion to occur?

    1. land contour
    2. poor crop selection
    3. excessive rain

4. all of the above

___

These questions stress the relationships between various elements recognized.[11] In a written communication, the stress is on interrelationships among ideas or major points. Has the writer been consistent in his point of view? How organized are the author's arguments? Are his arguments in line with his major premise? The first example requires the students to interpret the material at hand to determine the relationships of the elements of the statement to the general thrust of the statement. The second asks students to identify the key elements and their relationship to each other and to the over-all fact that erosion had occurred.

These questions require students to activate thinking skills such as determining the strength of an argument or claim or identifying ambiguous claims or arguments. All questions at the analysis level deal with what Beyer identifies as the micro-thinking skill of analysis.[12]

EXAMPLES:
Analysis of Organizational Principles

- From listening to the senator's speech, which of the following statements best describes it?

    1. It was a plea for giving others a chance to voice their opinions.

    2. It argued that dissent without reason is the greatest danger to our country.

    3. It made a case for treating dissent in historical perspective.

    4. It called for an overall strengthening of law agencies.

- Listen to the new symphony. How has the composer developed the piece to give the feeling of contemporary confusion?

___

Questions at the upper level of analysis are the most complex and difficult, asking students to analyze the structure and organization of a communication or of an event.[13] With regard to written material, students deal with the communication as a whole, centering on the interrelationships among ideas to determine which particulars are relevant to particular conclusions or judgments. They identify the main thesis of the written communication and recognize essential facts or assumptions. Students also attend to cause and effect relationships. These questions also can request students to identify logical fallacies in arguments. Questions at this level of analysis refer heavily to the major critical thinking skills noted in Chapter 1: distinguishing between verifiable facts and value claims, identifying logical fallacies, recognizing logical inconsistencies in a line of reasoning, determining the strength of an argument or claim.

Synthesis Questions

In contrast to analysis questions that ask students to break wholes into parts, synthesis questions, require students to put information obtained or considered at lower levels of learning into some new pattern or structure, new at least to the students. Bloom mentions that the emphasis is upon uniqueness and originality. "In synthesis . . . the student must draw upon elements from many sources and put these together into a structure or pattern not clearly there before."[14]

At this level, the student is challenged to combine information obtained from his or her inquiry and to produce a product—either a statement, a plan, or some general principle. In processing synthesis questions students draw on the lower levels of cognitive functioning. They must analyze situations, apply special skills, reflect on their understandings, and draw upon various aspects of knowledge.

Bloom has divided synthesis into three levels or subcategories, distinguished primarily on the basis of the type of product expected: *production of a unique communication, production of a plan or proposed set of operations,* and *derivation of a set of abstract relations.*[15]

EXAMPLES:

Production of a Unique Communication

- Write a paper expressing why all people should be given an equal chance to succeed in life.
- Write a paper defending the need for conservation.
- Think of a funny time in your life. Make up a story about it and tell what this period taught you.

These questions ask the student to create a communication uniquely his or hers and that presents certain ideas, experiences, and feelings. Students are to engage in creative thinking. While the resulting product need not demonstrate pure creativity, the students' individual thinking and personality should be evident. No precise prescriptions exist as to what the communications must look like. The student is free to generate his or her own. These ques-

REFLECTION

Comprehension questions, application questions, analysis questions are all essential for critical mindedness. Accepting this, such questions should be rather common in our classroom talk. However, research on classroom talk suggests that we are far off our mark.

Reflect on your classroom talk—your talk and your students' talk. Do you allow students to respond to and, perhaps more importantly, generate questions at these levels? Most of us tend to say, "Yes," but we may be fooling ourselves. Processing such questions takes some time.

Record your classroom talk in a particular content area and categorize the questions you ask, the questions your students ask. How many questions at each level are there? Do the same for another content area. Do you get a similar question profile?

Chat with a colleague about these three levels of questions and how they, especially analysis questions, are integral to critical thinking. You may want to arrange for peer coaching to increase the number of questions at these levels.

It is useful to get a reading of your questions at various points during the year; that way you can see if you are improving the questioning atmosphere in your classroom or, if it is already good, if you are maintaining it.

tions should be raised in all areas of the curriculum. It is likely that such questions will be raised in literature and creative writing classes.

EXAMPLES:

Production of A Plan or Proposed Set of Operations

- Each year hundreds of thousands of acres of good agricultural land are taken from agricultural production and used for building sites. Create a plan that would reverse this trend.

- Make a proposal that would increase the community support of public education.

- Create a proof for the following equation using what information you know about the binary system of numbers.

- Develop a procedure for making sea water into fresh water.

These questions differ from the first level of synthesis in that they focus the student's attention on a particular type of product: a plan or a proposed set of operations; the student's job is complete when the plan or proposal is created.

In a classroom where the thinking strategy of problem solving is emphasized, the teacher would raise such synthesis questions, especially at the problem solving step, and devise or choose a solution or plan.

<u>*EXAMPLES:*</u>

Derivation of a Set of Abstract Relations

- Consider how people use language in school and in the outside community. What general statement would explain the role of language in society?

- People are often unwilling to change their behavior even when they recognize that adjustment will be beneficial to them in the future. Develop a hypothesis that would serve to guide your study of this human behavior.

- Often people who work and play together have a tendency to make poor group judgments. Study the material on the actions of several groups and formulate a theoretical statement explaining such group action.

Questions formulated to get students to respond at this final level of synthesis, invite them to create or derive some type of statement or conclusion to explain or classify information from data or situations. Students are asked either to take data or phenomena and to either classify or explain them or to draw upon some basic propositions or conclusions and to deduce other propositions.[16] The questions are appropriate in several thinking strategies—in analyzing alternatives, which is part of decision making and engaging in the final step of conceptualizing, modifying concept attributes and structure.

Synthesis questions are essential to both teacher and student talk, for these questions foster active participation. Students must come up with their personal expressions; they must reflect and then produce.

Evaluation Questions

Evaluation is a process or cluster of processes that enables people to decide whether to accept, change, or eliminate something. In evaluation, people—in our case, students—concentrate on the relative values of whatever they are judging, obtaining information that they can employ to make statements of worth regarding the focus of the evaluation.[17]

Bloom states essentially the same thing: evaluation is "the making of judgments about the value, for some purpose, of ideas, works, solutions, methods, materials, and so forth. It involves the use of criteria as well as standards for appraising the extent to which particulars are accurate, effective, economical, or satisfying."[18]

If students are to enact the various thinking strategies noted in Chapter 1, such questions must be posed. The final state of problem solving is evaluate the solution; stages four, five and six in decision making (rank alternatives, judge highest ranked alternatives, and choose best alternatives), and stage six of conceptualizing, (modifying concept attributes/structure) all require evaluation questions. The critical thinking skills primarily evoke evaluation. To distinguish between verifiable facts and value claims requires evaluation questions. Such questions are used when determining the credibility of a source, identifying logical fallacies, or assessing the strength of an argument or claim. As mentioned in Chapter 1, critical thinking is primarily analysis and evaluation.

EXAMPLES:

Judgments in Terms of Internal Evidence

- Distinguish between the following statements those that are fact and those that are value claims:

  Boston is located in Massachusetts.

  No city should be allowed to grow larger than one million people.

  A strong central government assures all people of their rights.

  The Constitution was signed on Sept. 17, 1787.

- Consider the argument that the author gives for an extended school year. Has he used effective logic in making his case?

These questions require the student to analyze data or conclusions from standpoints such as logical accuracy, consistency, and other internal criteria. Students responding to or creating their own questions at this level are dealing with judging, appraising, or valuing.

EXAMPLES:

Evaluation in Terms of External Criteria

- Drawing on the criteria for a good question, how would you rank the questions you used in your research activity?
- Indicate why *Tom Sawyer* is classic literature?

■ The following statements are drawn from the position paper on world co-operation. Indicate which are significant to the argument presented.

Questions addressing this second level of evaluation focus primarily on having the student apply known criteria to judge various situations, conclusions, or documents he or she encounters or develops. To judge the quality of a painting, the student can apply criteria developed by a noted group of artists. If asked to judge why some piece of literature is a classic, the student can utilize criteria articulated by scholars of literature. Requested to determine the significance of various statements, a student can employ criteria drawn from logic.

Ideally, students encouraged and guided to be effective thinkers are aware of the necessity to apply criteria in making evaluation judgments; in judging the effectiveness of theories, or concepts, of various processes, or of particular solutions advanced. Critical thinking requires that criteria be brought to bear on all information encountered in school and out of school. While evaluation may be classified as a microthinking skill, it is indeed major in directing students in determining the worth of all that they do and encounter. Evaluation serves as the gate keeper in the academic game of questioning and thinking.

AFFECTIVE DOMAIN QUESTIONS

"What do you think of that?" In responding to such a question, we attempt to generate some answer that results from a cognitive processing of particular data. However, we also all react with some type of emotional response—a drawing to or a pulling away from the focus of the question. This is depicted in the indepth structuring model presented on page 53 dealing with the emotions. Actually, we cannot separate our values and emotions from our knowledge acquisition and thinking. While we all are more familiar with knowledge and thinking, the cognitive domain, we cannot ignore our values and emotions, the affective domain.

In Chapter 1, metacognition was discussed stressing that a crucial goal of the school was to get students to gain executive control over their processing of information. Equally important is the executive control we gain over our affective domain. We need to realize that there will be no cognition if we are unwilling to attend, to receive information or to respond to situations. This is the first stage of the affective domain. In striving to become autonomous learners, students must become skilled in the control of their attention.[19] They must become competent in generating feelings such that they feel positive about themselves and their learning. Being aware of one's feelings and

Activity

EVALUATE

Synthesis and evaluation questions are crucial to the critical processing of information. Contemplate the questioning in your classroom, then generate some general statements about it. Evaluate your conclusion drawing on both internal and external criteria regarding good classroom questions.

Share your evaluation with a colleague. If you have a peer coach with whom you feel comfortable, ask him or her to evaluate the questioning dynamic in your classroom.

Evaluating your own questions is not just a one-time activity. Get into the posture of conducting such statement making and evaluation at specified times during the school year. Are you getting better? Staying the same?

---

capable of controlling them to some degree rank as essential. In some ways, it supercedes having control over one's thought processes. The student who feels good is well on his or her way to becoming a good student, a fully functioning individual.

Questions in the Affective Domain

While various ways exist to classify levels of values and emotions, Krathwohl's taxonomy of educational objectives, handbook II dealing with the affective domain, is perhaps the most well known and most useful. The taxonomy identifies five major stages of the domain, each subsuming the lower levels.

Following is a brief overview of the various levels of the affective domain of the taxonomy of educational objectives.

As with the cognitive domain, we can get some assistance in forming these questions by considering key works and phases. Figure 3–6 lists these.

Questions at Various Affective Levels

Questions at the Receiving (attending) Level

"First, you must get their attention." These are familiar words. Even students realize that for them to do any learning, they first must attend to whatever it is they wish to learn. The first level of the affective domain, then, is receiving. Receiving has three subdivisions: *awareness, willingness to receive,* and *controlled or selected attention.*

Receiving (Attending)

At this level the learner is sensitized to the existence of certain phenomena and stimuli; he or she is made willing to receive or attend to them. This is the first and crucial step if the student is to be properly oriented to learn what the teacher has planned.

Receiving has three subsections.

AWARENESS. Awareness is almost a cognitive behavior. But unlike knowledge, the first level of the cognitive domain, the concern is not really with memory or the ability to recall, but that given the appropriate opportunity, the learner merely will be conscious of something and will attend to a situation, phenomenon, object, or stage of affairs.

WILLINGNESS TO RECEIVE. This second stage centers on getting the individual willing to notice a given stimulus, not to avoid it. Will he willingly react to data, situations presented in learning situations?

CONTROLLED OR SELECTED ATTENTION. The third level of receiving is concerned with the differentation of a given stimulus into figure and ground at a conscious or perhaps semiconscious level. This level specifically is asking the student to regulate his perception and to "shut" out distracting stimuli.

Responding

The concern at this level goes beyond merely attending to the phenomenon. At this stage, the teacher desires the child to become involved sufficiently in his work so that he will continue it minus guidance and formal class structure. This level also has three subdivisions.

ACQUIESCENCE IN RESPONDING. At this stage the teacher wants students to comply with a particular situation. This suggests encouraging a certain degree of student passivity so far as the initiation of the behavior is concerned. Compliance might be a better term, for there is more of the element of reaction to a suggestion and less of the implication of resistance or yielding unwillingly.

WILLINGNESS TO RESPOND. The capacity for voluntary activity is the key here. There is the implication that the learner is sufficiently committed to exhibiting the behavior not just because of a fear of punishment, but "on his own" or voluntarily.

SATISFACTION IN RESPONSE. This third stage gets at the feeling the student attains from responding to a question, a situation, or some type of material. It refers to reaction that causes a feeling of satisfaction, an emotional response, generally of pleasure or enjoyment.

Valuing

This third level refers to a thing, phenomenon, or behavior that has worth. The main thrust here is to get the individual to value so that his or her resulting behavior is sufficiently consistent and stable to have the characteristics of a belief or an attitude.

Figure 3–6

Affective Domain of the Taxonomy of Educational Objectives[20]

An important aspect of behavior characterized by valuing is that it is motivated not by the desire to comply or obey, but by the individual's commitment to the underlying value.

ACCEPTANCE OF A VALUE. At this level, we are concerned with ascribing worth to a phenomenon, behavior, object, etc. The term "belief" adequately describes what may be thought of as the dominant characteristic here.

One of the distinguishing characteristics of this behavior is consistency of response to the class of objectives, phenomena, etc., with which the belief or attitude is identified.

PREFERENCE FOR A VALUE. Behavior at this level implies not just the acceptance of a value to the point of being willing to be identified with it, but that the individual is sufficiently committed to the value to pursue it, to seek it out, to desire it.

COMMITMENT. Belief at this level involves a high degree of surety; it suggests conviction. In some instances it may border on faith, in the sense of it being a firm emotional acceptance of a belief upon admittedly nonrational grounds.

The person displaying such behavior is clearly perceived as possessing the value in that he acts to further the thing valued in some way, to extend the possibility of his developing it, and to deepen his involvement with it and with the things representing it. He attempts to convince others and to convert them to his cause.

Organization

As an individual successively internalizes values, she encounters situations in which she must (a) organize the values into a system, (b) determine the interrelationship among them, and (c) establish the dominant and pervasive ones. Such a system is built gradually, subject to adjustment as new values are incorporated.

CONCEPTUALIZATION OF A VALUE. This first subcategory allows the individual to create an abstraction or abstractions relating to the values she possesses. Here the individual functions at the level of conceptualization. She is attempting to clarify values identified and found useful into some manageable system.

ORGANIZATION OF A VALUE SYSTEM. Objectives properly classifed here are those which require the learner to synthesize a complex of values, possibly disparate ones, and to organize them into an ordered relationship with one another. Here the student is attempting to take identified values and incorporate them into a system for regulating further reactions and actions.

Characterization by a Value
or Value Complex

At this level of internalization the values already exist in the individual's value hierarchy and they are organized into some kind of internally consistent system.

Figure 3–6
Continued

The individual already has utilized values to regulate his behavior, and he functions quite calmly with these values unless his values are challenged or he is threatened for his views. This level has two substages.

GENERALIZED SET. This level gives an internal consistency to the system of attitudes and values that the individual has synthesized. It enables the person to respond selectively at a very high level. It is sometimes spoken of as a determining tendency, an orientation toward phenomena, or a predisposition to act in a certain way. The generalized set may be considered closely related to the idea of an attitude cluster, where the commonality is based on behavioral characteristics rather than the subject or object of the attitude. A generalized set allows the individual to simplify and order the complex world about him and to act consistently and effectively in it.

CHARACTERIZATION. This final level is the zenith of the internalization process and includes broad objectives relating to the phenomena covered and to the range of behavior comprised. Here we find those objectives which concern a person's view of the universe or philosophy of life. The objectives at this level are so encompassing that they tend to characterize the individual almost completely.

Before considering question examples you may find it useful to compare the levels of the affective domain with those of the cognitive domain.

Figure 3–6
Continued

EXAMPLES:

Awareness

- Please write what comes to mind when you hear the following names?

    Michael Jackson

    The Who

    The Grateful Dead

    Whitney Houston

- Fill in the missing blanks for the situation.

Situation	*Country*
The leading Asian industrial power	_____
The oldest republic in the world	_____
Gave us common law	_____

While these questions resemble very closely knowledge-level questions they differ in that they are not so much concerned with whether the student

Characterization
Are you willing
Are you confident
Explain how
Will you engage
Is that just
What did you do
Is that your philosophy
Indicate those

Organization
Have you judged
Does the statement imply
Have you weighed alternatives
Please explain

Do you agree
As you view
In your opinion

Valuing
Do you like
Do you participate
List which
Defend
Are you loyal to
Do you accept
Do you agree
Identify those
Rank order
Should the

Responding
Are you willing
Do you observe
Do you do
Do you practice
Are you interested in
Will you accept
Does it feel pleasant
Are you satisfied
Do you like
Indicate which

Receiving
Are you aware
Have you heard
Will you accept
Do you know
Do you prefer
Indicate whether
Do you appreciate
Do you recognize
Have you ever
Would you like
Are you interested

Figure 3–7
Key Words and Phrases for Affective Questions

can recall the information requested as to whether the student is merely conscious of something, that when given the opportunity the student will be willing to attend to some situation, some phenomenon, or object.

EXAMPLES:

Willingness to Receive

- Of the following five activities, which would you prefer to do first?
- If you had a free afternoon, which of the following activities might you do?

    Play ball
    Take a nap
    Visit a museum
    Go boating
    Read a book

- The following items present various activities that a person can do. After each item place an "A" if you really would like to do the activity; a "B" if you do not care one way or the other; or a "C" if you would really not like to do the activity.

    Go swimming in a swimming pool
    Join a mountain climbing club
    Belong to a book club
    Take dancing lessons

Questions at this second subcategory of receiving aim at determining if the student has a preference for and is willing to commit attention to the topic, task, or activity at hand. Will the student pay attention, or will he or she ignore the question and the topic to which it refers? Essentially, these questions ask if students will sit still to receive a given stimulus.

EXAMPLES:

Controlled or Selected Attention

- Are you keeping a list of things you wish to investigate?
- Would you like to engage in an independent investigation?
- Underline those activities that you like or would want to do?

    To attend lectures given by scholars in the field
    To have the opportunity to debate various positions on nuclear power

_____ To have a chance to determine my own curriculum

These questions place students in a type of forced-choice situation—either they would or would not be willing to attend. Students must express their preferences; they must indicate their willingness to attend consciously to various phenomena. These questions suggest to students that they can have some degree of control of their attention. Realizing this, students can work to improve their thinking and questioning; they can map out particular strategies to facilitate increased attention.

Questions at the Responding Level

In contrast to the first affective level, questions at the responding level direct students to go beyond merely attending to actually engaging in learning, in answering the questions. Students are on their way to becoming active students by doing something with the information. Like the previous major category, responding has three subdivisions: *acquiescence in responding*, *willingness to respond*, and *satisfaction in a response*.

EXAMPLES:
Acquiescence in Responding

- In responding to the following statements put a mark in Column 1 if you perform the activity on your own initiative, a mark in Column 2 if you do the activity but only with outside encouragement, and a mark in Column 3 if you do not engage in the activity.

	Column 1	*Column 2*	*Column 3*
Read fiction	_____	_____	_____
Go to ballet performances	_____	_____	_____
Attend special lectures at school	_____	_____	_____
Do your homework	_____	_____	_____

- Of the following two situations, in which would you rather be involved?

  Collecting money for a school fund drive

_____ Presenting a play for the school at a fund raiser

Questions at this level determine a student's willingness to respond to some stimulus, some situation, even though he or she might not seek it initially. Such questions seek to identify those concerns and areas of learning that the learner will at least tolerate, to which he or she would be willing to comply.

EXAMPLES:

Willingness to Respond

- In this next section of the unit, select from among the five major activities the one on which you wish to work.
- With regard to the following statements put a plus if you would do the following activities, a minus if you would not and a question mark if you are not sure.

    _____ Engage in discussion with friends about current issues

    _____ Do an independent study on a history topic

    _____ Question the teacher as to the accuracy of material

    _____ Defend your rights with fighting if necessary

These questions ask the learner to indicate if he or she is sufficiently motivated to action or reaction. Would the individual do some particular action voluntarily? While quite similar to the previous level of questions, these questions differ in that the asker is not attempting to put any pressure on the student, only to determine the student's stance—just what will the student do given free choice in the matter.

Teachers, skilled in asking these questions and knowledgeable about affective questions in general, realize that raising such questions can obtain from students a verbal indication of their willingness to respond, but whether the student actually does respond cannot be determined from listening or reading a response. The actual willingness to respond and deal with information in particular ways can only be determined through observation of interaction with a particular situation, content, or other individual. It is the behavior of an individual over time that really is the proof of the pudding.

EXAMPLES:

Satisfaction in a Response

- In reading a novel, indicate with 1 those aspects that really appeal to you,

2 for those aspects that have minimal appeal, and 3 those aspects that elicit negative reactions.

_____ Having exciting characters

_____ Having a high degree of suspense

_____ Having a carefully developed plot

_____ Having a great deal of dialogue

_____ Having characters with whom I can identify.

■ When observing a painting, indicate with "Yes" those aspects of the painting that have a great appeal to you, indicate with "No" those qualities that cause you to dislike a painting, and indicate with "Neither" those aspects that really don't elicit any reaction.

_____ The use of bright colors

_____ The use of abstractions

_____ The use of subdued colors

_____ The use of human form

_____ Stress on landscape

Questions dealing with satisfaction in a response are raised to ascertain whether in fact a student obtains some level of enjoyment from responding to or dealing with certain content areas, specific topics, or situations. Such questions essentially aim at having students articulate two aspects of indepth processing—the voicing of the emotions elicited by the thinking about information or a situation and a verbalization of their actual physical feeling. All questions at the responding level strive to get students to focus on and articulate their reactions to the leaning world. However, these questions are not designed to get students to articulate why they respond as they do. Such reflection is called forth by questions higher on the affective taxonomy scale.

Questions at the Valuing Level

Questions at this level are raised to determine if individuals accept a value or have a preference for it or a commitment to it. They are posed to elicit from students an awareness of how they judge the work of things, phenomena, and behavior, drawing on both internal and external criteria. These questions center on the markers that enable the student to employ his or her own criterion of worth.[21]

The valuing level of the taxonomy has three subdivisions: *acceptance of a value, preference for a value,* and *commitment to a value.*

Acceptance of a Value

- Decide what your reaction is to the following statements. If you agree, place A in the space; if you disagree place D.

    _____ Extra monies should be provided for students from minorities so that they are more likely to succeed in life.

    _____ Equal monies should be provided for both boys' and girls' sports in the schools.

    _____ Students who cannot affort to go to college should be furnished with free grants.

    _____ People who earn over a million dollars should be taxed at the rate of 80 percent.

- As a result of reading the novel, explain your reaction to the major lesson presented.

Questions at this level center on getting students to really place worth on some phenomenon, behavior, event, or object. Beliefs are being asked for. Krathwohl defines belief as "the emotional acceptance of a proposition or doctrine upon what one implicitly considers adequate ground."[22] When raised either by teachers or students these questions are posed to determine if one has consistency of response to a class of objects, phenomena, or people with which the belief or attitude is identified.[23]

Preference for a Value

- When you hear or read a conclusion presented by an authority do you:

    _____ Accept the conclusion with little thought

    _____ Look for ways in which the conclusion falls short of explaining all situations

    _____ Reject it outright unless it agrees with your own prior view

- Which person would you most wish to be like?

    President Bush

    Jim Wright

    Pope John Paul II

    Queen Elizabeth II

- Read the following paragraph about the place of women in the religious life. Indicate your reactions to the information by checking one of the following statements.

(paragraph given to students to read)

_____ This statement expresses my views.

_____ This statement states the opposite of my views.

_____ I am uncertain as to where I stand on this issue.

Questions at this level of valuing are raised to push just a bit on students or have students push themselves to go beyond just identifying their values. Students are urged to indicate openly their preference regarding values and to make efforts to attain the behavior couched in the identified value.

EXAMPLES:

Commitment

- Identify any "helping others" behaviors you have engaged in at least three times in the past week.
- Describe briefly how you have been a "responsible citizen" this past month.
- Indicate your response to the following activities:

  1. If you engage in the activity frequently (more than once a month)
  2. If you seldom participated in the activity

     _____ Read papers in which you disagree with the editorial policy
     _____ Listen to speakers or to other persons with whom you basically disagree
     _____ Develop a position on issues after reading as much information as is possible

- Should the press be allowed to publish criticism of an elected government official? Give the reasons for your response.

Questions at this level seek to determine whether students hold a firm emotional acceptance of a belief, a position, or a mode of operation. Often such questions seek to determine if students actually engage in activities that indicate their holding a particular value or value set. These questions attempt to uncover whether a student values something to the degree that its worth is attended to over a period of time. What is the level of drive and perseverance evidenced by the student's response? What proof is there that the student does indeed value?

Question at the Organizational Level

Values do not exist in isolation; students cannot process a value excluding it from other values held. Questions that address a value held by students essentially lead students to realize that the value being questioned exists and their response to it exists within a context. This being the case, it becomes necessary for the student first, to organize the values into a system; second, to determine the interrelationships among them; and third, to rank order them in light of their importance.[24]

Questions at the organizational level address the student's creation and articulation of a value system. Organization has two levels: *conceptualization of a value* and *organization of a value system.*

EXAMPLES:

Conceptualization of A Value

- Of the several characters in the story which ones possess basic assumptions similar to those that you hold regarding the democratic way of life?
- The following statements are expressions of opinion about which there is current controversy. Indicate your reactions (agree A, disagree D) to these statements.

    _____ The political beliefs of a candidate for the Supreme Court should be a key consideration in approving the nomination.

    _____ Freedom of choice is more important than the rights of the unborn in the abortion issue.

    _____ In deciding on the constitutionality of a law, the Court should hold paramount the rights of the individual over that of the group.

Questions at this first sublevel, conceptualization of a value, really demand that students identify and classify concepts, especially normative concepts. In some instances, the students will actually name the value, the normative concept, that is directing their response. Of course, the conceptualization may not always be verbal. In an art class, the conceptualization may be expressed in terms of composition of the painting. Questions at this stage meld both the cognitive and the affective, bringing together the indepth processing divisions of mental picture, linguistic information, and emotions. Students functioning at this level have to engage in thinking, specifically analyzing and synthesizing information. It is through analysis that students isolate the properties of the particular normative concept in question and through generalization bring the concept into relationship with the particular context in question.

EXAMPLES:

Organization of a Value System

- In observing the painting "The Night Watch" by Rembrandt, would your reaction to it be most characterized by

  1. An admiration of the technique
  2. A check for accuracy regarding the interpretation of the particular period in history
  3. A feeling of awe at the magnificence of humankind
  4. A reaction as to its wealth on the current market

- When listening to the song "America," which option best explains your reaction?

  1. A feeling of pride
  2. A feeling of responsibility
  3. A feeling of humility
  4. A feeling of thanksgiving

- The statement below is followed by particular views that one can hold. List these views in an order in which the most important is listed first, the least important last.

  People who have achieved financial success have certain obligations.

  1. They have obligations to themselves for their own happiness.
  2. They have an obligation to those who are less fortunate.
  3. They have a primary obligation only to members of their families.
  4. They have a minimal obligation to their country.

Questions asking students to engage in organization of a value system reflect a close relationship with questions that deal with analysis of organizational principles. These questions tie most closely to the thinking strategy of conceptualization noted in Chapter 1, especially step four, interrelate categories of attributes. Students in responding to these questions must bring together various values meaningfully linked to form a higher order relationship. At times, this arranging of concepts into a value cluster results in more than an existing context of values; in some instances, students responding to such questions actually synthesize a new value or value complex.[25] When this happens, the student is at step six of conceptualization, modifying conceptual attributes/structure.

Questions at the Level of Characterization by a Value or Value Complex

The major goal of raising questions in the affective realm is that individuals will, through guidance, attain a level of thinking and behaving that demonstrates an effective incorporation of affective understandings and skills into a personalized philosophy—into acceptance of particular values and the responsibility to live by them—a type of personalized credo to principles and ideals.

Students responding to such questions through both words and deeds draw upon values organized at the previous affective level. In viewing the student, the teacher and others begin to see that the student is acting in a particular way such that the individual's behavior can be described and the individual can be characterized as possessing particular beliefs, ideas, and attitudes; in short, adhering to a particular philosophy.

While such questions will be asked in the school classroom, we teachers need to realize that this level will not be attained to any great deal in the school.

> Realistically, formal education generally cannot reach this level, at least in our society. In all open and pluralistic societies ... the maturity and personal integration required at this level are not attained until at least some years after the individual has completed his formal education. Time and experience must interact with affective and cognitive learnings before the individual can answer the crucial questions, "Who am I?" and "What do I stand for?"[26]

This final level of the affective domain has two subdivisions: *generalized set* and *characterization.*

EXAMPLES:

Generalized Set

- People are collecting money and supplies for victims of a natural disaster that occurred in your state. Consider what you will do to help these people.

- You are walking through a park and see a larger boy picking on a smaller boy. Which of the following would you do?

_____ 1. Tell the larger boy to behave

_____ 2. Ignore the situation

_____ 3. Assuming you are bigger, begin to pick on the larger boy

_____ 4. Help the smaller boy fight back

Questions at this level focus on whether students have internal consistency with their system of attitudes and values at any particular moment. Queries are raised to ascertain the students' orientation and the consistency of those orientations toward some phenomena. Inquiries are phrased to isolate a person's predispositions to act in particular ways. These questions strive to determine what philosophy a student has in place. Ideally, students can ask themselves these questions to gain an awareness of their philosophies of life. While these questions do not allow students to reach final closure on their views of life, they do assist students in their decision making, especially when they are to choose best alternatives, the final step in the thinking strategy of decision making.

EXAMPLES:

Characterization

- Which of the following statements indicate basically what you believe to be the primary purpose of your life?

  _____ Relating to your family

  _____ Knowing your God

  _____ Being able to obtain happiness

  _____ Gaining a position of power

  _____ Being able to change with the times

- Which of the following beliefs would you say has the greatest power over your actions and thoughts?

Questions at the affective level of characterization address the zenith of the affective domain, that point of the internalization process in which all values and value stances, as well as emotional reactions, are organized into varied systems that enable the individual to function effectively in different situations. The characterization level is where the individual defines his philosophical orientation to life and responds according. An individual's responses to questions at this level are so broad that they tend to reveal the overall essence of the individual. The individual is characterized by what he or she

---

TRY IT

Get a reading on your affective questioning in your classroom. Record a classroom dialogue and determine how many of the questions deal with the affective domain. Most likely, you will find few affective questions. Of the few that you do record, what is their level?

Map out a strategic plan to increase the numbers of your affective questions. Monitor your questions over a two-week period to assess your success with them.

---

says and does, and how he or she feels towards his or her world. Responding to these questions, students and we only get an indication of the type of person he or she is at that point in time. There is no way to obtain a precise quantification of who this person is. All students are in a process of becoming; therefore, there is always the need for us and our students to recognize the incompleteness of one's values, attitudes, perceptions, and even one's knowledge at any particular point in time.

CONCLUSION

This chapter has presented numerous examples of both cognitive and affective questions. Awareness of these types and skill in formulating such questions serve both teacher and student well. Working with both cognitive and affective questions requires from us and our students careful observation and analysis of our questions and those of others so that we realize the impact of various types of questions and recognize those situations when certain types of questions will assist us in achieving desired goals.

We need to keep in mind that the cognitive domain deals with knowledge, understanding and the processing of information in ways that allow one to be active, competent, and reflective. The affective domain deals with emotions, interests, values, attitudes, and appreciations. While the questions have been discussed separately as members of two distinct domains, in the reality of the classroom both types will be asked together and many questions will have both cognitive and affective aspects. We cannot help but *think* about how we *feel*; likewise, we cannot escape *feeling* about *what* we think.

Questions classified according to the cognitive and affective domains are questions grouped as to their desired function. However useful such a classification scheme is, we need to realize that other classification schemes exist, specifically classifications as to question focus and question syntax. In the next chapter, these classifications will be presented.

REFLECTION AND ACTION

Reflect on how you encourage students to raise affective questions. If you do not, plot a way to encourage such questions.

Discuss with your students the importance of contemplating the affective realm of their learning. Directly teach students that they can raise various types of affective questions that will assist them in controlling their emotional and valuative responses to learning.

Schedule times for students to share how they are employing affective questions.

NOTES

1. Robert J. Marzano and Daisy E. Arredondo, *Tactics for Thinking* (Alexandria, Va.: Association for Supervision and Curriculum Development, Midcontinent Regional Educational Laboratory (Aurora, Col.: 1986).

2. Robert J. Marzano and Daisy E. Arredondo, *Tactics for Thinking.*

3. Robert J. Marzano and Daisy E. Arredondo, *Tactics for Thinking.*

4. C. Chen and S. Schweizer, *On-line Bibliographic Searching* (New York: Schuman, 1981).

5. E. E. Horne, "Questioning Generation and Formulation," *Journal of the American Society for Information Science* 34 (1): 5–15.

6. Benjamin S. Bloom, ed., *Taxonomy of Educational Objectives* (New York: David McKay, 1956).

7. T. C. Barrett, *Taxonomy of Reading Comprehension,* in R. Smith and T. C. Barrett, eds., *Teaching Reading in the Middle Grades* (Reading, Mass.: Addison-Wesley, 1976).

8. Benjamin S. Bloom, *Taxonomy of Educational Objectives.*

9. Benjamin S. Bloom, *Taxonomy of Educational Objectives,* p. 89.

10. Benjamin S. Bloom, *Taxonomy of Educational Objectives.*

11. Benjamin S. Bloom, *Taxonomy of Educational Objectives.*

12. Barry K. Beyer, *Practical Strategies for the Teaching of Thinking* (Boston: Allyn and Bacon, 1987).

13. Benjamin S. Bloom, *Taxonomy of Educational Objectives.*

14. Benjamin S. Bloom, *Taxonomy of Educational Objectives,* p. 162.

15. Benjamin S. Bloom, *Taxonomy of Educational Objectives.*

16. Benjamin S. Bloom, *Taxonomy of Educational Objectives.*

17. Allan C. Ornstein and Francis P. Hunkins, *Curriculum: Foundations, Principles, and Issues* (Englewood Cliffs, N.J.: Prentice Hall, 1988).

18. Benjamin S. Bloom, *Taxonomy of Educational Objectives,* p. 185.

19. Patricia M. Miller, "Metacognition and Attention," in D. L. Forrest-Pressley and G. E. MacKinnon, and T. Gary Waller, *Metacognition, Cognition, and Human Performance* (Orlando, Fla.: Academic Press, 1985).

20. David Krathwohl, *Taxonomy of Educational Objectives, Affective Domain* (New York: David McKay, 1964).

21. David Krathwohl, *Taxonomy of Educational Objectives.*

22. David Krathwohl, *Taxonomy of Educational Objectives,* p. 140.

23. David Krathwohl, *Taxonomy of Educational Objectives.*

24. David Krathwohl, *Taxonomy of Educational Objectives.*

25. David Krathwohl, *Taxonomy of Educational Objectives.*

26. David Krathwohl, *Taxonomy of Educational Objectives,* p. 165.

4

Question Types

as to Focus

and Syntax

Not diminishing the significance of the cognitive and affective classifications, questions can also be coded by the focus they command students to take and by the response demanded by their wording. This chapter discusses question types according to both focus and syntax. It is important to remember, however, that while we can classify questions as to focus and syntax, in the reality of question raising and answering, there is much overlap with cognitive and affective dimensions. For instance, questions serving a convergent focus function can also elicit certain types of affective and cognitive responses. Likewise, questions classified by syntax also trigger in students affective and cognitive responses. An educative question ferrets from the student, the respondent, a total response—an involvement of his or her total being. Considering question types as to focus and syntax gives us knowledge that will make more manageable our and our students' planning of questions and questioning strategies. The more numerous our classification of questions, the richer our understanding; the more likely it will be that our questions will become central in the learning process.

QUESTIONS AS TO FOCUS

Questions have the power to center a respondent's attention, to focus it. The question becomes a type by the nature of the focus it elicits in this person. One typing of focus is drawn from J. P. Guilford's model of the intellect.

Structure of Intellect

Guilford generated a construct that depicted the intellect or mental operations. It comprises:

1. Operations: mental operations dealing with the processes of certain content
    A. Evaluation (making assessments or decisions)
    B. Convergent thinking (creating relationships and analogies)
    C. Divergent thinking (creative thinking, elaborative thinking)
    D. Memory (recalling knowledge)
    E. Cognition (knowledge)

2. Products: mental operations related to the application of operations to content
    A. Units (figural, symbolic, and semantic data)
    B. Classes (categories of units)
    C. Relationships (connection between items)
    D. Systems (related bodies of knowledge)
    E. Transformations (constructed changes in pre-existing data)
    F. Implications (perceived association of previously unrelated items)

3. Contents: mental operations confined to information and comprehension
    A. Figural (material perceived by the senses)
    B. Symbolic (letters and digits organized in a general system)
    C. Semantic (a form of ideas or verbal meanings)
    D. Behavioral content (social intelligence or understanding of oneself and others)[1]

These dimensions of the structure of intellect Guilford displayed graphically in a 5 by 6 by 4 geometric model. Combining all of these dimensions presents us with 120 cells of what Guilford identified as distinct mental abilities. Presently, there are more than one hundred abilities recognized.

While Guilford's model is highly abstract, it does point out to us that questions aimed at stimulating the intellect can indeed elicit most complicated responses, many of which we and even the respondent can only vaguely recognize. But, Guilford's model allows us to classify questions as to operations—as to focus.

The two operations that give the greatest support to considering operations as essentially focus categories are convergent thinking and divergent thinking. For convergent thinking we phrase questions to direct the respondent's attention to some particular dimension of information. Convergent questions can be at any cognitive or affective level. For instance, the teacher can pose a question requesting that students converge on a specific fact. Such a question can demand attention at the analysis level, eliciting from students one or a few answers. Likewise, the teacher might ask students to furnish the one best interpretation of a particular reading. This question, at the comprehension level, serves to direct the student's attention.

Just as questions at any cognitive or affective level can serve to encourage or demand convergence of thought, questions can also be worded to focus students' attention to many situations, events, facts, objects. These questions get students to focus on divergent thinking or production. "What are several implications of the story?", a comprehension question, is a divergent question when grouped by focus. Furnish several general statements that can be drawn from the argument. A synthesis question is also a divergent question.

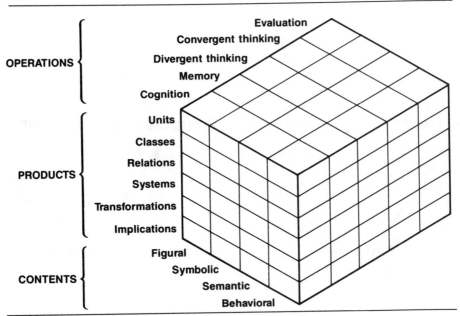

Figure 4–1
The Structure of Intellect
Source: From J. P. Guilford, *The Nature of Human Intelligence*
(New York: McGraw-Hill, 1967), p. i.

Diagramatically, the convergent and divergent foci of questions are presented in Figure 4–2 below.

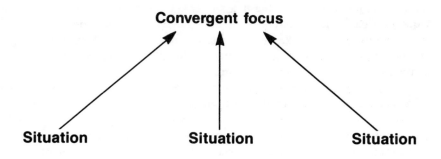

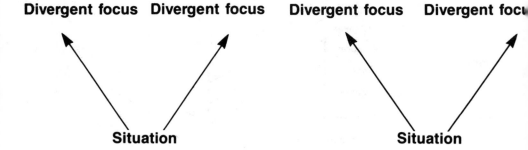

Figure 4–2
Convergent Divergent Foci of Questions

Gallagher and Aschner Focus Category

Gallagher and Aschner, drawing on Guilford's model, created a four-division category system by which we can classify questions: cognitive-memory; convergent thinking, divergent thinking, and evaluative thinking.[2]

Some people consider these as cognitive classifications, but convergent and divergent thinking really address question focus. The division is less clear with cognitive memory and evaluative thinking. Even so, one could argue that these questions essentially have students focus on facts and on matters of judgment and value.

Gallagher and Aschner's category has been popular due to its simplicity of categories, especially compared with Bloom's classification scheme. Roger Cunningham clusters these questions under conceptual-level questions, noting that such questions can have the focus of either being open-ended or closed. If open-ended, the questions are divergent, calling the reader to seek many responses, answers, to the question. In comparison, closed questions focus the respondent's reaction to just one or two answers.[3]

Cunningham, drawing also on the work of Wilen, notes that the openness (divergence) and closedness (convergence) of the questions can be identified by the designations of "low" and "high."[4] According to Cunningham, these designations help eliminate the confusion of attempting to classify questions with several different labels. However, it seems that while confusion may be eliminated, there may be a loss of precision in typing the questions. Essentially, one is mixing the focus of the question with its cognitive level.

Low-Convergent Questions

Low-convergent questions are at the lower end of the cognitive scale (knowledge in Bloom's taxonomy; memory and cognition in Guilford's; and cognitive-memory in Gallagher and Aschner's) focusing the respondent's attention on one or just a few answers. These questions suggest to those hearing them that there is a right answer, a "yes" or "no" that can be given. The student is to draw from memory the fact or concept or theory that will satisfy the question. No thinking is required other than is this fact, concept, the right one.

EXAMPLES:
Low-Convergent Questions

- What is the proper name for the neighborhood of animals and plants existing in a particular region?
- What explanation does the book give for the economic depression of 1929?

High-Convergent Questions

Questions so classified serve the same purpose—to focus students' attention on some aspect of their learning but call into play higher cognitive activity. With this classification scheme, we really do not know what cognitive function; it could be focusing on something by engaging in analysis or evaluation, or even synthesis. All that we can say is that these questions ask for a centering of attention and some type of thinking.

EXAMPLES:

High-Convergent Questions

- In the following material, which assumption is the key assumption?
- For this chemical reaction to occur, what is the necessary and sufficient condition?

Low-Divergent Questions

In general, divergent questions are open-ended and for that reason less predictable as to the types of potential responses and answers. An element of surprise may exist for both the question asker and the question answerer. Divergent questions in general exert a time demand that exceeds that of convergent questions. In dealing with divergent questions, whether at a low or high cognitive level, students require process time—opportunities to explore various avenues of investigation—to plot potential pathways of inquiry. They need time to travel these pathways and perhaps to negotiate detours when potential answers begin to emerge.

Specifically, low-divergent questions ask students to deal primarily at the knowledge level or initial levels of comprehension but to *focus* on many answers, many directions, many concepts, diverse interpretations. These types of questions could well be the dominant questions asked when first getting students into problem solving—looking at all aspects of the problem and even suggesting ways in which a problem might be classified, or even solved.

EXAMPLES:

Low-Divergent Questions

- Name all the ways in which the data before us can be classified.
- How many trends have been presented by our author?

High-Divergent Questions

These open-ended questions are asking students to engage in cognitive processes that bring in various aspects of thinking; the student is not just to retrieve from memory many bits of information, but rather to think through alternatives for the purpose of generating several answers or conclusions. An aspect of creative thinking is called for when asking questions with this focus.

In phrasing these questions, we as teachers give evidence that we have some faith in students' abilities. We believe they can, through various modes of thinking, produce diverse responses to these questions. Students can formulate many judgments; synthesize rich elaborations; make intuitive leaps, speculate; critically analyze numerous assumptions; and formulate varied generalizations.

EXAMPLES:

High-Divergent Questions

- Give a forecast of the future economy of the nation.
- If you were to manage this experiment, what processes would you employ?
- Name some major consequences on agriculture of a shift in the jet stream southward over the Gulf of Mexico.

Hyman's Question Types

Ronald Hyman advanced his classification of questions to represent cognitive process classifications, and certainly they are in as much as any question will always have a cognitive dimension. However, it seems that Hyman's classification is more a scheme for identifying question focus than cognitive function.

Hyman drew his four categories of questions from work by John Wilson: (1) definitional, (2) empirical, (3) evaluative, and (4) metaphysical.[5] Hyman points out that these categories imply no hierarchy; these are just four types of questions. The actual sequencing of the questions is the questioner's challenge.

The lack of hierarchy supports classifying these questions as to focus rather than type of thinking. Hyman asserts that definitional thinking is not a lower order of thinking than empirical thinking, and empirical thinking is not lower than evaluative. One can argue that these are essentially not specific types of thinking at all but rather the giving of focus to particular types of information.

Activity

You have just read about question level (high-low) and openness-closedness (divergent-convergent). While these classifications have been popular because they appear simple, creating questions at various levels of convergence does require some thinking and practice on our part.

Select a topic from one of your class units. Write two questions from each of the types dealing with this topic.

Low-convergent questions—my examples: _____

_____

_____

High-convergent questions—my examples: _____

_____

_____

Low-divergent questions—my examples: _____

_____

_____

High-divergent questions—my examples: _____

_____

_____

Have a colleague critique your questions. Do you both agree? If so, you are on your way; if not, discuss and defend your questions but keep an open mind.

Definitional Questions

In definitional questions, the focus is definitions—words, terms, phrases, classifications, concepts, even principles and generalizations. How one is to deal with these definitions is not elucidated. A student may just be asked to draw from memory particular definitions or to evaluate which facts before him or her are most relevant to the situation at hand. The cognitive aspect of such questions is inferred primarily from the context within which the question is framed. However, the wording of a definitional question can clue the student into what is needed when dealing with this particular focus. Essential for us to remember is that the question focuses the student's attention on words, terms, or phrases.

<u>*EXAMPLES:*</u>

Definitional Questions

- What is the meaning of biome?
- What is a bull market?
- What do we mean when we say that this animal is part of the reptilian family?

Empirical Questions

Empirical questions request the respondent to *focus* on the world—the world as perceived through the senses. It does not necessarily ask that one engage in any investigation, as the name empirical might imply; nor does it prevent it. The central point is that in responding, the student must perceive the world. Hyman notes that such questions ask for facts, comparisons, and contrasts among facts, explanations of events, and conclusions based on the analysis of facts.[6]

Hyman's comments regarding these questions support even further that empirical questions are essentially questions with focus rather than a particular cognitive level. Such questions can exist at the knowledge level focusing the respondent's attention to the reality of the world. In dealing with such questions the students may process the information comparing and contrasting, but the focus still is on reality as perceived through the senses. This processing need not be elaborate; it may be little more than going to the library to check the card index to determine who wrote the novel *Hawaii.* It may be just checking the evening newspaper to determine who headed a government commission.

Of course, there may be occasions when the processing of an empirical question will call for more elaborate mental action. The question may ask for the consequence of depriving particular types of plants of sunlight; the focus is to determine the consequence. Students may actually have to set up a week-long experiment to obtain the answer, but the truth of the answer will still be determined by reference to observations—utilization of senses.

Hyman posits that these questions may request observations about events that did not actually occur. For instance, what might have happened to the development of California if it had not been won from Mexico. Students have no way of verifying this by means of their senses, but they can logically consider the situation from an "if/then" stance. Students do have data from observing what has occurred in similar situations. While the focus is still empirical, there is a demand for some creative thinking.

EXAMPLES:
Empirical Questions

- Who wrote the novel *Hawaii?* (focus on fact)
- What generalization can you make about international trade? (conclusion based on analysis)
- What is the difference between a bull market and a bear market? (focus on comparison)
- What is the reason that the metal bar bends upward when heated? (focus on explanation of event)

Evaluative Questions

It is a bit more difficult to argue the case that evaluative questions are primarily classified as to focus. Still, as Hyman employs evaluation, such questions seem to focus students' attention on types of information rather than on having them evaluate information. Such questions ask students to center on attitudes, beliefs, or morals. The category does become fuzzy, for Hyman states that such questions require the respondent to give his own personal value judgment to the information in question. Even so, the questions focus more on the particular types of content or events than on evaluating situations or information.

EXAMPLES:
Evaluation Questions

- In dealing with the issue of people without adequate housing, what is the key value that seems to be behind the actions?
- Why do you believe that the legal drinking age should be lowered?
- Furnish support for a removal of aid to dependent children?
- What are your key values regarding freedom of speech?

Metaphysical Questions

Metaphysical questions center on metaphysical or theological beliefs. Such questions are usually absent from public schools but quite common in religious schools. While Hyman notes that such questions involve faith, questions could have this focus just asking students for knowledge or understanding of facts, events, and practices of various beliefs. In studying a particular culture, one could raise questions that focus on people's belief systems. So defined, they could be considered a specific type of empirical question.

In private schools supported by religious groups, metaphysical questions may strive to center (focus) students' attention on their belief systems. In responding to such questions, students may have to draw on their own faith. Hyman, noting the rarity of such questions, suggests ignoring this question classifier. However, we need not neglect this focus, since empirical questions can request gaining data about the religious dimensions of cultures. Of course, such questions requesting that students identify and explain their belief systems are not appropriate in a public school.[7]

EXAMPLES:

Metaphysical Questions

- What is the Hindu belief system?
- What arguments do people advance to support the presence of God?

Essentially Hyman has furnished us with three types of questions, their greatest value being that they can assist us in determining a particular focus for inquiry. As to which type of question to employ, the question raiser first identifies the focus of the lesson or situation. If the focus is on facts, then the questions are definitional; if the emphasis is on information that can be processed by the senses, then the questions are empirical; if the stress is on information that defines attitudes, beliefs, and values, then the questions are evaluative.

While having only three categories of questions may appear easy, this very briefness may be problematic. This is especially true with the empirical category; one could argue that almost all cognitive and affective types of questions can be clustered under this focus division. If so, the questioner still lacks guidance as to what specific questions to raise to get information considered and processed in particular ways.

Question Types by Realities Focus

Questions, classified as to focus, direct individuals' attention to particular aspects of their reality. How we look at reality depends in part upon the organizers we create and/or employ. We can organize reality as to facts about reality or statements about reality such as is implied in Hyman's empirical classification, but other ways exist.

Leila Christenbury and Patricia Kelly have furnished us with a useful way to determine question focus: the questioning circle.[8] Their schema contains

REFLECTION

Of the four types of questions discussed—definitional, empirical, evaluative, and metaphysical—perhaps you recognized ones you have employed in your class room. Which types do you most frequently use? Rarely use? What rationale regulates your questions? If you have never used such questions—although this is doubtful because it is hard not to ask questions that deal with facts, definitional questions—then answer as to why not.

Record your reactions to your reflections and date them. Later when reflecting on questions so classified, you can record your questions at this new time point. Are you remaining steadfast or changing your particular questions? What reasons have you for your questioning behavior? Such reflection makes us more aware of who we are as students ourselves; it allows us to participate in our own metacognition, our own thinking about questions.

three overlapping circles identified as matter, personal reality, and external reality. These circles represent major foci for questions.

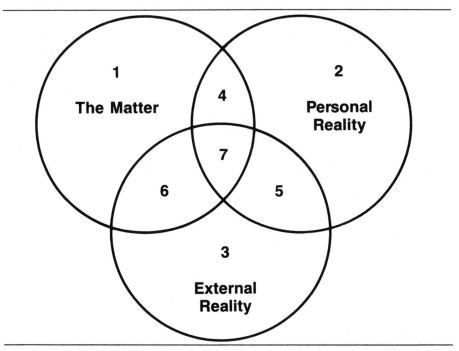

Figure 4–3
The Questioning Circle[9]

The first circle area, the *matter,* refers to the subject to be considered or questioned. The second circle, *personal reality,* deals with the individual's experiences, values, and thoughts. The third circle, *external reality,* centers on the world external to the individual. It subsumes the experiences, history, and concepts of other situations, peoples, and cultures.[10]

The questioning circle serves as a vehicle for contemplating the foci of the questioning process; essentially, it tells the person that he or she can raise questions about the subject matter at hand—the focus of the lesson. It also informs the questioner that questions can be posited about one's personal reality—one's affective responses to the subject matter. Finally, the circle lets the person know that questions can be raised that bring the outside world to bear on the subject matter under consideration.

While each circle denotes a definite focus for questions, the model shows that the foci or domains overlap. Essential to the model is the central overlapping of all three domains (#7 in the diagram). Christenbury and Kelly note that this meshing of the three circles denotes the most significant questions, those with the highest order.

Employing the model, the questioner realizes that there will be times when questions will focus on each circle (#1,2,3); times when particular intersections will be used to determine the focus (intersection #4,5,6); and times when the central intersection will be primary (intersection #7). Students, cognizant of this model, will realize that what main circles are called into play depends upon the subject area under investigation. For instance, in a mathematical lesson the *matter* being investigated may be the concept of "set." The *personal reality* would be that of the student's experiences with the concept, and the *external reality* would be authorities' views of set and various mathematical rules that relate to the concept.

A sketch of a social studies lesson on the family, having students employ the questioning circle strategy, is shown in Figure 4–4. The questions raised are noted as to the number of the circle, presented in Figure 4–4. Ideally, this lesson sketch would be done by students as they plan their approach to the lesson.

The goal in using these questions or in having students map out these questions is to get students to raise and process questions in circle area 7, the intersection of all three circles. Questions at this juncture call the students to focus their questions regarding the family drawing on the subject matter at hand, their personal knowledge about the family, and what authorities have to say about families. Essentially, the focus of these questions (#7) is on creating generalizable knowledge, generating universal content. In processing such questions students begin to possess rather complete understanding.

The example of the questioning circle dealing with the family shows that the actual names of the circles—the matter, personal reality, external reality—can be adjusted to fit the focus of the content under consideration. In the family example, the *matter* is the concept family, the *personal reality* is the student, and the world is the *external reality.*

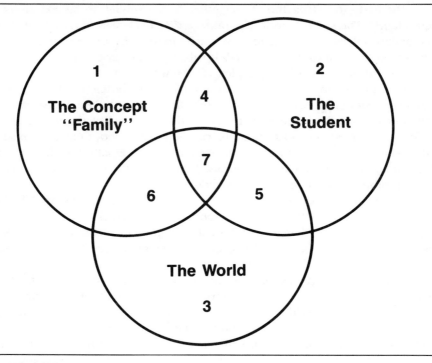

Topic: The Family
Strategy: Questioning Circle
Planning Stage: Question Sketch

Question 1. The Matter: How can we define the term "family"?

Question 2. Personal Reality: Do you live in a family?

Question 3. External Reality: What types of families exist in other nations?

Question 4. The Matter/Personal Reality: Is your family just like the definition of family?

Question 5. Personal Reality/External Reality: In what ways is your family like those in other cultures?

Question 6. The Matter/External Reality: In what ways are the families in other cultures like our definition of family?

Question 7. The Matter/Personal Reality/External Reality: How do you think people have modified the family group to function within their culture context? What general statement or statements can you make about families in the world?

Figure 4–4
Questioning Circle: Family Lesson[11]

Christenbury and Kelly furnish several examples of questioning circles with various contents. If the circle is to be used as a means of guiding questions in literature, it might look like the following Figure 4–5.[12]

Here the matter is the *text* under consideration, the particular story. Let us assume that the story is Hemingway's *Old Man and the Sea.* The *reader* refers to the student who is reading the story, and the *world and other literature* refers to examples and ideas that come from the positions and stories of other authors.

In planning questions for this literature class, the questions might resemble the following:

Question 1. The Matter (Text): What is the main reason that the old man sets out to sea?

Question 2. Personal Reality (Reader): Have you ever been in a similar situation as the old man?

Question 3. External Reality (World and other Literature): What other stories have pitted a person's determination against great odds?

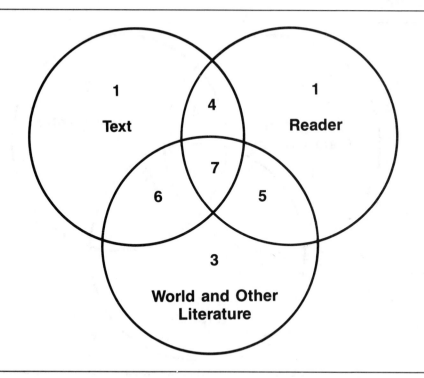

Figure 4–5
Guiding Questions in Literature

Question 4. The Matter/Personal Reality: What situations might cause you to act in the manner of the old man?

Question 5. Personal Reality/External Reality: Given the same situation, would you have acted as the old man did?

Question 6. The Matter/External Reality: What other novels present a similar story with regard to theme?

Question 7. The Matter/Personal Reality/External Reality: When is it more important to have made the effort than to have succeeded in the task?

The questioning circle can also be employed in denoting questions that apply to the processing of information; for instance, in conducting an experiment. Plotting out the questions becomes part of metacognitive activity, enabling the student to determine how questions will be processed during the various stages of the experiment.

In a science lesson dealing with the effects of sunlight on plant growth, the questioning circle can be diagrammed to show the subject, the experimenter, and the product expected, as in Figure 4–6 below.

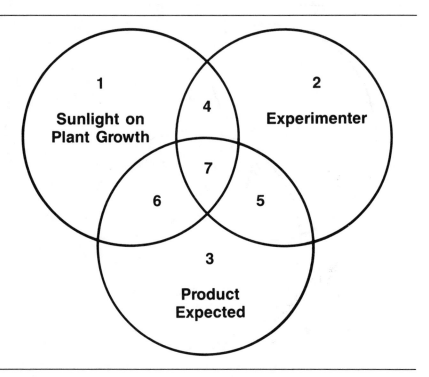

Figure 4–6
Questioning Circle in a Science Lesson

Questions then can be planned to deal with each circle and overlapping segment.

Question 1. The Matter: (Sunlight on plant)
What is my subject, my key question?

Question 2. Personal Reality: (Experimenter)
What do I already know about this subject?

Question 3. External Reality: (Product expected)
What type of report do I need to create for my audience?

Question 4. The Matter/Personal Reality:
What experience do I have with this area of investigation?

Question 5. Personal Reality/External Reality:
How can I use my prior knowledge to conduct this experiment?

Question 6. The Matter/External Reality:
What ways can I show that these plants are impacted by sunlight? What effects has sunlight had on plants in my garden?

Question 7. The Matter/Personality Reality/External Reality:
Which procedure can I employ that will enable me to answer my original question on the effects of sunlight on plant growth?

The questions in the previous example relate to the processing of the experiment. It is also possible for students to record particular questions that relate to the content itself. For example, on the matter, questions can be raised as to why "type of plant" is being studied; what its features are regarding its leaf structure. In the matter and external reality, questions in area 6 of the diagram could focus on the impacts various degrees of sunlight actually had on the plant. What occurs when I increase the sunlight? Decrease the sunlight? Eliminate it for one day, two days, five days?

What the questioning circle allows both teacher and student to do is to manage the focus of their questions in a consistent fashion. It enables the student and teacher to systematize their questioning so that all aspects of an investigation or educational activity are considered. It enables students and teachers to think more deeply about what they are doing in both teaching and learning.

Questions Defined by Conceptual Categories

The previous model allows classifying questions as to focus on three major categories. Richard Derr presents a question classification based on the

Activity

APPLICATION

You have become acquainted with classifying questions as to reality focus. Plan a lesson. Pick the content area, arranging your questions according to the circle focus. Make a diagram of the three circles for your particular lesson. Write at least one question for each circle or intersection of circles.

My Lesson:

Topic: _____

Circle diagram:

My Questions:

1. _____
2. _____
3. _____
4. _____
5. _____
6. _____
7. _____

Now try out your lesson!

conceptual presuppositions of questions. He defines conceptual presupposition as the logical antecedent conditions of questions.[13] Discussion of suppositions and presuppositions was presented in Chapter 1. Important to remember here is that all questions presuppose, assume, something to be true in order for the question to be processed.

Derr in making his point furnishes the example, Who was the author of *Hamlet?* This question presupposes that the play *Hamlet* did indeed have an author and also that the identity of the author is or can be made known. This question presupposes the concept of identity; therefore, the question is concerned with determining this identity.

The conceptual presuppositions are a crucial property of questions because they shape the content of the inquiry.[14] In other words, conceptual presuppositions determine the *focus* of the question. Knowing how we structure our world conceptually in turn structures our questions.

Derr identifies eight basic concepts that can serve as foci for our questions. Additionally, we can employ these conceptual foci in identifying the question type itself.

Category	Question example
I. Existence	Does X exist?
II. Identity	What is X? Who is X?
III. Properties	What are the features of X?
IV. Relation	How is X related to Y?
V. Number	How many X's are there?
VI. Location	Where is X?
VII. Time	When is X?
VIII. Action	What is X doing?[15]

While Derr does not rule out other categories, he seems to be fairly comfortable with the categories given. The important point for us as teachers and our students is that questions can now be named as to focus with some degree of precision. It is more powerful for students to realize that questions can have eight foci than only noting that questions can be identified as just definitional and empirical in focus or divergent or convergent in focus.

Several ways to type questions as to focus have been presented. While we need not use all of them, it is important to remember that there are several. Knowing this furnishes us with more precision in our question raising and responding. Also, the focus of a question identifies to a major degree the purpose of a lesson, the direction of an inquiry. Thus aware, the questioner realizes where he or she is going and can evaluate the direction of his or her questioning in light of the general direction desired. If questions are diverting one from a desired focus, then the questioning can be stopped and new questions posed to redirect the inquiry.

It would be so simple if there were only two types of questions—fact questions and process questions. But such is not the case. Questions are complex linguistic structures designed to engage individuals cognitively and affectively in processing particular contents. For this reason, even their identification as to type is challenging. Some have argued, however, that identification could be simplified if we just look at the key starting words of various types of questions—their syntactical beginnings.

QUESTION TYPES ACCORDING TO SYNTAX

In Chapter 2, the question was discussed as a specialized type of sentence possessing either an interrogative form or function. Kubinski stated that it is an expressed desire for information.[16]

Derr presents the question as a specialized expression designed to make a determination about some object in reality—a sentence that asks *about* something.[17] Derr contrasts questions with requests that, while also having question marks, do not ask about something but ask *for* something or permission *to do* something. "What is the atomic weight of lead?" is a question asking *about* lead, specifically its atomic weight. "May I please use the slide projector?" is a request, in this case *to do* something—use the slide projector. "Are you finished?" is a request essentially urging one to finish. Requests are often found in classroom dialogue as part of management talk. Questions, at least according to Derr, are separate from classroom management; questions are part of learning and information processing strategies.

Few would challenge that questions are particular types of speech—acts that trigger speech, acts of answering. The questioner can gain some assistance in determining the type of answer desired or required by looking at the wording.

Graesser and Murachver have noted that a question can be considered as comprised of three elements: a question function, a statement element, and a knowledge structure.[18]

Consider the question when was the Treaty of Paris signed?

This question can be divided into

Question function: When

Statement element: The Treaty of Paris was signed *"when"*

Knowledge Structure element: (history)

The question function, determined usually by the initial word of the question, provides the student with the clue as to what is to be done with the question; at what level it is to be processed cognitively and perhaps affectively. The student, instructed in questions, realizes upon seeing "when" that there are several potential ways for processing the question; it can be processed at a comprehension level or perhaps at just the knowledge level. The function also clues the student to focus. It also is a "time" question, drawing on Derr's classification.

The statement element, common to all questions, is a statement explicitly stated or implied: the completion of the statement is the answer to the question.

The knowledge structure refers to the information realm with which the question is dealing, the question's content. Realizing what the knowledge structure specifically is clues the respondent as to the content and meaning of the statement element. Usually, students do not have to consider this too deeply, as most teachers quickly reveal what is the subject matter of the lesson in which the questions are being raised. "When was the Treaty of Paris signed?" is asked in social studies. "What is the atomic weight of lead?" would be asked in a science lesson. However, there are times when the knowledge structure element is unclear. "Why did Mr. Jones give the speech?" does not have a self-evident knowledge structure. If the knowledge structure is politics, then there is a range of possible responses. If the knowledge structure is education, then other responses are suggested. If the knowledge structure is drama, a third realm of possible answers is plausible.

Both teacher and student need to realize that to answer a particular question, they must determine and reference the question's world knowledge structure. Doing this decides in part the nature of the content of the speech act. The actual level of functioning, however, will be determined by the question function, depicted by the initial word.

Question Categories

Lehnert in working with questions has identified several question categories that can be identified by the initial word of the question.[19]

Wh- Question Types

A majority of questions start with *wh* words: what, when, where, why, who, which. Much of the time, such questions can be classified as open-ended questions, suggesting several avenues to the respondent. Such questions cannot usually be answered with a simple "Yes" or "No." This contrasts these questions with those so worded that a "Yes" or "No" does satisfy the question. "What caused the market crash in October of 1987?" suggests several answers; therefore, it is an open question. "Did you invest money in the stock market in October?" is a closed question; "Yes" or "No" satisfies the question's demand.

Notwithstanding the above, classifying questions as "wh" questions lets ourselves off the hook too easily. Lehnert has categorized question types not only by initial wording but also by the question function suggested.

What Question Types

Causal antecedent—These what questions ask the respondent to determine what was the cause of something; what event or situation occurred prior to the situation denoted in the statement element. For instance, "What caused the investors to panic and sell large amounts of stock?" essentially asks students to produce an answer to the statement element, "the investors panicked and sold large numbers of stock." Something happened that *caused* the event to occur. What was that something or somethings?

Causal consequence—These questions, also begun with *what*, are concerned with what occurred *after* the statement element. "What happened after the drop in the price of the dollar?" requests information on what occurred after the "price of the dollar dropped," what was the consequence of such action? The student now looks for what resulted from this event.

Enablement—These what questions request the respondent to identify what facilitated something to occur. "What allowed the rush of stock selling to occur; what enabled it to happen?" The key function is enablement.

Judgmental—Questions with this function use *what* to ask the respondent to make a judgment as to some event. The question can be both cognitive and affective. "What do you think of how the government managed the stock market crisis?" In other words, "What is your view or judgment as to how the situation was handled?"

Feature specification—There are times when the what question asks the respondent to describe something, to denote its features. Lehnert classifies such questions as feature specification. "What does a Porsche 928 look like?" is requesting that the student indicate and describe the specific features of this particular automobile. "What is a mountain?" demands the denoting of the key attributes of a mountain.

Why Question Types

Goal Orientation—Questions with this function strive to get the question respondent to determine the reason or goal of some action. "Why did George Washington urge the new country not to become entangled in foreign affairs?" In processing the question, students might query themselves as to the goal that Washington had in making this statement. "Why was the school bond issue defeated?" also requests students to determine the goal for such action.

Expectational—These questions essentially ask students to extrapolate from information at hand. What would you expect might occur, or what were people's expectations in the event being considered? An expectational question might be, "Why would you argue against that particular plan of traffic control?" For the expectations of other people, the question might be, "Why did the United States decide to protect all American owned ships in the Persian Gulf?"

Requests—While Derr argues that requests differ from questions, Lehnert does have requests as a question category. This should not really produce problems for us; all we need to do is realize that requests are special types of why questions: asking individuals *to do* something or requesting something from individuals. In the question "Why don't you write a position paper on recycling waste?" it is evident that the student is being asked *to do* something.

Where Question Types

Locational—Frequently, when phrasing "where" questions, we are requesting an indication of where some event occurred or where some phenomenon is located. "Where was the Treaty of Paris signed?" "Where is the largest city in the world located?"

However, locational questions may relate to process, where one might initiate action. For instance, "Where would you begin to solve the problem?", meaning what would be your first step in enacting a solution, is a commonly heard question. "Where would you locate a nuclear dump?" is also asking for location but only after the student had engaged in some problem solving. This does point out that while we can classify these questions as to their initial wording, some ambiguity still exists as to the exact types of intellectual processing being requested.

Where questions might also ask for an identification of the place where an argument is made or logic broken. "Where in this paper does the author present her argument?"

Which Question Types

Identification—Questions beginning with the word *which* are essentially after identification, to get the respondent to point out a person who did something, or a place where something happened, or an event that caused something. Examples of such questions are: "Which President signed into law social security legislation?", "Which city hosted the 1986 World's Fair?" or "Which event served as the rallying point for the Spanish American War?"

There are times when which questions focus students' attention on a process or process segment. For instance, the teacher might ask, "In light of this situation, which solution might be the most appropriate?" One might also pose, "Which of the following questions might be the most appropriate in light of the central problem confronting us?"

When Question Types

Time Identification—*When* type questions are special types of identification questions requesting one to place in time some event, person, thing, or process. If we want to know the time span of some famous person's life, we would most likely ask, "When did Mozart live?" "When did the United States officially enter the Second World War?" refers to the time placement of that event. Time identification can be future oriented, as in the question, "When do you think we will balance our federal budget?"

Convention—These questions ask students to identify some understandings of a particular convention. "When is it proper to address someone as Reverend?" refers to some aspect of the convention of etiquette. "When is it proper to eat with one's fingers?" also tests a person's knowledge of table manners. In a language arts class teachers often phrase convention questions: "When do we start a new paragraph?" "When do we capitalize the first letter in nouns?"

Who Question Types

Person Identification—Differing from *which* identification questions, these questions solely deal with the identification of persons: "Who shot Abraham Lincoln?" "Who was the first American to walk on the moon?" "Who was King John?" "Who was Albert Einstein?"

Such questions, however, are more than just identifying a person. Sometimes they ask students to identify the person who could or should perform some activity; for instance: "Who should be selected to manage the world trade center in light of its current problems?" or "In light of our classroom, who could do the best job of representing us at the student council?"

H- Question Types

Few types of questions begin with an "H" word. *How* and *have* are the two key ones.

How Question Types

Procedural—Many questions beginning with the word *how* request an indication of the manner in which something should or would be done. For example, "How would you solve the problem?" requests an elaboration of steps necessary for enacting a procedure. "How did the people adapt to the Civil War?" asks for the ways (procedure) that people employed to survive.

Quantification—Frequently, we hear questions such as "How much is our national debt?", "How much money do you have?" "How much does the television cost?" These questions request an indication of some quantification.

I- Question Types

The prominent I-type question begins with the word Is.

Activity

ANALYSIS

There are many types of "wh" questions. Take one of your textbooks and record the "wh" questions in one chapter and classify them as to syntax.

Textbook questions (wh)	Question type

What is the major type of "wh" question? Is this type consistent with your goals for this chapter? If these questions do not reflect your emphasis in teaching this material, what other types of "wh" questions could you create. Generate some samples.

Sample "wh" questions for this chapter to address my goals.

_____

_____

_____

Is Question Types

Many times questions begin with the word "Is": "Is this your mother?" "Is this your social security number?" "Is this the correct spelling of your name?" "Is the prime minister of New Zealand a conservative or liberal?" Several types of questions can be grouped under this category.

Verification—Such questions as "Is this your social security number" are raised to verify the accuracy of some number, name, situation, event, or person. "Is California the largest state in the nation?" is phrased to gain confirmation of some fact; in this case, the size of California.

Permission—"Is it all right to speak at this meeting?" is not an uncommon question. The person raising it is requesting permission to do something. In a way, it is a request for an indication that some action is appropriate. There are times when permission questions are "Is" questions in spirit but worded with "May I" such as "May I speak at this meeting?" The intent of the question has not been altered.

Disjunctive—The question, "Is the prime minister of New Zealand a conservative or liberal?" is disjunctive, for it requests clarification of an "either-or" situation. "Is Canada larger than the United States in area?" is another example.

The "is" question can vary a bit with the tense of the verb. "Is the prime minister conservative or liberal?" can be phrased, "Was the prime minister conservative or liberal?" if one were interested in a past prime minister. Such "is" questions might begin with "where," as in "Where are all of the king's men sitting at the table?"

Comments on Question Syntax

The many question categories discussed under syntax, drawn from Lehnert's work, reveal a rich variety of question types. However, most questions classified according to syntax can also be classified globally as cognitive questions. Such questions can also have affective components. "What are your feelings on the matter?" is an affective question; it is also a judgmental question. "How would you handle the situation?", while asking for procedural knowledge, also has an affective component—requesting one to make known his or her value stance regarding the particular situation. "Why do you think that is appropriate?" is definitely an affective question.

While syntax provides us with general guidelines for classifying questions, it also alerts the skilled language player to the uncertainty of question classifications. Questions are contextual; chameleon in nature. For example, "What are the consequences of reducing Medicare benefits?" may at first seem to request identification of the causal consequence of that action; however, a class may have been dealing with the issue of responsibility for others and thus the question has an affective dimension—actually asking the person to make known his or her value positions regarding Medicare reduction.

CONCLUSION

This chapter presenting question types as to focus and syntax furnishes information that will allow the question user, whether teacher or student, to play the language game with more finesse, with more understanding of the complexity of these specialized types of speech units. We do not lack for categories: the focus categories suggested several types; the conceptual categories further increased our list; and the syntax categories identified various options for our questions.

While the reader should not feel compelled to employ all of these categories, he or she should be cognizant that they exist and that students should

Activity

You now have an awareness of the myriad ways to classify questions, but we all need to be able to play the game of questioning, not just talk the game. Selecting any content area, create a lesson in which you use at least four types of questions. Keep the lesson to around forty minutes, a bit shorter if you teach at the early elementary grades. The lesson plan should have your major questions written out and sequenced. Your plan can follow a format similar to the one presented.

My Lesson

Topic: _____

Grade: _____

General Objective: _____

Questions

_____

_____

_____

_____

_____

Invite a colleague to view the lesson. Explain your questioning purpose. Ideally, your colleague also has read this chapter and the previous one. Ask him or her to watch you teach and record the questions you are using to determine if you are adhering to your plan. After the lesson, debrief. Ask your colleague for examples of questions he or she would raise in a similar lesson.

Perhaps try a dry run; re-teach with no pupils present to get your questions down.

Offer your coaching services to your colleague to encourage his or her questioning.

Record your perceptions from this practice and date them to create a program record.

If you cannot get a colleague to coach you, video tape your lesson and engage in self-coaching.

know of them. Possessing knowledge about questions and questioning strategies empowers students to recognize questions encountered and to determine the manners in which they should or could be processed. Such knowledge enables students to create more thoughtful questioning strategies, heightening their chances of reaching their learning objectives and facilitating their types of thinking.

For the teacher, such detailed understanding of question types will facilitate his or her thinking, thus contributing to a classroom environment in which students are indeed paragons of reflective inquiry, of critical mindedness. How to go about creating such questions for the dynamic classroom is the content of the next chapter.

NOTES

1. J. P. Guilford, *The Nature of Human Intelligence* (New York: McGraw-Hill, 1967), p. i.

2. Mary Jane Aschner, James J. Gallagher, Joyce M. Perry, and Sibel S. Afsar, *A System for Classifying Thought Processes in the Context of Classroom Verbal Interaction* (Urbana, Ill.: University of Illinois, 1961).

3. Roger T. Cunningham, "What Kind of Question is That?" in William W. Wilen, ed., *Questions, Questioning Techniques, and Effective Teaching* (Washington, D.C.: National Educational Association, 1987).

4. William Wilen, *Questioning Skills for Teachers,* 2nd. ed. (Washington, D.C.: National Education Association, 1986); Roger T. Cunningham, "What Kind of Question is That?" in William W. Wilen, ed. *Questions, Questioning Techniques, and Effective Teaching.*

5. John Wilson, *Language and the Pursuit of Truth* (Cambridge: Cambridge University Press, 1953); Ronald T. Hyman, *Strategic Questioning* (Englewood Cliffs, N.J.: Prentice-Hall, Inc., 1979).

6. Ronald T. Hyman, *Strategic Questioning* (Englewood Cliffs, N.J.: Prentice-Hall, Inc., 1979).

7. Ronald T. Hyman, *Strategic Questioning.*

8. Leila Christenbury and Patricia P. Kelly, *Questioning, A Path to Critical Thinking* (Urbana, Ill.: National Council of Teachers of English, 1983).

9. Leila Christenbury and Patricia P. Kelly, *Questioning, A Path to Critical Thinking* (Urbana, Ill.: National Council of Teachers of English, 1983), p. 13.

10. Leila Christenbury and Patricia P. Kelly, *Questioning, A Path to Critical Thinking.*

11. Francis P. Hunkins, "Students as Key Questioners," in William W. Wilen, ed., *Questions, Questioning Techniques, and Effective Teaching,* p. 170.

12. Leila Christenbury and Patricia P. Kelly, *Questioning, A Path to Critical Thinking.*

13. Richard L. Derr, "Questioning and Information/Library Science," *Questioning Exchange* 1: 2 (May 1987): 107–10.

14. Richard L. Derr, "Questioning and Information/Library Science."

15. Richard L. Derr, "Questioning and Information/Library Science."

16. Tadeusz Kubinski, *An Outline of the Logical Theory of Questions* (Berlin: Akademie-Verlag, 1980).

17. Richard L. Derr, "Questioning and Information/Library Science."

18. Arthur C. Graesser and Tamar Murachver, "Symbolic Procedures of Question Answering," in Arthur C. Graesser and John B. Black, eds., *The*

Psychology of Questions (Hillsdale, N.J.: Erlbaum, 1985), 15–88.

19. W. G. Lehnert, *The Process of Question Answering* (Hillsdale, N.J.: Erlbaum, 1978). Lehnert reference drawn from Arthur C. Graesser and Tamar Murachver, "Symbolic Procedures of Question Answering."

5

Creating Effective

Questions and

Questioning Strategies

A poor questioner cannot be a good teacher, ... and a good questioner cannot fail altogether as a teacher.[1]

We are all natural questioners. Despite this, not everyone poses questions in ways that get either oneself or others to reflect, to ponder, to process information in ways affording new insights. It seems from listening to ourselves that we are more inclined to be unskilled questioners than skilled. To become skilled questioners, careful thought and careful planning are required. As noted in a previous chapter, educators are not concerned with everyday questions but with educative questions, and such questions demand great care.

The question does not occur to our mind, we must find it. It does not take on a shape, we must give it form. It does not deliver itself, we must present it. We prepare a question to be educative. We conceive it, formulate it, and pose it. To conceive an educative question requires thought; to formulate it, requires labor; and to pose it, tact.[2]

To be an effective questioner and to get our students similarly skilled requires planning. This is axiomatic; all teachers plan. No teacher enters the classroom lacking forethought as to what to do. The type of plan teachers create, however, varies greatly in format and detail. Some plans are mere sketches, little more than an indication of the topic to be covered and time of presentation. Many plan books foster such sketches. In contrast, some lesson plans are detailed noting specifically the organization of the topic, its sequence, and manner of presentation—even noting materials to be used.[3]

Most educators accept the maxim that sound planning contributes to effective teaching. If disagreement exists, it is over the procedures one might employ in planning rather than the fact of whether one should plan. Teachers' approach to planning can be influenced by their teaching style or personality. Teachers who are methodological tend to create highly structured plans to be followed with little variation. Persons considered concrete sequentials in their learning will often create plans favoring an ordered presentation of information to students. Individuals who are more laid back, more spontaneous in nature, more abstract random, may generate plans that are more open, containing more options or numerous avenues for investigation.

There is no one way to plan. Even the way to plan suggested in this chapter is not *the* way. Rather, it is one suggestion that hopefully will trigger contemplation of planning and encourage commitment to it. Educational lesson planning does not become lesson planning by virtue of particular stages, but rather by purpose of the activity—such planning consists of a teacher's activities designed to create and organize teacher and learner behavior within a specialized environment. Planning is the recorded orchestration of a teacher's and students' actions, materials, environments, and particular contents. Planning resembles choreography—recording various moves for individuals in classroom theater. Some lessons may be like a ballet, requiring rather extensive detail. Others may mimic spontaneous jazz dancing, leaving room for breaks from the main routine.

We can conceptualize planning in numerous ways. The more we reflect on planning, the more we appreciate its complexity, recognize its challenge. If this were a book dealing with all instruction, this chapter would address approaches to planning and consider all of the variables extant in the classroom. However, this book focuses on questions and questioning within the context of thinking. Therefore, this chapter presents ways in which we can plan our questions and ways of getting students to question so that our and our students' goals and objectives have a greater likelihood of being attained.

PLANNING EFFECTIVE QUESTIONS AND QUESTIONING STRATEGIES

Why focus just on planning questions? Why not deal with questions within the context of total classroom planning? Most of us know how to plan a lesson in general terms, even if we do not always follow our own advice, and questioning is commonly used at all grade levels.[4] Despite our common knowledge of planning and questions, however, research indicates that we are more inclined to be ineffective than effective questioners; more inclined to overuse questions at the knowledge of specific facts level and to underuse questions that trigger deep reflection, indepth processing of information.[5]

Planning as Decision Making—as Thinking

Planning is a special type of thinking in which we or our students engage in a mental processing of situations in relation to a goal or goals for the purpose of choosing appropriate alternatives. In Chapter 1, the thinking strategy of decision making was identified. To reiterate, the stages of decision making were defining the goal, identifying alternatives, analyzing alternatives, ranking alternatives, judging alternatives, and choosing best alternatives.[6] Essentially, planning is decision making. As such, it requires some degree of reflection and ultimately the making of particular choices.

We must remain mindful that decision making is a complex process despite the apparent clear-cut steps presented in this book. Reality is much less certain. The difficulty becomes apparent when we note that planning has stages; we make decisions about these various stages, and the decisions made at each stage also have steps that can guide our action. Stufflebeam and others note that decision making has four major stages: (1) becoming aware that a decision is needed, (2) designing the decision situation, (3) choosing among alternatives, and (4) acting upon the chosen alternative.[7] These stages are similar to Beyer's.[8] Stufflebeam's stage one can be related to Beyer's step one: defining the goal. Stufflebeam's Stage 2 can be related to Beyer's Steps 2, 3, and 4. Stage 3, choosing among alternatives, is similar to Beyer's Stages 5 and 6. The fourth stage of Stufflebeam, acting upon the chosen alternative, seems to be an added step, a most important step for one needs to do something with the best alternative chosen.

In planning as in decision making, there are several assumptions about the person involved in the process as well as about the process itself. It is assumed that the person planning has sufficient information to make necessary choices. If the person lacks requisite information, it is taken for granted that the information can be obtained by means of one or several ways or avenues.

Second, it is assumed that the planner has sufficient sensitivity—sensitivity to the situation and to the person involved in the situation. This sensitivity is a type of awareness, an ability to perceive that which is necessary in order for something or someone to be successful.

A third assumption is that the decision maker is rational. He or she believes in the power of the mind, cognizant that particular thinking strategies can be employed to maximize something.[9]

Most books that discuss planning tend to portray it as a self-evident logical process, a process that will allow one to just look at the situation, consider the data available, and then utilize clear-cut steps to attain desired goals. Actual planning, however, is more intuitive, more affective, less precise—at least with regard to steps. We are emotional beings, and our planning of questions and strategies will be greatly influenced by the emotional templates we bring to the task. Rather than carefully following steps, almost in a blind adherence, we more or less follow an evolutionary, somewhat naturalistic, planning approach. Flexibility is present in our actual planning. Rather than managing precise variables in predefined sequences, with clear awareness of impact, we seem more often than not to be managing chaos, managing productive messes in the classroom in which uncertainty coexists with certainty as classroom guest.

The above furnishes us with a caution: These are steps but not *the* steps to be taken; this is a sequence to consider but not *the sequence* to be followed without question. In other words, the steps of planning questions and strategies should be read in a thinking, questioning fashion. The information provides the grist for reflection, the nudge for action, but we must make the process of planning questions personally ours.

Formulating Effective Questions— Questioning Strategies: Steps to Consider

Become Knowledgeable

The effective planner knows about that which he or she is planning. While it is impossible to be completely informed on the content, the person who wishes to raise significant questions in meaningful strategies to get students to process information in a thinking manner must have more than an adequate understanding. While Stufflebeam and others note that awareness is the first step in decision making, the good planner is more than aware. He or she *knows* the types of questions possible; he or she knows the various research studies that have been done on questions and questioning; he or she is cognizant of the various functions that questions can serve; he or she grasps the essence of the various instructional strategies and realizes not only their instructional benefits but also their nurturant qualities.

There is much to be learned about questions and questioning; much to be comprehended about thinking. It is a lifetime challenge, a continued search to gain command of our craft: teaching. Certainly, we should be better this year than last, realizing that we are still not as competent as next year. The educator aiming to become master questioner and to facilitate such competence among his or her students realizes that he or she must first be a student of the question and its use. In becoming knowledgeable, we realize the necessity of continuing to inquire into the realm of the question—to reflect on just what we know, to question our assumptions, our competencies, and to map out ways of addressing our concerns.

You as reader might react that this first step is stating the obvious— everyone knows that the first step in doing anything is having the requisite

YOUR KNOWLEDGE BASE

It is important to ascertain our levels of knowledge about any subject before we plan to use that information. We need to document what we know we do not know. Reflect on your knowledge base. Hopefully, your readings of the previous chapters have not only answered some questions but also raised some. Perhaps share these answers and questions with a colleague.

Has there been any shift in your thinking on planning? If none has occurred, jot down why not.

knowledge. So it would seem, but few among us have focused in great depth on the question. Even when we speak of ways to get students to think, we do not usually mention specifically the questions to be employed. Research indicates that we need to spend more time on this first step: becoming knowledgeable

Engage in Analysis

Engaging in analysis differs from becoming knowledgeable in that analysis refers to becoming acquainted with the specific educational situation in which we find ourselves. It is where we define our particular situation to get a feel for our students regarding their background, their readiness for particular types of learning, their interests, both present and potential, their needs, and their learning styles.

Before thinking of particular types of questions and strategies that one might employ, students' identities must be made clear. We learn about our student audience and co-inquirers through reading anecdotal records, studying test results, observing student behavior in class encounters, and noting students' questions and questioning behavior.

From such analyses we begin to identify student needs and desires, noting those which can be met in class through certain types of thinking and questioning strategies. We commence identifying those needs that can be addressed as a class group and those that can be processed individually through independent study. We start to sense a type of balance necessary in our classroom between teacher presentation and student interaction; between content and process.

In analyzing the current situation, we articulate the situation for our lesson or lessons. What are the particular schedules or teaching arrangements within which the lesson will be taught? How much time is available for high-level questions? What facilities are at our disposal? Do we have sufficient space for meaningful student interaction? Is the educational environment conducive to cooperative learning or large group instruction? Are the necessary materials in the classroom or in the school?

In analysis, we direct our attention to the educational environment and to the student actors within that environment. While our actions and questions are not completely influenced by our surroundings, we must consider our facilities. If we wish students to ask questions stressing synthesis, specifically formulating generalizations, the educational situation must enable students to discuss or consult with fellow students and to consult resource materials, view filmstrips, view maps, or engage in responding to a computer program. The educational environment cannot be sterile. It should inform the student who is to question, who is to think, that the necessary materials and appropriate spaces are at hand.

This step may cause us as teachers to realize that before we can really start a lesson we must return to the first step, becoming knowledgeable. Analyzing the situation and the demands of our class may point out that we really have insufficient information regarding questions and questioning strategies. Often from engaging in this second stage, we identify our own areas of need regarding questions and questioning strategies.

In the first two steps of planning, we become aware not only of needs for our students and ourselves but also gain cognizance of potential opportunities for using questions in particular sequences to trigger thinking. Recognizing possibilities in light of needs leads to the third planning step—considering goals and objectives.

Consider Goals and Objectives

Much has been written and debated on goals and objectives; some would argue that too much has been said. These debates are not going to be resolved here. Neither is this author going to take a particular stand on the merits of general objectives or precise instructional objectives. Readers are free to seek their own levels of comfort on these points. Nevertheless, it seems we can all achieve consensus that we do require some means of guidance toward some perceived end point or points.

Education is purposeful, and goals and objectives are guidepoints along the avenue of purpose used to direct our development, implementation, maintenance, or evaluation of our educational programs. In the case of questions and questioning, we employ these statements to influence our creation of questions and questioning strategies and their delivery.

Considering goals and objectives is closely related to the previous major planning step. We might even engage in both steps simultaneously. After acquainting ourselves with our students and their needs and interests, and defining our teaching situation and facilities, we need to reflect on the basic goals of our school, of education.

Today a major school goal is developing in students skill in thinking in diverse and productive ways. Aligned with that goal is one indicating that students will possess the knowledge, ability, and disposition to question effectively within various thinking processes.

"To enable students to be competent questioners" is a most worthwhile goal; it is essential, yet it is rarely stated explicitly. Granted, it is implied in much of what we support. From the research, however, it appears that in not explicitly stating this goal, we are not attaining it. Students are not becoming competent questioners—knowledgeable of types of questions, their functions, or of their diverse strategies. Giving conscious attention to goals in our planning should help to fill this gap.

Once goals have been defined, we can then consider objectives. Again, we need to think of objectives as guides, even behavioral objectives.[10] A majority of educators has accepted the view that specific statements are the most effective for educational objectives. A meaningful objective states outcomes in terms of observable behavior expected of students after instruction. With regard to questions, a behavioral objective might read:

> After direct instruction in analysis questions, the student will be able to raise such questions in light of a particular paragraph and identify the key assumptions in the paragraph. The student will be able to use analysis questions correctly (that is identifying assumptions in written material) 80 percent of the time.

We can, however, opt for nonbehavioral objectives, objectives somewhat general in their wording. The above objective rewritten in nonbehavioral form would read: "The student would be able to employ analysis questions when such questions are required in the reading." Which objective format is the teacher's choice; however, we cannot ignore this stage of planning. We must be cognizant of our purposes for using or having students use questions and questioning.

In this third planning step, our actions are related to what Stufflebeam would call the design stage of decision making. In writing or selecting objectives, we are designing the direction for our actions, for our questions, giving shape to our planned educational encounter, at least with regard to our questions. We are making choices about end-points, deciding to travel this avenue rather than that one. We are in the early stages of formulating decision alternatives.[11] The actual alternatives are selected at the choice stage of decision making.

In creating or selecting goals and objectives, we are drawing on our sensitivity to the situation, our students, and ourselves. The appropriateness of our goals and objectives depends in part on just how successful we are at being sensitive.

Once goals and objectives are determined, we are well on our way to considering specific types of questions for possible use in class dialogue. Now we are ready for the next step: considering question types and strategies.

Considering Question Types and Questioning Strategies

In becoming knowledgeable of questions and questioning strategies (step 1), we focused on the general field of questions. In considering question types and strategies, we focus on particulars—what questions might we use in this situation, what strategies could be appropriate for attaining goals and objectives identified. This is the stage at which we contemplate the major assumptions relating to questions. We begin to consider the criteria of the good question.

The specific types of questions we will consider and the particular strategies we will tentatively opt for will be guided by our goals and objectives. If we wish students to deal with the upper levels of thinking, then the questions contemplated, if you are using Bloom's taxonomy, will be analysis, synthesis, and evaluation questions. If you are employing the syntax of the question, you may consider "Wh" questions, especially what questions dealing with causal antecedents, causal consequences, enablement, and judgmental. (The reader is referred to Chapter 4 where such questions are discussed in detail.) If your preference for classifying questions is by conceptual categories (see Chapter 4, pages 109–113), you may want to weigh questions that deal with properties and relation, especially if you are stressing critical thinking. How is X related to Y is a key aspect of analysis, which is a primary feature of critical thinking.

The types of questions contemplated while influenced by one's goals and objectives will also be impacted by one's preference for a particular classificatory scheme. You might be partial to classifying questions as to openness and closedness. Ideally, one should employ several ways of classifying questions. Such classifications should also be shared with your students so that they eventually engage thoughtfully in planning their questions.

The important point is that in reflecting on our possible questions and potential strategies we are striving to increase the likelihood of successfully attaining our objectives. Lesson purpose will determine question types. Emphasizing using questions and questioning strategies to get students to think effectively does not exclude the use of questions at the lower end of the cognitive taxonomy or at feature specification. There are no poor questions or, for that matter, good questions; there are only appropriate and inappropriate questions, their appropriateness determined by the purpose they are to play rather than their wording. Do the questions address the goal or objective of the lesson? If the lesson is to enable students to gather a data base for initial understanding of the field of study, then the questions selected and sequenced should emphasize knowledge and at most comprehension. Questions at the analysis level might well be inappropriate. Similarly, if one plans a lesson in which the objective is that students will draw warranted conclusions from material presented, then questions at the knowledge level only stressing definitions are inappropriate. Remember questions should be designed to do that which you want them to do. If they do what you want them to do—and students need to know this—then the questions are proper. Even the best written analysis question will be a poor question if all you want to know is the name of the president of Mexico.

Criteria Considerations

Considering question types does not guarantee questions of the best type possible. To be sure that we have the most effective questions of each type desired we need to consider certain criteria. If we want students to gain a knowledge base, we want appropriate knowledge level questions. Similarly, if students are to synthesize information or determine causal consequence, questions at these levels or having these foci must be employed.

A key criterion is that the question must address the content and activities under consideration. A science lesson about snails should contain questions geared to that content. If in this lesson students are to study the behavior of snails in particular environments, then questions should trigger in students observation.

The question "What can you tell me about life forms?" is inappropriate for this lesson, failing to deal specifically with snails. Also, a correct answer to the question is "I can tell you nothing." A question more to the point, "To what animal classification do snails belong?", informs students that the lesson focus is on snails and their classification. Still this may not be the best question. Usually, it is hard to determine if a question, standing in isolation, will allow students to attain the lesson's objective. Even so, we can assess whether the question is in the ball park, whether it will contribute along with other questions to students processing information successfully.

A related criterion is that the question suggests the activity for processing the information. Referring to our snail lesson, if we desire students to observe, then some questions in our class talk must suggest the activity. The question "Find out all that you can about snails" will not meet this criterion for it is unclear in informing the student as to what "find out" means. It could mean go to the library and read a book, observe a snail in the school terrarium, ask someone who is a snail expert, or something else. A much better question would be, "Look at the snails in our class terrarium and record their actions over a fifteen-minute period." Here the question informs students that they are to look for patterns of behavior.

A key assumption of questions mentioned in Chapter 2 was that questions suggested an answer. Indeed, the answer statement is the other half of the question sentence. Appropriate questions suggest the content and also denote tentative answers. The questions about looking at snails and recording their actions implies an answer form such as "Snails spend their time _____" or "Snails engage in doing _____."

Perhaps the key criterion of the effective question relates to its wording. Does the question's wording make clear what it expects, both cognitively and affectively, from the student? Can the student grasp the question's meaning? Will the question's wording enable the student to perform the desired task?

This criterion of clear wording is a bit complicated. For instance, questions beginning "How" or "Why" may not always herald high-level thought responses. For instance, you may ask the student, "How was the area settled?", wanting the student only to name who came into the region to homestead. [The student who realizes the context in which the question is raised replies correctly that the region was settled by farmers who wished to take over the range land.] If you wish high-level thinking you might phrase your question, "Knowing what you know about resource utilization, judge whether the original settlers made good use of the land?" In this situation, the student knows that the question focus is on effectiveness of resource utilization.

Likewise, when and where questions are not always low-level questions. Students after reading a particular document might hear the teacher ask, "When was this poem written?" The question appears low-level requiring as the answer only a date. However, assume that the poem employs a certain poetic form and makes certain references that place it in a particular time period. In responding, the students have to analyze the poem as to its style and mechanics and then identify those references that place it in time. In order to produce the date, students actually have to think critically.

In another lesson, the teacher asks, "Where will you find the shopping center?" Again, the question appears simple, only asking for a one-word knowledge response—the location. However, in this lesson students have not been told where this shopping center is. Rather they have to study a map and determine where the shopping center might be. The students have to apply location theory and engage in a type of problem solving. True the answer may be brief, such as "at the intersection of Broad Street and Highway 9," but students have actively produced the response.

A well-worded question encourages students to respond with optimal productivity. Students know what is expected, so no need exists to follow the original question with a second rephrased one to get students started. The well-worded question provides adequate directions within it. The question about resource utilization directed students to judge whether original settlers made good use of the land. Furthermore, they were to judge drawing on what they already knew about resource utilization—the students received a clue as to what criteria to employ in making their judgments.

In stating "knowing what you know about resource utilization," the question tied its focus to others previously raised about resource utilization. An efffective question will often, through its wording, enable the student to see the relationship of this question with ones previously asked.

Our wording of questions depends upon more than just the content and experiences to be provided. We must take into consideration our students' learning styles and the level of the lesson. We may want closed questions at the beginning of a lesson and with students who are concrete sequential (Note: The terms concrete sequential, concrete abstract, concrete random and abstract sequential are coined by Anthony Gregoric).[12] This will furnish structure for our students. In contrast, if our students are rather sophisticated and random abstract and the lesson is appearing in the middle of a well-developed unit, we might word our questions to be open-ended, allowing students more choice in how they will process them.

A well-worded question considers students' intellectual and experiential maturity. With students just beginning a unit on culture, most likely it would be unwise to ask, "Who can tell me what culture means?" However, we often do hear such questions posed at the outset of a unit. Students with no prior experience with this concept, at least at an intellectual level, are not likely to respond productively. Also, "tell me" is a bit vague—does the teacher want students to express their thinking on culture, someone else's thinking, or what the book states? With a class unfamiliar with culture, it might be more effective over a week's period to ask specific questions about people's actions and then to request students to classify these actions. After this, the teacher might indicate to the students that the classified actions represent what certain scholars call culture. In this class, the questions served to build a knowledge base and then directed students to analyze the knowledge base looking for patterns. The teacher then told this class that these things, actions, can be included under what people call culture.

If, however, the teacher had had his or her class studying culture for six months, then an initial question might have been, "From all of our previous considerations of culture, what might be a powerful description of culture?" Students in responding can, in this situation, draw upon previous learnings, realizing that the action requested is a grand synthesis of previously processed material.

Writing or Selecting Questions: Questioning Strategies

In planning as decision making, the final stage is action, the actual writing or selecting of questions and questioning strategies for our lessons. Several sub steps exist in the writing, selecting process: (1) reflecting on the content about which you wish to question, (2) writing or selecting a tentative list of questions, (3) judging the tentative list for appropriateness, and (4) revising the questions and forming strategies for the particular lesson.

Activity

MY QUESTIONS TYPES, MY QUESTIONING STRATEGIES

A major stage in planning is contemplating possible types of questions for our classes and ways to organize them into strategies. However, in the planning process, prior to considering question types we must engage in analysis. We need to analyze our questions in our classroom talk. The results of this will influence what question options we consider.

Think of your own classroom talk and analyze it. Is it generally effective? What about your questions? Are they on target, addressing your goals and objectives? Are the types of questions you employ similar to the types mentioned in the previous two chapters?

In twenty-five words or less jot down what you think about your questions. Perhaps share your statement with a colleague who knows your teaching. Is there agreement?

Reflecting on the Content

Making sure that our questions are educative requires that we take time to think. In the previous major stages of creating questions, we have been reflecting on questions in general; now we reflect on the specific lesson content. What are the demands of *this* lesson content? What questions might arise from students considering *this* content? What do I want my students to know? What information do I think my students will want to know from studying this content?

Related to reflecting on the content of *this* lesson is considering possible student activities appropriate for this lesson. What activities can my questions suggest to facilitate my students comprehending this content?

Such reflection leads us to the next, second action stage.

Writing or Selecting Tentative Questions, Questioning Strategies

The teacher, knowledgeable about questions and questioning, in thinking about particular lesson content will automatically think of potential questions and ways to sequence them. Frequently the teacher jots these questions down.

In this second substage of planning, the jotting of questions is made more systematic. The teacher ponders each major lesson topic. For each topic, possible questions are noted that will focus students' attention and get them to consider the content in certain ways. From this pool, the teacher can obtain the most appropriate question. Regardless of whether one is going to write his or her own questions or select them from school materials, one needs to be mindful of the goals and objectives of the lesson.

Not all questions have to be created from scratch. At times, we will just select questions from our instructional materials; for instance, our textbook.

We do not want to delude ourselves into thinking, however, that just because the questions are in commercially prepared instructional materials they are automatically appropriate. We need to study such materials and their questions. Are the questions effective in relation to our lesson's objectives? Can the questions in the text stimulate interest with our particular students? Can our students deal with these questions productively? Do we have adequate time to process these questions? Are these questions of comparable cognitive or affective emphasis with those we have been using in our class dialogue? Are the text questions so sequenced as to complement our questioning?

Often, upon analyzing text questions, we find a dominance of one type of question that may conflict with our lesson's general goal. We may still check off those questions, however, that at least reflect our lesson's focus and then revise them to reflect the cognitive or affective emphasis of our class. For example, if the text section contains mostly knowledge questions, we may wish to revise them into analysis questions, still taking some cues from these knowledge questions.

In revising text questions, remember that they should facilitate the attainment of the stated objectives and relate to pupils' readiness and interests. Again, consider the time schedule. Do the revised questions meet the relevancy criterion? Are the revisions clearly worded without giving undue clues? Do they reflect the intended cognitive or affective level? Mindful of such considerations, we should create a good tentative list of questions drawn from texts, articles, games, or even the curriculum guide. We can at this juncture tentatively select particular strategies into which we can plan our questions.

Judging the Tentative Question List—
Potential Strategies

Making some tentative revisions already engages us in judgment; it activates a type of formative evaluation. Here in substep three we are now doing a final evaluation of our questions and strategies. Here we are applying the criteria of an effective question: relates to the content; depicts the activity clearly to the student; is clearly worded; is appropriate for the student's learning style; appeals to the student's interests and capabilities; is feasible to process in terms of time and resources. A final criterion, not previously mentioned, is that the question has the potential to trigger additional questions, further inquiry.

Drawing on these criteria, the teachers check off those questions to be used without modification, those with potential but needing revision, and those not appropriate for their class and or the topic. This leads us to the final substep: revising.

Revising the Questions and Strategies

What actually needs to be accomplished with questions requiring revision depends upon the flaw identified in the question. The flaw of a question is situation dependent sometimes; for example, a question's focus may be appropriate but, for a particular lesson, is at the wrong cognitive level. This does not mean that the question is a bad question, only that the cognitive level is not suitable for the lesson. In this instance, therefore, the revision is to rework the question to enhance its cognitive level. For instance, a textbook question on the American Revolution read, "What were the causes of the Revolution?" The question has value, but as it relates to the textbook it is only comprehension. Wanting students to analyze the causes, you revise the question to read, "Of the several causes of the American Revolution listed in the book, which can be classified as major?" To respond, students must now analyze, think about the causes given in the book and determine the importance of each to the Revolution.

Occasionally, questions on the tentative list just require tighter wording. "How many participated in the Continental Congress?" may be reworded as "Which individuals represented the various colonies at the Continental Congress?" The question is clear in that the information desired is the names of the representatives at the Congress. The first question exhibited some confusion as to what was meant by participation.

Often, when considering our lesson's questions, we decide when they should be raised in class dialogue—their sequencing, their inclusion in particular strategies. (Particular strategies will be discussed in later chapters.)

In reviewing our tentative list of questions we may conclude that certain ones should precede others.

Perhaps our tentative list has a sequence suggested by the development of the questions in the textbook. We may wish our students to process the information in a different sequence, employ a different strategy. Perhaps, the book presented the material deductively, with questions related to a general idea. We may aim to encourage our students to think inductively. To accomplish this, we may reverse the question sequence, inquiring in our lesson about the particular and concluding with questions directed at the general.

At times, it is valuable to have a colleague react to our tentative list of questions and our first attempts at revision. A colleague can bring a fresh perspective to the topic. A colleague can serve as a coach. If we wish to use our colleague in this way, it is valuable to involve him or her early in our planning. This should not be threatening. Developing effective questions takes time. Colleague cooperation provides mutual benefits with all parties gaining.

At the conclusion of this substage, we possess a list or map of questions arranged in particular orders or strategies that quite likely will facilitate our students in processing information in desired ways. This list of final revision, however, is not a dialogue script to be followed rigidly. Rather, it is a guideline proposing types of questions and their sequencing. Ideally, the questions generated will suggest additional questions aimed at getting students to think deeply about information confronting them.

Certainly, questions in our class dialogue will resemble those on our guidesheets (lesson plans). If we are new to this lesson topic or new to questions, we may even stick rather closely to our questions and their sequence. Our first teaching of this lesson may serve as a type of guided practice. We may even have a colleague present to observe our class actions and perhaps to provide coaching suggestions on how we can improve. As we get more knowledgeable about and skilled in questions, we should be able to engage our students in questioning and thinking without colleague assistance.

Following these planning steps will not guarantee success on all educational fronts, but it certainly will increase the likelihood that our questions and questioning strategies will have the potential to heighten the thinking and information processing of our students.

Students in the Question Planning Process

"In a certain fundamental sense, it is these individuals' ability to answer questions that characterize them as experts...."[13]

"Good thinkers are willing to think, and may even find thinking enjoyable."[14]

All educators want students to be expert questioners and thinkers, to find the processes of inquiry and thinking enjoyable to such a degree that they as individuals will be self-motivated and take pleasure in lifelong learning. For our students to attain some degree of questioning expertise, some proficiency in thinking, such that they possess a fairly sophisticated grasp of information and a continuing desire for study, we need to share with them our knowledge about thinking and questioning.

All of the information presented in this book should eventually be taught to students. Some of the teaching may be direct in lessons apart from a certain subject's content. Some can be indirect or woven into the processing of certain subject matter. The entire emphasis on metacognition is to make students aware of what they are doing when thinking, when questioning, when processing information such that they not only have executive control over their processes but can continue to perfect their thinking, their questioning.

The stages of planning questions and questioning strategies that have been presented in the first part of this chapter can be directly taught to students.

Activity

YOUR TURN

You have just read about the four substages involved in actually writing or selecting questions. Select a topic to teach and employ these four steps in planning a questioning sequence for your class. Perhaps have a colleague review your questions.

Did you personalize the planning steps in any way? How? Why did you do that? Remember, the steps are suggestive; feel free to be creative but have a reason for making modifications in the planning procedure.

Try out your lesson using your questions. How did the lesson work? Did you use most of your questions? Yes, good! No, why not?

You should get into the habit of planning all your questions in a similar fashion until it becomes second nature. Remember: good plans, good questions, good lessons.

Students can learn about the types of questions, the assumptions behind questions, the dynamics of questions as specific linguistic devices. Students can be shown how to and given opportunities to analyze the various types of questions they will encounter either in people's speech or in materials confronted in and out of the classroom.

If students are to generate a question, they must be conscious of their level of knowledge regarding a particular topic. This is the second major stage in planning: analysis. Chapter 2 noted that we all need to possess a certain level of information to ascertain what we do not know, our level of ignorance. This level of prior knowledge is obtained in the first planning stage of becoming knowledgeable. The necessary data may be furnished students through our direct instruction. From this analysis stage, students not only get a feel for what declarative knowledge is required, but also begin to grasp what they need to learn about procedural knowledge, about questions, about thinking. From analysis, students are able to flesh out their goals and objectives.

In step three of planning, considering goals and objectives, students create a stake in their own learning, their own thinking; the goals and objectives, at least some of them, are their goals and objectives. There may be times when students' goals and objectives for a lesson differ from ours, but both sets need not be incompatible. For instance, we as teachers may have a goal for a language lesson that students upon receiving a particular instruction have an understanding of the various uses of language in the modern world. Students, while not ignoring our objective, may have their own objective, "By studying the various uses of language, I will gain prestige with my class colleagues." The objective has been personalized; the student has ownership.

Students with the "uses of language" lesson may raise questions more in the affective realm: "With which use of language do I feel most comfortable? How do I feel when my friends engage in using language in particular ways?" In contrast, we as teachers may have planned for this lesson the following questions: "How many uses of language are available to us? Why are particular uses of language found in certain professions?" Ideally, if both we and students have consciously planned the lesson, then class questioning is enriched, broadened.

The fourth step in planning, presented earlier for the teacher, can also be directly taught to students. With such instruction students realize that they must consider question types with regard to the content at hand. They need to consider questions mindful of the criteria for good questions. At this stage students are gaining information that will make them better questioners.

These first four planning stages, while crucial, will be for naught if students lack opportunities to write or select their questions—to engage in the four substages that teachers themselves have utilized: (1) reflecting on the content, (2) writing or selecting a tentative list of questions, (3) judging the appropriateness and value of the list, and then (4) revising the questions and strategies for a particular lesson.

In a time of knowledge explosion, we need to teach procedural knowledge to our students. Yet we have still been rather vague in outlining to students the details of how one actually does process information. Engaging students in question planning and in critiquing their planning allows these youth to gain a command of their learning.

This general framework (heuristic) for planning questions and questioning strategies is useful regardless of the content being studied. Students should realize that this general planning method can be employed in planning particular questioning strategies and in engaging in various questioning activities. In Chapter 8, attention will be given to specific ways in which students can actually plan, utilize and assess their questions. For now, it is sufficient to know that these general stages can allow students to gain command of "knowledge how."

Central to fostering in students expertise in questioning and thinking is having them participate in the process of learning. Effective inquirers require opportunities to see the question as an effective tool. We teachers as exemplars must model effective questioning. Do our questions stimulate pupils to engage in searches? Do our questions serve as handles by which students attain increased understanding?

For students to become proficient thinkers and questioners, time should be scheduled into each day for planning, for asking questions, for challenging classmates and even the teacher. Students need opportunities to react to various data and then to generate significant questions. They need occasions to discuss their selections with their peers. Explaining to classmates why certain questions are crucial may be more useful in the learning process than the actual answers generated.

To become a fully functioning learner, the student needs detailed knowledge of process. Development of this knowledge must be started in the early grades. This awareness results from not only asking the student what he or she knows but from asking how he or she got to know such information.

Awareness of process, knowledge how, can foster in students an aggressive attitude toward learning and an eagerness to understand themselves within this world. Armed with this attitude students develop an acceptance of their conclusions as tentative, realizing that with all information there is uncertainty, thus the need for continued inquiry, additional thought.

CONCLUSION

Planning increases the likelihood that what we desire will occur. This chapter presented a planning heuristic that we in education can employ to create effective questions and questioning strategies. It does not guarantee that results will be positive, but it does increase the probability that such will be the case.

Planning was presented as a complex process, a type of decision making engaged in to stimulate optimal learning. It is generalizable in that the steps presented can be employed when planning questions in any subject matter field.

Few among us would argue against careful planning, but not all of us might agree that students should be privy to knowledge about the planning steps. However, the case was advanced that students need to be knowledgeable of ways of planning their questions and questioning strategies if they are to control their own learning and develop an enthusiasm for inquiry. Such student awareness can develop informally in the classroom, but direct instruction in the planning process as well as the nature of the question also needs to occur. Ideally, whatever we as teachers know about questions and questioning should also be possessed by our students. True thinkers, true questioners will not occur accidentally; such individuals result only from conscious effort by the parties involved in learning—teachers and students.

NOTES

1. Herman H. Horne, *Story-Telling, Questioning, and Studying* (New York: The Macmillan Co., 1916), p. 66.

2. J. T. Dillon, *Teaching and the Art of Questioning* (Bloomington, Indiana, Phi Delta Kappa, 1983), 7–8.

3. Richard Kindsvatter, William Wilen, and Margaret Ishler, *Dynamics of*

Effective Teaching (New York: Longman, 1988).

4. Ambrose A. Clegg, Jr., "Why Questions?" in William W. Wilen, ed. *Questions, Questioning Techniques, and Effective Teaching* (Washington, D.C.: National Education Association, 1987), 11–22.

5. Meredith D. Gall and others, "Effects of Questioning Techniques and Recitation on Student Listening," *American Educational Research Journal* (1978) 15, 175–199.

6. Barry K. Beyer, *Practical Strategies for the Teaching of Thinking* (Boston: Allyn and Bacon, Inc., 1987).

7. Daniel L. Stufflebeam, *Educational Evaluation and Decision Making* (Itasca, Ill.: Peacock, 1971).

8. Barry K. Beyer, *Practical Strategies for the Teaching of Thinking.*

9. Irwin D. J. Bross, *Design for Decision* (New York: The Free Press, 1953).

10. Allan C. Ornstein and Francis P. Hunkins, *Curriculum: Foundations, Principles, and Issues* (Englewood Cliffs, N.J.: Prentice Hall, Inc., 1988).

11. Stufflebeam, *Educational Evaluation and Decision Making.*

12. Anthony Gregoric, information gained in workshop and in conversation with Gregoric, 1984.

13. James R. Gavelek and Taffy E. Raphael, "Metacognition, Instruction, and the Role of Questioning Activities," in D. L. Forrest-Pressley, G. E. MacKinnon, and T. Gary Waller, *Metacognition, Cognition, and Human Performance,* Vol. 2 (Orlando, Fl.: Academic Press, Inc., 1985), 118.

14. Allan A. Glatthorn and Jonathan Baron, "The Good Thinker," in Arthur L. Costa, ed., *Developing Minds* (Alexandria, VA: The Association for Supervision and Curriculum Development, 1985), 51.

6

Questioning

Within the

Classroom

Teaching engages one in various verbal and non-verbal actions designed to stimulate thinking and learning in students. Integral to these specialized actions are questions. These actions are called strategies or teaching methods. From Chapter 1, we recall Hyman's definition of a strategy: "a carefully prepared plan involving a sequence of steps designed to achieve a given goal."[1]

The previous chapters have pointed out the place of questions within the realm of thinking, the nature of questions, the various ways to classify questions, and the steps necessary in planning questions. This chapter presents information on general strategies that can be used in our classrooms and also directly taught to students so they gain executive control over their own learning, their thinking.

GENERAL STRATEGIES, TEACHING METHODS

We teachers have several general strategies into which we can incorporate questions: lecture, discussion, demonstration, and inquiry. Each strategy is generic; that is, applicable to any and all subject matter. Lecture and demonstration are teacher dominated; discussion often involves influence sharing by both teacher and students, and inquiry ideally is managed primarily by students. We consider these strategies as general in that besides being applicable to any and all subject matter, each involves a recurrent patterning of teacher behavior and/or student behavior, each can be employed by more than one teacher, and each contributes or has the potential to contribute to student learning.[2]

The Lecture Method

Some might wonder about discussing the lecture method in a book dealing with questions; after all, the lecture method just presents large amounts of information. There are times, however, when we do want to present information to students; for this purpose, the lecture method is most productive. Perhaps the lecture method will be better regarded if we perceive it as a directive strategy or exposition, an explanation of information. Certainly, a good lecture directs students' attention to the information being considered and offers explanation. When well done, it contains junctures where questions are posed.

We may be better disposed to lecture as a method if we realize that it is a type of direct teaching that can lay the foundation or set the stage for pupils in their processing of information. Lectures can involve students interactively. We can start a lecture with a question, a problem, or even a controversy. Commencing a lecture in this way captures students' interests and encourages the raising of questions that can serve as advance organizers for the information to be received.

Students can and should participate in a lecture. For this to happen, the lecture must be planned carefully following various rules. Nekrasova, cited by McLeish, has presented eight basic rules that can guide students from passive receivers of information to reflective thinkers: (1) the lecturer should start the lecture with a presentation of problems and rules or indications of methods for solving them rather than a finished conclusion; (2) the lecture should sometimes include controversial subjects, and time should be allowed for *raising questions* about these subjects and debating them; (3) the presentation of material in the lecture should follow systematically psychological principles that indicate how students form perceptions and process information; (4) the significance of the information being presented is made clear by relating it to the students' realities; there is a connection of theory to practice; (5) *there are significant questions posed throughout the lecture with time allowed for questions by the students;* (6) the lecture should support various points with the citation of various experiments and demonstrations; (7) the lecture presents problems that either arise from the lecture itself or from the school materials; and (8) the *students are actively encouraged to pose problems and questions to the lecturer that will be processed at the conclusion of the lecture.*[3]

When well done, a lecture arouses in students active interest in the content. It furnishes a foundation upon which students can build independent comprehension. For students new to information, the lecture introduces them to the field, presents information requisite for gaining an initial grasp of the information. At first consideration the lecture seems inappropriate for teaching a skill. If we think of the lecture as a type of directive strategy, however, then even the lecture can be so employed; we can present a lecture to get students skilled in raising particular types of questions or learning the rudiments of ways of thinking.

Beyer notes that with novice students, it may be more suitable to use a rather didactic introductory strategy, a directive strategy.[4] Assuming students are to gain skill in using particular kinds of questions, the teacher presents some information about the nature of questions and the ways in which questions can be classified. The teacher indicates that raising effective questions is a problem, but a problem worth solving. (This is the first rule of creating a good lecture: presentation of problems.) The teacher encourages students to pose some questions about the presentation of this information. Drawing on these questions, the teacher presents additional information relating to the skill of questioning. All the while, the teacher is making reference to the importance of questions in students' school and out of school lives (Rule 4 of Nekrasova's list). The various ways of questioning are then presented to lay the foundation for later processing of questioning.

Rule 6 of a good lecture states that the lecture should support the various points with the citation of various experiments and demonstrations. Drawing on this rule, the teacher takes time to furnish examples of the various types of questions or particular strategies that could be used. Again, with lecture, the information presented is to acquaint the students with questions, to make them expert questioners.

In concluding the lecture or exposition, the teacher encourages the students to reflect on what has been presented, to review the information, the skill. This is basic lecture Rule 8. What the lecturer has done is move through various steps: (1) stage setting, (2) development and explanation, and (3) concluding. Figure 6–1 shows these steps with the substeps.

The substages under the lecture-exposition strategy are suggestive. One need not employ them all or follow the sequence noted every time. There will be times when only a portion of the strategy might be used; for instance, Step 1 and a bit of Step 2. The conclusion might be traded for a demonstration or discussion instead. Important to remember is that throughout this strategy, significant questions are presented. The level of questions presented in the stage setting will influence the level at which students receive the information. If initial questions direct students just to look for particular facts, then students will listen only for such information. If, however, key questions urge students to consider the place of questions in their lives, then information heard will be thought about at a higher level of thinking.

Step 1: STAGE SETTING

Presentation of examples, problems, rules

Allowing for any student questions

Tying the lecture, exposition, to students' previous experiences

Pointing out the worth of questions and questioning.

Step 2: DEVELOPMENT AND EXPLANATION

Presenting information on the skill of questioning

Relating importance of questions to students' school and out of school lives

Presenting examples of various ways of questioning, pointing out situations when particular questioning strategies might be employed

Allowing students to question the information, skill being presented.

Step 3: CONCLUDING

Presenting a review of information presented

Encouraging students to reflect on the information presented

Encouraging students to reflect on ways in which and when the information can be used.

Figure 6–1
Stages of Lecture—Exposition Strategy

The Discussion Method

Contrasted with the lecture method, which is primarily a teacher-centered group of behaviors designed to present information, the discussion method is a variety of classroom interaction patterns involving both teacher and student.[5] Essentially, it is a social activity, a cooperative engagement of people relating to a topic in a rational, purposeful manner.[6] This method postulates five attributes: "The discussion method occurs when (1) a group of persons, usually in the roles of moderator-leader and participant, (2) assembles at a designated time and place, (3) to communicate interactively, (4) using speaking, nonverbal, and listening processes, (5) in order to achieve instructional objectives."[7]

A discussion likens itself to a purposeful group conversation managed by the teacher for the purposes of attaining a great many educational objectives. While demonstration as a general method is closer to lecture in degree of teacher domination, discussion is being considered at this juncture for discussion and lecture often are combined by the teacher in a general classroom approach. Lecture sets the information stage; discussion enriches the students' understanding of the material presented.

Activity

SELF-CRITIQUE

We all lecture in our classrooms. There is nothing wrong with that provided they are good lectures and we don't overuse them. On page 144, eight basic rules developed by Nekrasova were noted:

1. lecture starts with presentation of problems, indicates method of solving them
2. lecture sometimes includes controversial subjects and allows time for raising questions
3. lecture follows systematically psychological principles
4. lecture relates information to students' realities
5. lecture poses significant questions throughout it
6. lecture cites various experiments and demonstrations
7. lecture presents problems that arise from lecture or from school problems
8. students actively encouraged to pose problems and questions.

Using these criteria, tape a class lecture of yours and rate it using the following checksheet. Place a check in the appropriate space. Pay particular attention to those criteria relating to questions.

Criteria	High Marks	Average	Low Marks
1			
2			
3			
4			
5			
6			
7			
8			

How did you do? Where do you need to improve? Reflect on why you have the profile you do.

The first attribute of discussion, describing group behavior, suggests that the number of persons in a group will influence the effectiveness of a discussion. Certainly, we can manage a discussion with thirty students; however, it is more effective if the group contains from five to eight students. Small numbers tend to enhance the quality of discussion for the group is a cluster of interacting persons behaving in certain ways partly in reaction to others' behaviors. In smaller groups members have more opportunities to interact, more chances to modify their thinking.

A small group is also easier to manage logistically in terms of space, easier to assemble: the second attribute. However, the time spent in discussion can vary, from a few minutes to over an hour. With adults, discussions sometimes last several hours. Today, with interactive video, students can assemble to discuss electronically. This may enrich the discussion by bringing together students from a much greater diversity of backgrounds. The richness of the group in terms of their experiential backgrounds and levels of interests regarding a topic enables students to stretch their thinking, their questioning.

The key attribute of discussion is interactive communication—the chance to converse with fellow students, to challenge them, to question them. Ideally, the teacher also participates as a fellow student, albeit an expert student.

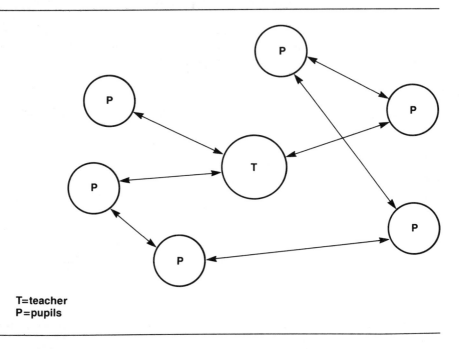

T=teacher
P=pupils

Figure 6–2
Dynamics of Effective Discussion

Interactive communication involves speaking and listening. Through discussion teacher and students make statements and raise questions that both structure their information worlds and disrupt their worlds. Participants learn to raise questions that both organize and reorganize perceptions and understandings.[8] Good discussions are dialectic in nature,[9] based on the notion that learning is more than just accumulating information at increasing levels of abstractness; it is more than just raising questions at increasing higher levels to have more sophisticated understanding of knowledge. Good discussions are arguments in the best sense of that word in that they introduce to students contradictory activity, the disruption of existing behaviors resulting in new behaviors, new understandings. Well done, a discussion allows students to formulate new conceptualizations, raise new questions, engage in novel thinking. By engaging actively in interactive communication students place themselves in conforming and non-conforming behaviors. A discussion occurs "between two poles: activity intended to mold relatively stable behaviors, on one side, and activity intended to disrupt these behaviors in order to allow for new ones, more effective and refined than previous ones, on the other side."[10]

Good discussion follows Socratic questioning. First, questions focus students' attention on the topic, the level of the question depending upon the purpose of the particular phase of the discussion. Once purpose has been achieved, students possess a particular understanding or mind set; now the teacher, or even another student, raises a question that breaks the mind set and asks if there is perhaps another way of considering the information. If this is the case, what might be the case if another situation arose?

Socratic questioning encourages students to challenge their own structures, to disrupt them, to contemplate alternatives, consider consequences to the alternatives. The questioning asks students to judge the worth of their positions and then to assess the value of their new positions. It demands that they analyze the bases for their arguments, critiquing the means of their analyses. In good discussion, students realize that questions accompany the making of statements so as to refine the statements, stimulating additional questions. This making of statements, refining of statements through questioning, generating additional questions, and challenging questions and their resulting answers leads to the attainment of the teacher's instructional objectives: the fifth attribute of the discussion method.

While some people identify various types of discussion, it is this writer's view that there is only one type—reflective discussion[11]—the reason being that all discussion aims, or should aim at engaging students in high-level critical and creative thinking. Certainly, the degree of structure of a discussion under the teacher's management will vary from highly structured, useful for students new to discussion or new to the topic, to rather free-wheeling, for students skilled in discussion techniques and quite familiar with the lesson focus. Initially, the teacher may be the time keeper, the major questioner, and the presenter of positions. As time passes, however, the conversation should become more open-ended among students and teacher, with time to raise questions that redirect students in their dialogue and contemplation.

What makes the discussion method interesting and challenging is that the interaction pattern of this conversation is flexible in both structure and in particulars of its enactment. It can go from highly structured with the teacher furnishing guidance, initiating most of the questions, and managing who responds to the questions, to very open-ended in which the students share with the teacher the direction of the discussion, the questions raised, and who participates. The less teacher involvement there is, the more student participation.

If a discussion is too structured with the teacher just going around the room asking questions, the method is really recitation. Not that recitation is unimportant, but recitation is a teacher-dominated procedure to ascertain students' levels of information; it is not designed to facilitate student questioning, reflection, intellectual productivity. Recitations resemble quiz shows with students vying for opportunities to demonstrate that they have the right answers. It is convergent in orientation, stressing knowledge of specifics, not thinking.[12]

Openness is central to good discussion. The skilled teacher fosters this openness by employing and encouraging students to utilize open-ended divergent questions at upper cognitive levels. Bridges elaborated on this characteristic of discussion openness:

> (a) the matter is open for discussion; (b) the discussants are open minded; (c) the discussion is open to all arguments; (d) the discussion is open to any person; (e) the time limit is open; (f) the learning outcomes are open, not predictable; (g) the purposes and practices of the discussion are out in the open, not covert; and (h) the discussion is open-ended, not required to come to a single conclusion.[13]

This writer would also add, the particular questioning strategies employed are open; that is, varied. Effective discussion leaders realize that engaging a variety of questioning strategies will increase the probability that their instructional objectives will be achieved.

Discussion Foci

We discuss for several reasons: for elaboration or further explanation of a topic; for problem solving, for summation; for problem generation; for question answering; for question raising; for forecasting future events, for policy determination—the list is endless. If we can think of it, we can discuss it. Of course, discussion is not sharing ignorance, not what Roby calls a "bull session" in which people share ideas without supportive data.[14] A good discussion builds on a knowledge base that may have been gained through a lecture or exposition or some other means, perhaps from an initial reading done in response to a key question.

Good discussion can guide students to consensus and uniformity of thought, but more often than not it leads students to divergence of conclusions and idiosyncracy of thought. When concluding an effective discussion, students, while having some answers to initial questions, should have even more questions. Good discussion serves as a door through which students can pass to additional inquiry, additional thinking. It is not primarily used as a vehicle for bringing students to a nice, certain, secure conclusion. If we always bring students to consensus, then we are engaged in a behavior "antithetical to the spirit and practice of critical thought."[15] Good discussions serve as send-offs to thinking, inquiring journeys.

Steps in the Discussion Process

Essentially, there are four phases that structure the discussion method: commencement, confrontation, challenge, and conclusion.

Commencement

Obviously a method, any method, must begin—commence. At this juncture one gains the attention of the group either by making some statement or statements or by presenting a set of questions. This first stage gets students aware of the nature and purpose of the discussion. Students may be informed through various statements as to the problem, issue, or topic to be discussed. Small discussion groups might be formed at this point. Teachers at this time may elicit from students their concerns; this is especially important if students are to gain some degree of executive control over their own learning. Students need opportunities to determine the purpose of the discussion or the questions to be addressed.

Confrontation

In confrontation, the teacher tells the students the rules of the discussion game. This is what we are going to do; these are the procedures we are going to follow. Confrontation is required even after students are skilled discussion participants. Students themselves need to realize the necessity of confronting themselves. Just what is the issue for discussion? What are the required questions? Why is it important to consider this issue in this manner?

In confrontation, problems can be classified and topics or issues elaborated, made clearer. Students can clarify how they are to process the topic in focus. Perhaps the teacher at this point states that in our discussion we are going to determine all the reasons for having a particular view. In another discussion, the pupils are challenged to gain support for an opposing view.

Challenge

The challenge stage is the actual discussion—issues have been identified, rules presented; now we are into interactive communication about the issue. Here teacher and students raise questions that stimulate thinking about the issue or problem. Here teacher and students through their dialogue create structures and challenge through questions these structures, breaking and reconstructing them as necessary. Here students contribute their ideas, raise questions, suggest solutions, justify recommendations, make predictions.

The teacher as skilled discussion leader gets students first to reflect on their data base and then to critique their own statements and questions. The teacher uses adequate wait time; students require time to reflect, to think, to question, to change directions in their information processing.

Time must also be provided so students can challenge each other, questioning their classmates' positions and conclusions. In a discussion, students can work as team members, discussion members, not just as individuals. Research has shown that the quality of products produced by groups is superior to those produced by individuals in proportion of the correct solutions to problems and the time required to reach solutions.[16]

A key technique for both teacher and students to use in discussion is the probe—the further questioning of students regarding their responses, the challenging of them to explain their thinking, expand their thinking to additional situations, issues, or problems, to clarify their statements. "When you say that people have to live within their means, what do you mean? Do you mean financial resources? Do you mean within their abilities? How can we determine what are the boundaries of our intellectual means?"

Probes for expanded detail and clarification force students to think. They call them to activate the various critical thinking skills outlined in chapter 1. In a discussion challenge, students may have to defend the credibility of a source of their statement, may have to reveal unstated assumptions, and may have to admit to having a certain bias. Certainly, they will have to determine and defend the strength of any argument or claim made.

In the challenge stage, there are nonquestion alternatives that can trigger student thinking and engagement. Dillon has found that such nonquestion alternatives can enrich a lesson. These nonquestion alternatives are: declarative statements, reflective restatements of students' comments; invitations for students to furnish elaboration, wait time (deliberate silence), and statements of encouragement.[17] More attention is given to these nonquestion alternatives later in this book.

Concluding

The concluding phase closes the discussion. It is really a partial close, however, for students should realize that there are still questions to be answered, further directions for exploration. Even so, one does have to come to some tentative ending. A main action here is to have the students draw conclusions and, perhaps more importantly, put these conclusions into some type of context with their previous classroom learning. Here the students make known the new ways that they have structured their knowledge as a result of this interactive communication; perhaps furnishing brief defenses of their new knowledge arrangements.

The conclusion in some ways sets the stage for the next discussion—providing grist for launching into new avenues of thinking, of questioning. At this final stage, students and teachers alike participate in summarizing where they have been (good for developing metacognitive awareness) and what they have concluded—where they have achieved consensus, where they have uncovered divergence, the insights gained regarding the topic and their manner of dealing with the topic. Also, at this stage, the teacher and students can specify where their conclusion can relate to other clusters of knowledge, other situations.

To summarize, the discussion method has four generalizable steps:

- Commencement

    Gaining attention of the group

    Clarifying purpose of the discussion

    Creating discussion groups

- Confrontation

    Presenting rules of the discussion game

    Classifying specifically the problem

- Challenge

    Raising questions to trigger appropriate thinking about the topic

    Contributing ideas

    Raising challenges to fellow students

    Raising nonquestion alternatives

- Concluding

    Bringing the discussion to a close

    Drawing conclusions

    Defending conclusions

    Setting stage for next discussion

    Attaining consensus

Discussion is specialized talk, engaged in to enable students to attain educational objectives. When well done students gain a sense of excitement

Activity

CHALLENGE

Sometimes we seek the safe road. The discussion method, however, offers us and our students opportunities to live a bit dangerously; that is, to explore and debate ideas somewhat controversial, ideas that push our boundaries, and wrest us from our comfortable ways of thinking.

One of the steps in planning a discussion is confrontation. Think of a topic that will challenge your thinking and your students' thinking and map out a discussion strategy following the steps presented in this chapter. Share your plans with a colleague and then with one or two students whose opinion you value. Get their reactions to your plans. Is the discussion really as controversial as you think? How might you add spice to it, to expand students' views of the topic? How do you react to your colleagues' suggestions; your students'?

Try out your challenge discussion with a small group of students, informing them that you are really engaging in a trial run with this approach. Besides enjoying being involved, students may well begin to view themselves differently, as persons who have something to contribute to the teacher.

Have a colleague view your mini-discussion and then debrief. What should you continue or change?

---

about being students; about raising questions, their questions; about doing their own thinking.

Demonstration

Demonstration, a teacher dominated method, aims to show students how something works or should be performed. A variation of the lecture it presents information employing visual and behavioral aids. With demonstration, the teacher may explain how a particular simple machine works. Instead of verbalizing, the teacher has a model of the machine and, as he or she talks, activates the model to reveal its operation. Sometimes with demonstration, the teacher explains what is occurring in a picture; other times, the teacher comments on the showing of a motion picture. At times the demonstration actually takes the students into the community for on-site viewing of some action or event, with the teacher explaining what is happening. This might be the case when the class visits a legislative session to observe the legislative process in action. Field trips can be viewed as demonstration orchestrated by the teacher in which people outside of the school perform some action.

When we wish our students to gain command of a particular skill, we can use demonstration. Students, upon hearing about a new skill such as critical thinking, may want to be shown how to use it. For example, if we want our students to be skilled in determining the factual accuracy of a statement, we can show how we would look at statements, classify them, what questions we would raise to determine the accuracy, what criteria we are employing.

We could demonstrate this skill by telling the students directly what we are thinking as we ask ourselves, "Is this statement accurate?" If the statement is "The Hungarian Revolution occurred in 1956," we could demonstrate how we determine the correctness of the statement: Where is this statement reported? Is it hearsay or can I discover it in a reference book? (Yes to reference book) Is this statement reported in any other book? (Yes) Is the term revolution a fact or an interpretation in this instance? (Essentially an interpretation) What might a Soviet historian say about the event? (Might say it was a police action, not a revolution) and so forth.

The final conclusion might be that if one takes a western orientation, then the statement is correct. However, if one takes a Soviet or Eastern Block orientation, then the statement needs qualification.

By demonstrating the process of questioning, the student sees how one applies the skill of determining factual accuracy.

We can exhibit to students how one actually employs a thinking strategy. Wishing students to gain some skill in problem solving, we might schedule a role playing situation in which the teacher and a student colleague act out the steps of the thinking strategy. The demonstration begins with the setting of the problem stage. Perhaps the objective is to have students realize how they can select an effective means of communicating particular situations. For example, the class is dealing with the issue of recycling waste materials. The teacher informs the students that the problem is to convince the public of the importance of recycling. The challenge is to determine how best to do this.

In role playing, the teacher and student colleague raise questions about waste materials. What types of waste material do we have? How do we now process what we have? Are our means of disposing waste the best possible? Are we running out of places to put our waste? Additional questions can be raised. In showing students what types of questions to raise, the class comes to realize that we are running out of places for dumping waste, and the dump sites now in use are chemically contaminating ground water.

The next step of the strategy is representing the problem or identifying the particular aspects of the problem and sub problems. With this example, the teacher states that the problem has aspects that deal with the physical properties of waste—waste takes up space—and aspects that are chemical—dangerous chemicals seeping into ground water systems or gases rising into the air. At this stage the teacher talks aloud what he or she is thinking, sharing this with the student colleague.

Once the problem has been defined in its various dimensions, the teacher indicates that he or she will demonstrate the next step: devising or choosing a solution. The teacher raises questions with his or her student colleague such as: "If we are running out of physical space, are there ways to reduce the volume of the waste so it will take less space?" The student colleague, role playing, responds, "We can burn it." The teacher replies, "Yes, that will reduce its mass, but will the ash of the waste contain toxins that when buried will also contaminate ground water?" The student colleague responds, "Well, that would still be a problem."

The questioning demonstration continues until the teacher and student colleague devise a plan that addresses all or most of the concerns. The teacher then directly tells the students that the next stage after choosing a solution or plan is to enact the plan. The teacher might here show a film where recycling has been done which shows the execution of the plan. The teacher informs the students that the final stage of problem solving is evaluating the solution. This final stage could be explained by having the teacher tell the students what questions would be raised at this final stage, the criteria being employed by the problem solver.

This example of demonstration is rather complex and might involve several class periods; however, not all demonstrations need to be long. Indeed some will be very brief, perhaps only five or ten minutes, done in response to a student's inquiry of "How do I do this?" In this instance, the demonstration contributes clarity into the lesson; it gives an immediate response to a student's question or concern.

Thinking and questioning are skills, and we need to do more than talk about them. We need to show, to demonstrate how to perform them. We may need to repeat our behaviors several times to get students comfortable with the steps. If we desire our students to generate analysis questions, we need to demonstrate such questions with material related to the class unit or lesson. If the focus to analyze alternatives is on asking questions, we need to act out this skill, pointing out the questions being raised as we consider options.

Demonstration is a type of direct teaching in which the information or skill presented is under the teacher's control. Students observe, and observe carefully. However, we want students to do more than just know the steps of thinking or questioning—we want students to actually think and question. Therefore, there may be times when we will do more than model particular skills for our students; after our modeling, we will actually coach students in these skills. Thinking and questioning skills, like all skills, are acquired only through actual use. Coaching students is common in physical education. Students are not going to perform tennis serves with any degree of skill unless the teacher first demonstrates how to do it and then furnishes time for students to practice serving with the teacher coaching the student, offering suggestions, and further demonstrating the technique. Coaching students to think, to question, is a bit novel, however. Certainly, thinking is more complicated than serving a tennis ball, but it is still a skill.

In our example of dealing with waste material, the teacher, after demonstrating how to problem solve, might ask students in teams of two to work through the strategy. The teacher might go around the classroom observing each team at work. If students fail to ask questions that will furnish needed information, the teacher might say, "Here, let me show you a type of question that might get you a handle on the problem. Now you come up with a similar question. Fine? Any other questions that might get you the same types of information?" The students now try out some new questions with the teacher observing. If the questions miss the mark, the teacher coaches the students in some other strategies. Just as with a football game, the coach shows a game plan for the day. If the team is losing at the half, the teacher coach and the student players discuss modifying their strategy. If students are having difficulty determining the proper solution to a problem, the teacher may work with the team in generating another game plan that might be more promising.

The key to coaching is that while the coach offers suggestions, the players actually play the game. The coach can suggest questions to ask, or steps to employ, but the students must produce their own questions. The teacher coach can call "Time," but the game cannot be cancelled. In coaching a skill, we can draw on our reserve players, other students, to come in to play the game. We can call on other students to get their ideas as to how they might solve a problem. We can ask other students to suggest questions. The coach gives examples, explains strategies, and, perhaps most importantly, offers encouragement—You can do it, can think, can question.

Demonstrations and coaching situations have the teacher in control, but students are not passive. They are listening, observing, questioning, and thinking. Demonstration is a most effective general strategy that when combined with other general strategies advances students in their thinking and questioning behaviors.

Demonstration has several general stages that give the strategy some form. These stages are indicated in Figure 6–3.

These steps are suggestive and generalizable to any and all subject areas in the school curriculum. As with any method, it is essential to make clear the skill or strategy that is to be demonstrated and to tie this skill into the overall lesson. Demonstration needs adequate time. Hurrying through the stages or rattling off various types of questions will only serve to frustrate rather than enlighten and make students skilled.

Inquiry

Of the four generic methods, inquiry involves students most extensively in their learning, challenging them to participate in information making in

- *Orientation*

  Setting the stage for the demonstration

  Identifying the skill or strategy that is to be demonstrated

  Tying the skill to be demonstrated into other learning

- *Demonstrating*

  Performing the demonstration

  Raising questions about aspects of the demonstration

  Allowing students to raise questions about the demonstration

- *Student Practice (This may or may not be done with a demonstration.)*

  Allowing students to practice the skill that has been demonstrated (Here coaching is employed.)

  Debriefing on the student practice

  Redoing the demonstration if necessary

Figure 6–3
Stages of Demonstration

contrast to information receiving. Inquiry addresses students' inquisitiveness, their thinking, focusing most directly on their critical mindedness. A smart educator contains within his or her instructional repertoire this particular generic method to furnish students with opportunities to build upon their natural curiosity and need to explore. If effectively managed, this method enables students not only to gain procedures for obtaining knowledge but also through their interactions with content and their questions to develop a valuing of knowledge and a zest for its pursuit.[18]

Inquiry is well suited to teaching problem solving, decision making, and conceptualizing—the three major thinking strategies that Beyer outlined (see Chapter 1). Indeed, many classify inquiry as synonymous with these thinking strategies. Others cluster inquiry methods under the terms inductive teaching, deductive teaching, and discovery.[19]

The key characteristic of this strategy is student involvement—getting students to process information in particular ways to arrive at some insight or conclusion. However, students are not just left to fend for themselves. Kindvatter and his colleagues classify inquiry as to the extent of teachers' involvement—much teacher involvement being guided inquiry, slight teacher involvement being open inquiry, and no or very little teacher involvement being individualized inquiry.[20] Ideally, individualized inquiry is the ultimate, having students so competent in thinking and asking questions that they can indeed inquire, process information, autonomously. Of course, there will be

Lecture → *Demonstration* → *Discussion* → *Inquiry*
   exposition
Teacher dominated   *Student dominated*

Figure 6–4

little individualized inquiry when we have young children or students new to some information, but there will be some. Students will and should be given time to investigate and inquire without teacher supervision. We all need time to explore information making—to make our own mistakes. Skilled teachers assist pupils in changing mistake making into productive learning.

Inquiry is both inductive and deductive. In the past, some educators felt that inquiry could only be inductive. The thinking strategy of conceptualizing presented in Chapter 1 suggests that induction is the "only way to process the information." Not so. Figure 6–5 shows both the inductive and deductive aspects of inquiry.

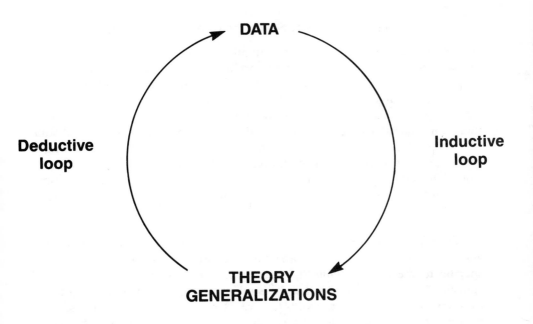

Figure 6–5
Aspects of Inquiry

At times we will wish our students to commence inquiry dealing with specific data, events, situations (induction). Likewise, there will be times when we wish students first to think about general information that has been presented.

Morine and Morine many years ago distinguished between inductive discovery (inquiry) and deductive discovery. They even introduced the term transductive (nonlogical) discovery.[21]

Types of Inquiry

Inductive Inquiry—Inductive inquiry engages students in dealing with specific situations or events, collecting and reordering data so as to formulate a category, concept, or generalization new at least to them. Such inquiry closely resembles the thinking strategy of conceptualization; it also parallels the scientific method. It is very similar to Dewey's model of reflective thinking.[22]

1. Identify and formulate the problem
2. Generate hypotheses (represent the problem in Beyer's schema)
3. Engage in data collection (execute the plan in Beyer's schema)
4. Interpret the data
5. Formulate conclusions (evaluate the plan in Beyer's schema)

The degree of focus in inductive inquiry can vary. It might be wide open in that students are just processing information for the sake of creating categories, or it may be somewhat structured with pupils being guided by the teacher to attain a certain conceptual understanding. But the key is that the data are just spilled onto the classroom floor and the pupils must see what is there, raise questions, think about what they see, and then put the spilled stuff into categories, looking for patterns, raising general questions, determining a way of processing the information, doing it, and finally making some conclusions. The conclusions resulting from such inductive functioning may produce surprises for students. They may exclaim, "Wow, I really had no idea that is what caused that event!"

Deductive Inquiry—Traditionally, we distinguish between induction and deduction, noting that the former involves an individual in going from the specific to the general while the latter guides one from the general to the specific. Both are inquiry in that the student is not being told what to think or know as is often the case with lecture. Here, the student is challenged to process the information, to raise questions, to think. In induction the thinking, the questioning, is done to arrive at some conclusion of the student's own making, although sometimes with the teacher's help. In deduction, the student processes questions that lead him or her to formulate a logical conclusion based on the information presented. If information is presented about a certain nation, students are challenged by the teacher to raise questions so that a conclusion can be deduced about this nation.

Deductive discovery is a variation of the Socratic method. In such a method the teacher controls the data, guides the inquiry, and raises questions to elicit from students propositions that most likely will lead logically to certain conclusions. For example, if we wished to employ deductive inquiry to teach the thinking skills of conceptualization, we might first present a particular concept—say, "nation"—and then define the attributes of this concept. We might tell students why the attributes are classified in particular ways. Perhaps we note that the concept nation suggests the following attributes: has a history, has a shared culture, occupies a similar geographic region, has a means of governing. Presented with this information, students might then be challenged to inquire into the various nations of the world and to formulate conclusions as to what is a strong nation, a weak nation.

Frequently, inquiry is both inductive and deductive; that is, students might be challenged to formulate inductively their own categories and concepts and then employ them deductively in processing additional information. Or perhaps students might be challenged to produce particular properties of some information by observing specific data. From these, students could be asked to construct deductive chains of statements; in this instance, students through inquiry could actually be engaged in theory formation.

Transductive Inquiry—In Chapter 1, we noted that creative thinking is an essential skill. Inductive and deductive inquiry tend to focus on the critical thinking realm—the logical, the rational; transductive inquiry focuses on the creative realm—the nonlogical, the nonrational. Attention on the transductive, the nonlogical, while new perhaps in our emphasis on creativity, is not really a new concept. Piaget, many years ago, defined transductive thinking as connecting sets of information in nonlogical ways.[23] In contrast to inductive (particular to general) and deductive (general to particular), transductive reasoning is particular to particular. In such reasoning, the pupil relates or compares two particular items or situations and notes their similarity in one or more ways. Such reasoning is employed in metaphoric thinking. For instance, a student might say "The ship knifed through the water" or "The fog came in on angels' wings." The student is comparing the particular ship to the particular characteristic of knife or the characteristics of fog to the characteristics of angel's wings.[24]

Transductive thinking is similar, if not identical to, what Edward deBono calls "lateral thinking."[25] Lateral thinking, not constrained by convention, may leave some things undefined, but it focuses on the similarities among things in one or more ways. The teacher might say, "pocket book," and the child says, "kangaroo." The particular feature of pouch and kangaroo are compared. For making analogies, students need skill in transductive thinking.

Transductive inquiry engages students in inquiring into ways that particulars can be compared. Students are challenged to think, to question similarities among particulars; to think imaginatively or artistically, to produce a specialized conclusion—an analogy or metaphor. In guiding this type of inquiry, we strive to get students to process information artistically. Many creative writing lessons will bear fruit if conducted through transductive inquiry.

Inquiry Stages

As with the other generic models, inquiry can be organized into various stages: (1) confrontation, exploration; (2) focus, hypothesis formation; (3) experimentation, fabrication, and (4) realization, drawing conclusions.

Stage 1: Confrontation, Exploration—Inquiry begins with students confronting a puzzlement, so presented that they are invited to explore, to investigate, to question, to begin mapping out a strategy or strategies of investigation. It is axiomatic that for inquiry to commence, we must first realize the existence of a problem or challenge. As noted in Chapter 1 we must first become somewhat certain as to what we *do not know.* Good thinkers, good questioners, possess this ability to perceive problems, issues. Our challenge as teachers is to develop this ability in all our students to such a state that eventually they do not need our assistance to inquire.

In this first stage, we engage students in "playing" with the situation, with the information. It is a time for them to interact with ideas, events, objects that are relatively unfamiliar to them. It is a time when raising questions is encouraged; a time when students commence getting a general sense of what they might do. Students begin to get a feeling for the rationale for the potential investigation; ideally, they come to discover the reason for the potential inquiry and the worth it might contain. If time is short, however, the teacher in this phase can furnish the students with the objectives and the rationale and guide them into the next stage.

Important at this stage is that students should begin to wonder why something is as it is, to experience discomfort because they do not yet have an idea or ideas or answers to this something.[26] The effective teacher nourishes this state of wonderment and works to activate in students doubt and suspicion in the good sense of these words—to foster inquisitiveness and an unwillingness to accept the views of others without careful consideration of data presented.

As teachers, we have several ways to stimulate wonderment, inquisitiveness, willingness to inquire, to think. One way is to present to students what appears to be discrepant events, or mysteries. In science, Suchman many years ago suggested getting students to inquire by presenting them with situations that contradicted expectations: water that seemed to boil when held in the hand; mysterious pieces of metal that bent in strange fashion when heated.[27] We need not have orange grass, however, to pique interest. We can simply encounter some situation and ask, "What happened here?"

We may also stimulate a willingness to inquire by presenting students with ideas that people currently argue about, querying, "Why is there such divergence of opinion?" Students could spend several weeks investigating the bases for people's differing views.

Inquiry can also be stimulated by having students indicate the needs people currently have, focusing on why these needs exist and then analyzing the means for addressing them. The current world does not lack for problems. All peoples' behavior is in response to some need. Our new discoveries have resulted from addressing needs. In this first stage, students can explore how some need has been addressed over time and whether currently it is adequately satisfied. Students can list all those needs currently unmet.

At this first stage, students develop a heightened sensitivity to their world and their place within it. They view their experience with a questioning posture, further refining their critical mindedness.

Stage 2: Focus, Hypothesis Formation—After students have explored the situation or situations, they come to focus on their inquiry. Here students realize just what is the nature of the problem before them, what are the challenges confronting them. This second stage aims to clarify what we are going to do as to direction and to then formulate some hypotheses, some questions to guide our efforts. Hypotheses are tentative explanations for events observed or data presented; they suggest answers to questions raised in the first stage of inquiry. They are, however, tentative answers—answers to be tested by the data, to be processed in the next general stage.

At this second stage, students decide what is the actual nature of the thing into which they are to inquire: Is it a problem, an issue? Does the situation demand an answer that is a product or a process, or both? Some inquiries request students to produce a product in the form of a new meaning to some concept; for instance, students may be inquiring into a situation that represents interdependence. They may not know this at first, but in stage 2, they should realize that this is their focus. The purpose of this inquiry is to generate a statement or statements that will explain those situations in which interdependence of actions is necessary for effective functioning. The product requested in this inquiry is a statement or statements.

In contrast, there may be times when the thing requested is process, a suggestion of how something might be done. In mathematics, a problem can be the focus of the inquiry lesson; students are challenged to create a process for solving a particular problem—the solution procedure is the result desired.

We can engage students in hypothesis formation in groups or individually. Ideally, we should do both. Students need competencies in working cooperatively and independently. During hypothesis formation, students need guidance to consider the assumptions they bring to their inquiry, the questions that will frame their efforts.

Stage 3: Experimentation, Fabrication—This stage is the actual conducting of the inquiry, the data gathering, data manipulation. It is the processing of data necessary to answer questions. Here, students invent categories for their data and analyze these clusters to determine relationships, connections, possible conclusions.

As teachers we counsel our students in identifying sources of evidence, questioning the natural evidence, and showing them means of collecting data. The degree of our involvement depends partly on whether we are engaged in inductive or deductive inquiry and the level of maturity of our students and their skill in inquiry. If working inductively with mature students, the inquiry most likely will be fairly open-ended with students free to proceed as they wish. However, if we are employing deductive discovery with students new to inquiry, we might at first be greatly involved in presenting data and the major premise to the investigation, as well as heavily involved in guiding students in their analyses of specific data.

The actual nature of the experimentation is determined in part by the content being investigated. If the content is mathematics, then the inquiry most likely will be deductive, investigated logically by observing relationships among the mathematics problem being questioned. In contrast, if the lesson is science dealing with physics, the inquiry might be inductive with the experiment being a testing out by observation, not by logical argument. In a history lesson, there might well be a combination of approaches; for instance, in inquiring into the disappearance of the Jumano Indian tribe, students could work logically analyzing the various documents written about the tribe and also work by observing evidence produced by anthropologists. Students might actually go on a simulated archaeological dig into the areas where the Indians last lived. The important point is that one is striving through inquiry to produce some conclusions. Students need to recognize early on that conclusions, and defense of conclusions, will be arrived at and defended by logic in some cases, such as mathematics, and by observation such as in a physics experiment to show how different metals react to different temperature variations, and in some instances by a combined approach such as investigating a social science problem—for instance, the disappearance of the Jumano Indian tribe.

In experimentation, students process innformation, raise questions, think about answers in ways that will either support or dispute their hypotheses. Students can arrange their data in columns that could be labeled "Support Hypothesis," "Refute Hypothesis", and "Data Uncertain." When the data have been so arranged, students can question why the information is so classified.

In arranging data, students are devising ways of looking at and processing the data and are inventing questions that will guide them down particular questioning avenues. Ruggiero states that one of the most useful things individuals can do in experimentation, in investigation, is to reopen their file of experiences and observations. "What have I learned that can help me solve this problem or issue?"[28] It is a time when we establish numerous cross references. In essence, the student is focusing on the "world knowledge" dimension of the question. What can I bring from my own prior experiences to this situation?

Students are also asking themselves how they can restructure the information to bring out different points of views, different relationships. Or it may be the teacher who through questions is asking students to reflect on previous experiences, previous ideas, even previous questions. Students are asked to consider "What if?" What if we looked at the information in this manner? What if we added to the experiment? If we subtracted from it? Much creative thinking centers on ferreting from students new ways of looking at situations, at information. We can employ questions to make the familiar appear strange to students and the strange appear familiar.[29]

Such questions not only get students to process data creatively but to be mindful of their procedures, important if we are to enable students to gain executive control over their learning.

Stage 4: Realization, Drawing Conclusions—The final stage of inquiry is the discovery, formulating, of conclusions that either support or reject the hypotheses raised, or answer or do not answer the questions posed at the outset of the inquiry. At this point, students might also modify their hypotheses or initial stances.

Realizing answers and drawing conclusions is the natural ending for the previous stages. However, we and our students should not be too quick to accept our answers. Conclusions should be considered tentative. Sometimes students, especially those new to inquiry, tend to accept the answer or conclusion and look toward another lesson.[30] "We have finished that now." "Not really, questions raised in this inquiry should serve as openers to further inquiry."

Ruggiero reports that early ideas are more common and less creative than later ideas. The reason for this is not entirely known; it may be due to the fact that the "familiar, safe responses lie most closely to the surface of consciousness and therefore are considered first."[31] Or it may be that the categories comfortable to us drawn from our prior learning experiences serve as organizers to the data processed; we tend to accept uncritically that which agrees with our mindsets.

At the drawing conclusions stage, we want to, through our questioning, get students to challenge their comfortable conclusions, to think of alternative ways, other conclusions, other uses for conclusions. We should challenge

---

TRY IT

Inquiry Turned Inward

Inquiry is a most powerful strategy for students to employ in the classrooms. It involves students; it involves us.

Inquiry demands of us a real shift in our self-view as teacher and demands of our students modification of their perception as students. In inquiry, the metaphor of salesperson is inadequate; we do more than sell information to students. Realizing we should use some method, however, and actually employing it takes commitment, awareness of our affective reaction to the strategy. In books, authors present information; rarely do they ask their readers to react affectively to the material and inquire into their feelings.

Let's do it. Engage in a bit of autobiographical analysis. Inquire into how you view inquiry. What in your past and present makes you view the strategy as you do? Are you nervous to explore too deeply; why? Excited; why? Does this method conflict with your view of teaching? With your teaching style? With your learning style? Have you found administrative support lacking when you have tried similar strategies?

Effectiveness with any strategy requires knowing ourselves as well as our content. Try the strategy on yourself; inquire into your personal reactions to inquiry. Share your feelings with a colleague if you like.

---

our students to think of the uncommon—to process their conclusions and evaluate them thinking creatively. For instance, students investigating a food shortage problem may have suggested that to solve the problem we need only to increase the land devoted to cultivation and add new fertilizers. The teacher might demand students to think of strange ways of increasing agricultural production. "Why not expand the area under cultivation by growing plants in air?" might serve to trigger students to search for uncommon responses, novel conclusions.

To obtain novel conclusions, students need to employ lateral thinking, to focus on particulars, to engage in free association, to participate in metaphoric thinking, to indicate responses that represent plus good points, minus bad points, and interesting points.[32]

This final stage has two words in it: realization, and drawing conclusions. Realization assumes that students in their investigation discover information that has been already uncovered by others. Students discern a procedure for solving a mathematics problem that is really already known to mathematicians; students uncover an interpretation of a particular social science concept also already known to the scholars in the field. Discovery assumes that out there is some information and that students through their questions and thinking come to encounter this already known information.

Drawing conclusions may mean the same to many of us, but it can mean that students do more than just discover that which is already known. They engage in a creative synthesis, restructuring information in ways somewhat novel, at least to them. It is a type of boundary pushing—going beyond what the authorities have said and generating a different twist to the information, a twist that could be input for later inquiries. Questions raised about conclusions can serve as door openers—you have not arrived, you have just reached a place where further questioning is appropriate, where additional thinking is necessary.

The final substage of discovery and drawing conclusions is evaluating the conclusions and polishing them. Have I answered my hypotheses? Are my judgments warranted from the data gathered and processed? Is my solution appropriate for the problem noted? Will it work?

If any of the answers to these questions is "No," then the students need to consider how to modify the conclusions, how to make those refinements necessary for at least tentative acceptance. It is very evident that critical thinking skills are engaged throughout inquiry and especially at this final stage, determining the adequacy of a statement or conclusion. It is also apparent that this stage resembles the final stages in problem solving, decision making, and conceptualizing—evaluate the solution, choose the best alternative, and modify concept attributes.

The major steps are not absolutes to be followed uncritically; rather, they are suggestive stages that can heighten the likelihood that students will inquire productively. Figure 6–6 shows these various steps.

CONCLUSION

Zvi Lamm has argued that what makes educators educators is not what they actually do in the classroom but what they do *before* coming into the

---

Stage 1   Confrontation and Exploration
   Presentation of puzzlement
   Presentation of rationale for inquiry
Stage 2   Focus, hypothesis formation
   Presentation of focus
   Formulation of hypotheses
Stage 3   Experimentation, fabrication
   Data gathering

Data manipulation
Data analysis
Stage 4   Realization, drawing conclusions
   Realizing, drawing conclusions
   Evaluating conclusions

Figure 6–6
Stages of Inquiry

classroom; in other words, their planning, their decision making.[33] While questioning is part of all peoples' speech, our questions are special in that they are educative questions, linguistic devices resulting from careful planning.

Our educational talk, our questions included, draws from a rich instructional base. This chapter has presented information on this base, specifically on four generic strategies: lecture, discussion, demonstration, and inquiry. These powerful strategies, rich with tradition, can be used in all subject areas. Given this, we do not need to argue their legitimacy; that is accepted. We do need to instruct ourselves, however, in the intricacies of these generic strategies, become familiar with the assumptions each brings to the educational drama, and gain expertise in using questions within each to maximize student learning and heighten student interest.

It is evident that the various thinking strategies can be incorporated into each of these generic strategies. The strategies we choose to emphasize depends greatly upon our goals and objectives for our lessons.

Selecting instructional strategies is challenging for we are selecting among strategies all potentially effective in instructing. However, these strategies nurture different things; some nurture acceptance of authority, some independence, some passivity, some comfort. The nurturant effects of these four generic strategies demand our consideration in our selection process.

These four generic strategies provide a framework for the verbal games we and our students will play in the classroom. The next chapter presents more specific strategies designed to engage students in questioning, in thinking.

NOTES

1. Ronald T. Hyman, *Strategic Questioning* (Englewood Cliffs, N.J.: Prentice-Hall, 1979), xiii.

2. Richard J. Shavelson, "Teachers' Decision Making," in N. L. Gage, ed. *The Psychology of Teaching Methods,* The Seventy-fifth Yearbook of the National Society for the Study of Education, Part 1 (Chicago: University of Chicago Press, 1976), 372–414.

3. John McLeish, "The Lecture Method," in N. L. Gage, ed. *The Psychology of Teaching Methods,* 252–301.

4. Barry K. Beyer, *Practical Strategies for the Teaching of Thinking* (Boston: Allyn and Bacon, Inc., 1987).

5. Meredith D. Gall and Joyce P. Gall, "The Discussion Method," in N. L. Gage, ed. *The Psychology of Teaching Methods,* 166–216.

6. Ronald T. Hyman, "Discussion Strategies and Tactics," in William W. Wilen, ed. *Questions, Questioning Techniques, and Effective Teaching* (Washington, D.C.: National Education Association, 1987), 135–152.

7. Meredith D. Gall and Joyce P. Gall, "The Discussion Method," in N. L. Gage, ed. *The Psychology of Teaching Methods,* 168–169.

8. Richard Kindsvatter, William Wilen, and Margaret Ishler, *Dynamics of Effective Teaching* (New York: Longman, 1988).

9. Zvi Lamm, *Conflicting Theories of Instruction* (Berkeley, CA: McCutchan Publishing Corp. 1976).

10. Zvi Lamm, *Conflicting Theories of Instruction,* 64.

11. Richard Kindsvatter, William Wilen and Margaret Ishler, *Dynamics of Effective Teaching.*

12. T. Roby, "Commonplaces, Questions and Modes of Discussion," in J. T. Dillon, ed. *Classroom Questions and Discussion* (Norwood, N.J.: Ablex, 1987).

13. D. Bridges, *Education, Democracy and Discussion* (Berks, England: NFER Publishing, 1979), cited in Richard Kindsvatter, William Wilen, and Margaret Ishler, *Dynamics of Effective Teaching.*

14. T. Roby, "Commonplaces, Questions and Modes of Discussion," in J. T. Dillon, ed. *Classroom Questions and Discussion.* Reference drawn from Kindsvatter, Wilen, and Ishler.

15. Vincent Ryan Ruggiero, *Teaching Thinking Across the Curriculum* (New York: Harper & Row, Publishers, 1988), 101.

16. Constance J. Seidner, "Teaching with Simulations and Games," in N. L. Gage, ed. *The Psychology of Teaching Methods,* 217-251.

17. J. T. Dillon, *Teaching and the Art of Questioning* (Blooming, In.: Phi Delta Kappa Educational Foundation, 1983).

18. Harold Morine and Greta Morine, *Discovery, A Challenge to Teachers* (Englewood Cliffs, N.J.: Prentice-Hall, Inc., 1973).

19. Richard Kindsvatter, William Wilen, and Margaret Ishler, *Dynamics of Effective Teaching.*

20. Richard Kindsvatter, William Wilen, and Margaret Ishler, *Dynamics of Effective Teaching.*

21. Harold Morine and Greta Morine, *Discovery, A Challenge to Teachers.*

22. John Dewey, *How We Think* (Lexington, MA: Heath, 1910), cited in Kindsvatter, Wilen, and Ishler, *Dynamics of Effective Teaching.*

23. John J. Flavell, *The Developmental Psychology of Jean Piaget* (Princeton, N.J.: D. Van Nostrand Company, 1963); Morine and Morine, *Discovery, A Challenge to Teachers.*

24. Harold Morine and Greta Morine, *Discovery, A Challenge to Teachers.*

25. Edward de Bono, "The Direct Teaching of Thinking as a Skill," *Phi Delta Kappa* 64, 10 (June, 1983), 703–708.

26. Vincent Ryan Ruggiero, *Teaching Thinking Across the Curriculum.*

27. J. Richard Suchman, "The Elementary School Training Program in Scientific Inquiry," Report to the U.S. Office of Education, Project Title VII. (Urbana, Il: University of Illinois, 1962).

28. Vincent Ryan Ruggiero, *Teaching Thinking Across the Curriculum.*

29. William J. J. Gordon, *Synectics* (New York: Harper & Row, 1961).

30. Kindsvatter, Wilen, and Ishler, *Dynamics of Effective Teaching.*

31. Vincent Ryan Ruggiero, *Teaching Thinking Across the Curriculum,* p. 41.

32. Edward de Bono, "The Direct Teaching of Thinking as a Skill," *Phi Delta Kappan.*

33. Zvi Lamm, *Conflicting Theories of Instruction.*

7

Specific

Questioning

Within the Classroom

In contrast to the previous chapter in which we dealt with questions within four generic strategies, this chapter centers on specific questioning strategies useful to both teachers and students that can stand alone or can be incorporated into the generic strategies. It is useful to again reflect on Hyman's definition of a strategy: "... a carefully prepared plan involving a sequence of steps designed to achieve a given goal."[1] While there is order to these strategies, it need not necessarily be linear; it can be modified by the student to even be circular. In employing these strategies students need to realize that they are not apart from their questioning or from the situations in focus. Certainly, there will be times when they can attain some distance, be objective observers and processors of information, but their objectiveness is always partial, never complete. One can never divorce oneself from one's questions. World views and one's values influence one's questions, one's selection of strategies, one's acceptance of answers. Questioning is a very human process.

SPECIFIC QUESTIONING STRATEGIES

Educators possess specialized pedagogic knowledge employed to attain certain goals and objectives. Good teachers have mastered this knowledge to a degree that they can deliver with skill and sensitivity strategies that enable optimal student learning. Good teachers have command of more than one educational tune; they are masters of many tunes, many strategies, and experts in orchestrating them productively.

While the specific questioning strategies presented in this chapter each follow a sequence, it should not be implied that the sequence is unalterable. Neither must we assume that all of these strategies must be employed during the course of the year. All of the strategies are good, meaning they all possess the potential to get students to process information to attain understanding of and commitment to particular knowledge.

Our planning task would be easy indeed if we could ascertain that certain strategies are inappropriate, actually produce negative learnings; however, all strategies are potentially effective. Having to choose from among good strategies makes selection much more problematic.

If performed well, all strategies, specific or generic, have the direct effect of instructing. Thus, in choosing which strategy to employ, we need to attend to what Joyce and Weil have called the indirect or nurturant effects of instruction as well as the direct or instructional effects.[2]

The direct effects of the strategy to lead or facilitate learners in learning is fairly straight forward. The direct effect of a lecture is that it delivers information for student consideration. Discussion directly involves students in talking about particular topics. Inquiry also instructs. The specific strategies of this chapter also instruct.

Equally important to direct effects are nurturant or indirect effects. Some strategies at times may actually nurture negative effects. For instance, lecture, very effective in delivering content to students, may make students overly dependent upon authorities and their thinking. It may cultivate a passivity potentially disarming to students in a world that demands participation. It may stifle a willingness to question. Being mindful of these potential effects we should not overwork the lecture method. This may appear obvious regarding the lecture. But, even inquiry if not carefully managed, can nurture in students a false sense that all information gained via one's own efforts is always of equal value to that produced by authorities.

The direct and indirect effects of our methods can be situational—sometimes lectures will nurture passivity among certain students and a heightened curiosity and a desire to learn among other students, depending upon their backgrounds. We must remember to list instructional and nurturant effects of our strategies when planning.

Certainly, we want all our strategies to present or assist students in attaining understanding of knowledge, and skill in thinking and questioning. This does not mean always having more inquiry than exposition. Lectures done well trigger thinking, questioning; inquiry done poorly can stifle such skills.

Strategy selection and their placement in lessons depend upon our goals and objectives. Our own teaching depends upon our goals and objectives, our teaching styles, our students' learning styles, students' backgrounds, the type of content to be taught, the time and resources available, and even the mores of the community. All this presents challenges to teachers.

The model in figure 7–1 suggests a definite cause-effect relationship. However, we cannot always be certain what is cause and what is effect. In many classrooms an apparent effect, a learning, a question may actually be the cause to the strategy selected; causes and effects may trade places at certain times. The parts of the models should be viewed as interactive: I use a particular strategy, get particular effects; I perceive these effects; those effects in turn influence (cause) my management of the strategy or perhaps lead me to another strategy. In classrooms the dynamics looks more like Figure 7–2.

These dynamics and the assumptions behind these strategies should be kept in mind as you read the specific questioning strategies.

The first several strategies are essentially designed for the teacher, although students can certainly be taught them directly. In the latter part of this section, discussion will center on strategies that can be classified more as student strategies.

Bloom's Taxonomic Strategy

Bloom's Taxonomy of Educational Objectives, besides being a useful guide to classifying objectives and questions, suggests ways of sequencing questions, both inductively and deductively.[4] Commencing with knowledge questions and proceeding through the various levels of the taxonomy to evaluation engages us and our students in an inductive strategy, going from the specific to the general. The various levels inform us as to the types of questions to employ. We realize that we can use each increasingly higher level of

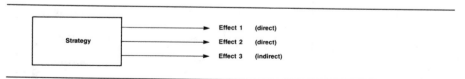

Figure 7–1[3]
Denotes the Relationship of the Teaching Strategy to Its Effects

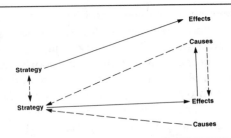

Figure 7–2

questions to raise students to a higher cognitive level. At each level, both open and closed questions expand and direct students' perceptions and understanding of the information to increasingly higher cognitive levels. At the final step, the students arrive at some conclusion or generalization, which is then evaluated as to worth and supportability. Throughout each of these steps, students engage in critical thinking, especially employing microthinking skills.

Reversing the steps, proceeding from evaluation to synthesis down to knowledge engages students in deduction. The lesson begins with students presented with a general statement, principle, rule, hypothesis, and then requested to utilize it in processing data. Students, assuming the general premise true, process information so as to arrive at another conclusion. The students' thinking is deductive; that is, information is processed from the general to the specific.

The value of Bloom's strategy is its ease of employment either inductively or deductively. Figure 7–3 shows this dual nature of the strategy.

When planning Bloom's strategy, teachers, or students for that matter, can develop a question map recording their key questions in a flow chart showing the major questions and the intersections or branches where related questions

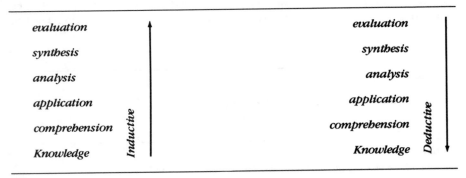

Figure 7–3

Activity

REFLECTION

All instructional strategies have nurturant effects. Often, these effects are part of the hidden curriculum. Hopefully, these effects are good; that is, they contribute to empowering students to be effective learners.

Think of the strategies you most commonly use in your classroom. Jot them down and then list at least two nurturant effects for each one.

My Strategies		*Nurturant Effects*	
1. _____		1. _____	
		2. _____	
2. _____		1. _____	
		2. _____	
3. _____		1. _____	
		2. _____	

Do you want to make any changes in your strategy use? If so, record how you might make those changes.

_____

_____

_____

_____

_____

_____

---

either enter into or flow from the central questioning. Assume students in a junior high school are challenged to analyze the issue of management of fisheries as a resource. The purpose of the lesson is to have students process the information, raise questions, and think inductively to generate a generalization about this resource. As teacher you inform the students as to the purpose of the lesson: to produce a conclusion that could be generalizable.

For this lesson you may have created a question map noting the key questions at each level of the taxonomy. The map is arranged inductively.

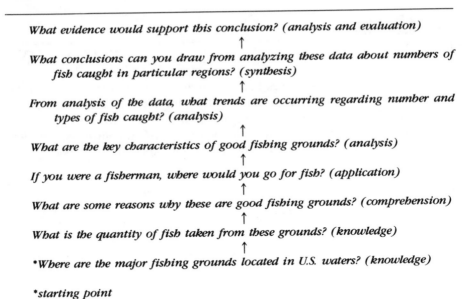

What evidence would support this conclusion? (analysis and evaluation)
↑
What conclusions can you draw from analyzing these data about numbers of fish caught in particular regions? (synthesis)
↑
From analysis of the data, what trends are occurring regarding number and types of fish caught? (analysis)
↑
What are the key characteristics of good fishing grounds? (analysis)
↑
If you were a fisherman, where would you go for fish? (application)
↑
What are some reasons why these are good fishing grounds? (comprehension)
↑
What is the quantity of fish taken from these grounds? (knowledge)
↑
*Where are the major fishing grounds located in U.S. waters? (knowledge)

*starting point

Figure 7–4
Question Map for Fisheries Resources

Certainly, the map can have other questions; however, these are the major ones. Viewing the map reveals that the students first must deal with knowledge of specifics. Then, they must comprehend the meaning of fishing grounds (Question 3). Eventually, students draw some conclusions, noting appropriate evidence.

In proceeding deductively, a similar question map is constructed. First, the teacher presents the class with a conclusion about fish resource management, challenging the students to gather evidence to support this general statement. Students proceed down the map, analyzing information, applying information, determining their understanding of fishing grounds, eventually gathering specific information to build a knowledge base. Finally, they would have one or more responses to the key question, "What is the evidence that would support the particular conclusion?"

Regardless of whether students proceed inductively or deductively, students do think and think critically. We have not just presented information to students; rather, we have raised questions demanding students to obtain their own information. This requires time, and while the map may appear to indicate that we as teachers just ask these questions in a definite sequence, we must allow adequate time for information processing. Such a lesson might take six days, each day centering on questions at a specific level of the taxonomy. When raising questions at each level, we need to furnish time for students to process the information, either to read to get the answer or to discuss with their classmates both questions and answers.

A Variation of Bloom's Strategy

At first glance, Bloom's strategy suggests definite linearity of processing information; one either goes through the questions inductively or deductively. Once started it appears that there is no going back, no returning to earlier stages. In the real classroom, however, if one is processing comprehension questions, one still can go down the scale and pose some knowledge questions. Perhaps in trying to respond to a comprehension question directed at understanding why certain areas have good fishing grounds, one has to ask additional knowledge questions to build the knowledge base.

Once additional facts have been obtained, students, realizing that they have sufficient understanding, apply this understanding in solving a puzzle such as, "Where might I go to fish if I were a fisherman?" After responding, students might raise questions at the analysis level, possibly looking for key elements that impact fish as a resource. Maybe students are stumped with this level of questioning; if so, they go down the scale again to process questions at lower cognitive levels to enrich their understanding of fishing grounds and fishing as economic activity. Once sufficient information has been obtained, they continue up the scale to analysis questions, proceeding to synthesis questions.

Diagrammatically, the jumping up and down the cognitive scale appears as follows in Figure 7–5.

If you traced the question pathways in your classroom, most likely they would resemble this figure more than the nice neat one on page 176. Our processing of information, responding to questions, is dynamically interconnected. What we do at one level will impact our actions at other levels; our thinking is interactive. While we may think we proceed in a neat fashion, inductively from specific to general, we actually may go from specific to general, general to general, specific to specific, general to specific. We may proceed in some other sequence. When we claim to be questioning inductively, we really mean that in our processing of information we are tending to travel the inductive avenue. Even so, there are lots of rest stops, side trips, retracing of steps, diversions and detours in our questioning, thinking journey.

Taba Strategy

Almost as well known as Bloom and his work is Hilda Taba and her general strategy designed to involve students in processing information inductively. Her strategy evolved from her extensive work in investigating children's thinking.[6] While there have been attempts to generate more stages in the strategy, the three original stages are still the most useful: concept formation,

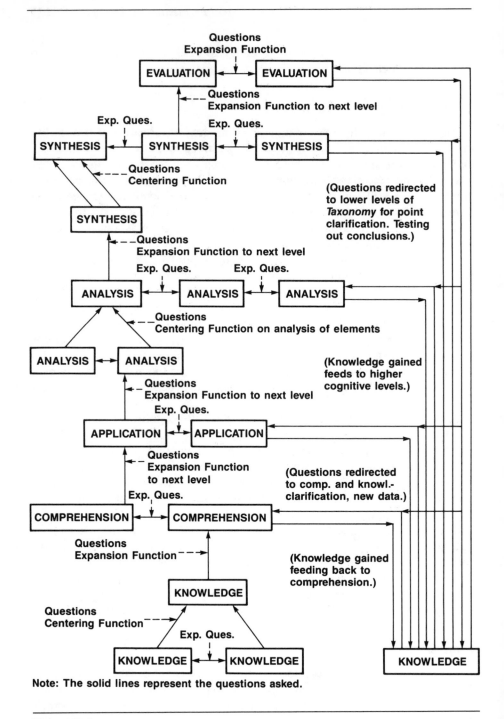

Note: The solid lines represent the questions asked.

Figure 7–5
Variation Strategy[5]

Activity

TRY IT

All right, you now have some information on how to arrange questions following Bloom's guidance. Select a topic you wish to teach and arrange questions that you would ask students to consider following either an inductive or deductive sequence. Consider this arrangement of questions as a type of map to guide you.

Ideally, try out your lesson with your class. Audio or videotape yourself to determine how closely you followed your lesson plan. If everything worked well, ask yourself why you had success. If things were a bit shaky, try to determine the reasons.

Practice this strategy several times, perhaps getting a colleague to coach you.

Lesson topic: _____

Strategy: Bloom's Strategy

  Question Map

   List your questions in the order you will employ them.

Self-critique on strategy utilization:

_____

_____

_____

_____

_____

_____

---

interpretation of data, and the application of principles. These three stages essentially involve students in three major thinking strategies: conceptualizing, problem solving, and decision making.

Concept Formation

Concept formation guides students through three steps: (1) identifying and enumerating data relevant to a situation or problem, (2) clustering data according to some common attribute, and (3) creating categories and labels for the clustered data. To guide students through these steps, Taba developed a sequence of questions to elicit from students particular types of thinking. The sequence repeated essentially at each of the three major stages involved the following questions: "What?"; "Why?"; "What does it mean?"

In concept formation, students begin by answering the question, "What did you see?", which results in information being listed. Then the teacher asks, "What belongs together?" In dealing with what belongs together, students group information or form patterns. The final question, "What would we call these groups?", requests students to name or classify the information according to attributes identified, resulting in labels for the information. Essentially, students identify and/or "create" concepts. (Such creation is really not the production of new information, only information new to the students.)

This stage of concept formation is shown in Table 7–1.[7]

While we are presented with pedagogical questioning moves, "What, why, what does it mean?" we still lack specifics as to types of questions to employ. Chapters 3 and 4 present us with much information to enable a more precise classification. The "what" questions can be classified as knowledge questions (Bloom); definitional questions (Hyman); matter questions (Christenbury and Kelly); or feature specification questions (Lehnert). Pick the classification most useful to you. We can do the same with the "why" questions, and "What does it mean" questions picking that classification most useful to us. In doing this, we can speak with more precision about our questions. We can say, if we prefer Bloom's scheme, that to engage students in concept formation, we sequence questions as follows:

Concept Formation
Overt Activity

1. enumeration listing

2. grouping

Questions to be asked

knowledge questions
comprehension questions

application questions
analysis questions

Table 7–1 Concept Formation

OVERT ACTIVITY	COVERT MENTAL OPERATIONS	ELICITING QUESTIONS
1. Enumeration, listing	Differentiation (identifying separate items)	What did you see? hear? note?
2. Grouping	Identifying common properties, abstracting	What belongs together? On what criterion?
3. Labeling, categorizing	Determining the hierarchical order of items super- and subordination.	How would you call these groups? What belongs to what?

SOURCE: Hilda Taba, *Teacher's Handbook for Elementary Social Studies* (Reading, Mass.: Addison-Wesley Publishing Co., Inc., 1967), p. 92.

3. labeling, categorizing   analysis questions
                                                synthesis questions
                                                evaluation questions

If we find Lehnert's syntactical schema more to our liking, we can sequence questions using that scheme.

Concept Formation

Overt Activity	*Questions to be asked*
1. enumeration	feature specification
	enablement
2. grouping	goal orientation
	expectational
3. labeling, categorizing	causal antecedent, consequence
	judgmental

This additional information not only furnishes us with more precision but also allows us to obtain a better grasp of what questions are designed to do and an indication of the type of cognitive operations likely to be elicited by the questions. For instance, we attain more precision in saying, "I asked a *what* question to engage in enumeration to specify features," than just to say, "I asked *what* questions to get students to enumerate." There are a lot of "what" questions out there. Which ones did you use?

Interpretation of Data

As with the first stage, the second stage, interpretation of data, contains three steps: (1) identifying critical relationships, (2) exploring those relationships, and (3) making inferences. Essentially, in responding to "what" questions, students interpret information before them and analyze the links between and among the various concepts denoted in concept formation.

Exploring relationships is a response to those "why" questions requesting students to infer and to analyze the data before them to link clusters of information and to extend given information. At this juncture, students are asked to see how information presented holds together; they are asked essentially to comprehend the interrelationships identified in substep one. In replying to "why" questions, students recognize facts and assumptions essential to the information before them. They are to look for cause-and-effect relationships.

The third substep, making inferences, is perhaps misnamed for students do more than infer from material read and discussed or situations analyzed. They are to engage in formulating generalizations, generating conclusions, to produce defensible statements. In problem solving, this is the step—devising a solution; in the strategy of decision making, this is choosing the best alternative. Making inferences is essentially synthesizing information to interpret data accurately—all this from just asking "what" questions.

It is evident that the "what" questions of this step are different from the "what" questions identifying critical relationships and the "what" questions raised in concept formation. These differences make clear our need to realize the classifications behind "what" questions. These "what" questions are essentially synthesis questions, derivation of a set of abstract relations questions if we draw from Bloom's categories; essentially causal consequent and expectational questions if we employ Lehnert's scheme.

Interpretation of data is presented in Table 7–2.[8]

Utilizing some of the other classification schemes, we can appreciate that the question sequence in this second stage is more complicated than at first appears. Using Bloom's categories, interpretation of data has the following questioning sequence.

Interpretation of Data
Overt Activity   *Questions to be asked*

1. Identifying critical relationships   Comprehension questions
                                                        analysis of elements, relationships

2. exploring relationships   analysis of relationships

3. making inferences   synthesis questions,
                                                        derivation of set of abstract
                                                        relationships

Embracing Lehnert's classifications we would use the following sequence of questions.

Interpretation of Data
Overt Activity   *Questions to be asked*

1. identifying critical relationships   what (causal antecedent)
                                                        what (causal consequent)
                                                        why (expectational)
                                                        what (enablement)

Table 7–2 Interpretation of Data

OVERT ACTIVITY	COVERT MENTAL OPERATIONS	ELICITING QUESTIONS
1. Identifying critical relationships	Differentiating	What did you notice? see? find?
2. Exploring relationships	Relating categories to each other Determining cause-and-effect relationships	Why did this happen?
3. Making inferences	Going beyond what is given Finding implications, extrapolating	What does this mean? What picture does it create in your mind? What would you conclude?

SOURCE: Hilda Taba, *Teacher's Handbook for Elementary Social Studies* (Reading, Mass.: Addison-Wesley Publishing Co., Inc., 1967), p. 101.

2. exploring relationships   causal antecedent,
                                              causal consequent
                                              enablement

3. making inferences   causal consequences
                                              enablement
                                              concept completion

   With Lehnert's classification, the exact sequence of particular types of questions is not as clear as with Bloom's. Even so, it is still more illuminating than just saying, "Ask 'What, why, and what does this mean?'"

Application of Principles

   In Taba's final stage, application of principles, questions are designed to get students to apply their information, to link it to other information and situations. Information created in step two is now to be used to generate additional information, to elaborate conclusions. As with the previous two stages, application of principles contains three substeps: predicting consequences and generating hypotheses; explaining and/or supporting predictions and hypotheses; and verifying predictions. Here, students further their inquiry, apply what they have learned to other situations, and employ generalizations developed or hypotheses created to gain greater understandings.

   Table 7–3 depicts these steps of the final application of principles.[9]

   In the first phase students, drawing from previous information gained, make forecasts or predictions from data analyzed to explain new information in light of previous conclusions or hypothesize why some event happened.

   In the second phase, students respond to "why" questions to explain or support their recently made predictions: "Why do you think this will happen?" If students, drawing on previous information have forecast an economic recession to occur in the next year, they are challenged to explain the

Table 7–3   Application of Principles

OVERT ACTIVITY	COVERT MENTAL OPERATIONS	ELICITING QUESTIONS
1. Predicting consequences, explaining unfamiliar phenomena, hypothesizing	Analyzing the nature of the problem or situation, retrieving relevant knowledge	What would happen if . . . ?
2. Explaining and/or supporting the predictions and hypotheses	Determining the causal links leading to prediction or hypothesis	Why do you think this would happen?
3. Verifying the prediction	Using logical principals or factual knowledge to determine necessary and sufficient conditions	What would it take for this to be generally true or probably true?

SOURCE: Hilda Taba, *Teacher's Handbook for Elementary Social Studies* (Reading, Mass.: Addison-Wesley Publishing Co., Inc., 1967), p. 109.

basis for the prediction. They are invited to identify the key elements affecting the market, the links between those elements, and the reasons why such interactions will trigger a recession.

Such questioning leads to the final substage in the Taba strategy, verifying the prediction. Here students, again responding to "what" questions, must draw upon logical principles or knowledge about the dynamics of particular situations to verify the prediction, to defend it. In the case of the expected recession, students must explain the internal logic of the market place, perhaps drawing on various economic laws regulating supply and demand.

Again, we can employ Taba's basic framework and insert questions classified according to other schema. Drawing on Bloom's work the sequence of questions would appear as follows:

Application of principles
Overt Activities

Questions to ask

1. predicting consequences

analysis of relationships
application questions
(of rules, principles),
synthesis (hypothesis formation)

2. explaining, supporting
predictions hypotheses

analysis of organizational principles
analysis of relationships

3. verifying prediction

evaluation of internal and external
  evidence
analysis of organizational principles

With Lehnert's scheme, the questions sequenced might be as follows:

Application of Principles
Overt Activities

Questions to Ask

1. predicting consequences

what (causal consequence)

2. explaining, supporting
predictions, hypotheses

why (expectations)
what (enablement)

3. verifying the prediction

what (judgmental)
what (causal consequence)

Managing the Strategy:

Taba was very specific how teachers were to use her strategy. The approach was not to be a random posing of questions, but rather a precise going up a ladder, one step or rung at a time. Each major rung (step) had three levels of questions—What? Why? and What does it mean? No rung was to be skipped.

Taba noted that questions at one particular level (rung, step) were to be distributed to most, if not, all pupils.[10] One would not phrase a question at a higher cognitive level before all students had processed questions and grasped information at the previous, lower level. This careful sequence was to be respected within each major step. For instance, one would not raise categorizing questions before students had successfully processed questions at the listing and grouping levels. To proceed otherwise, Taba argued, would frustrate students who had not mastered that step and who were now required to process information at an even higher level. This frustration, growing incrementally, would nurture negative feelings. Before students could be lifted to a higher intellectual plain, they all had to have attained success.

Questions at each particular level had to involve even the slowest students, lest they be lost in further interactions. Students not having the opportunity to participate at one particular plateau of questioning would lack requisite understanding to respond effectively to higher levels of questions. Being unsuccessful in early stages of inquiry or discovery spelled future failure in later dealings with higher questions.

While the strategy appears somewhat complicated, it can be used with pupils at any age. The author employed this strategy with fourth grade children to get them to generate conclusions about life in their community. The lesson started with all children placing one shoe in a pile in the center of the classroom. Responding to stage one, students listed their shoes, grouped them, and categorized them. Some resultant categories were sports shoes, dress shoes, work shoes, school shoes.

Once students accepted their categories, they proceeded to step two, interpretation of data. To begin, students had to respond to their categories. "What did you notice about these shoes?" Some answers were that they were of different colors, of different materials. "Why do you suppose these shoes are so different?" keyed pupils to explore relationships. Answers appeared such as, "Well, we wear shoes when we do different things. Perhaps we only had certain types of material for making our shoes. I think teachers tell us what types of shoes to wear."

After most students had accepted their answers as plausible, they were asked to make inferences, "What conclusions can we make about shoes? About why people wear them?" Students replied, "We have soft feet. Our feet would catch cold. Shoes help us do different things, like play sports or run. Shoes help us look nice on special occasions, like going to church."

For the last step, application of principles, children were asked, knowing what they now knew about shoes and people, could they answer the question, "What would happen if we all had our shoes stolen?' Replies were, "We would have sore feet." A favorite response was, "We would not have to come to school." Explaining this prediction raised other responses, "Well, we would not be able to come to school because we would hurt our feet on the way. We would look funny. We would all catch cold and have to stay home." The last questions asked children to verify their prediction, to defend it. "What would have to happen for us to all act as we have said if we all lost our shoes?" "We

Activity

STRATEGIC PRACTICE

Practice makes perfect, so the saying goes. When we first try out a new behavior, a new method, however, we are a bit uneasy, awkward. We stumble a bit, but in time we do get better.

Take a lesson that you have taught before and this time plan the Taba strategy into it. Remember that you will have to go up the ladder. You will have to plan your lesson, specify the questions you will ask at each stage (each substep). Share your total strategy with a colleague. Perhaps your colleague will suggest some modifications in your questions or their arrangement.

Now try out the strategy. Whether your colleague knows the strategy or is a novice, it is good for this person to be there to coach you in applying the strategy. Remember that it will take a while to go through all three major stages.

Schedule time to debrief with yourself and your colleague after each major stage has been used.

Once you have used the strategy effectively in one subject area, plan to employ the strategy in another subject area.

---

would still have to have soft feet. The supplies for shoes would have to still be out (out of materials)."

While the lesson was fun, it was also important for it engaged students in processing information. They created their answers, their conclusions. The teacher had not presented them with information, but rather, through specific questioning, enabled students to generate information. The pupils were in the driver's seat for the lesson.

Questioning Circle Strategy[11]

Both the Bloom and Taba strategies are essentially sequential and suggest a hierarchy. In Chapter 4, a classification scheme for questions developed by Christenbury and Kelly was presented. While their work provides us with ways to classify questions, it also suggests a questioning strategy and one that, they contend, is an alternative to sequential and hierarchical questioning. They suggest that questions can be grouped in the form of overlapping circles representing different areas or foci of concern, and raised in various sequences. The three key circles are: (1) the matter, (2) personal reality, and (3) external reality. As noted in Chapter 4, matter refers to the subject of discussion or the focus for the questions. Personal reality directs the questioning and thinking to the individual's experiences, values, and ideas, and external reality, directs questions to the world external to the individual. Attention is given to experience, history, and concepts of other situations, peoples, and cultures.

Figure 7–6 shows the arrangement of these circles.

In addition to informing the user of the focus of questions to be employed, the strategy implies possible sequences for questions. For example, one can sequence questions as follows: (1) questions on matter, (2) questions on personal reality, and (3) questions on external reality. Unlike the Taba strategy, this is not a required sequence. Students do not first need to process all *matter* questions before advancing to personal reality questions. Questions quite possibly could be sequenced (1) matter, (2) external reality, and (3) personal reality. Another possible sequence could be (1) external reality, (2) personal reality, and (3) matter.

We can further vary the sequence by considering the various overlaps (4, 5, 6, 7) in the circles. We might construct the strategy as follows: (1) the matter, (2) matter and personal reality and external reality. While the sequence of the questions can be varied at will, it should result from our thinking about what we want students to do. Ideally, we want our students eventually to process questions represented by the interactions of all three circles, questions at intersection #7.

In Chapter 4, pages 107 through 109, there are several breakouts of placing questions according to the questioning circle. While those examples were presented to show different types of questions, they also reveal questioning sequences. Those sequences, however, are all the same; that is, having questions start with circle one, the matter and proceeding through circle two, three, and then intersection 4, 5, 6 concluding with seven. The following example shows an alternative arrangement.

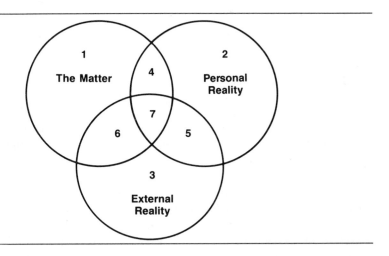

Figure 7–6[12]

<u>*LESSON:*</u>

Types of Mountains

Question 1. Considering the mountains in our region, how do you think
(7)
they were formed? (The matter, personal reality, external
reality)

Question 2. Are there mountains similar to ours in other parts of the
(3)
world? (external reality)

Question 3. Describe what our mountains look like?
(4)
(matter, personal reality)

Question 4. What signs do mountains have that clue us as to how they
(1)
were formed? (matter)

Question 5. Have you ever seen these signs close up?
(2)
(personal reality)

Question 6. Have geologists who have studied mountain formation arrived at similar ways of determining mountain formation?
(6)
(the matter, external reality)

Question 7. (REPEAT OF QUESTION ONE)

The above sequence instead of being 1, 2, 3, 4, 5, 6, 7 is essentially 7, 3, 4, 1, 2, 6, 7. Most important to remember is that the nature and purpose of the questioning as well as students' backgrounds will influence our questioning sequence.

In the example just given, note that the first question, Question 7 as to type, is employed as an advance organizer to trigger students' thinking about the topic of investigation. At this point, a response is not expected. Rather the question sets the stage for processing the other questions. Once students have processed these other questions, they are ready to answer Question 7, thus its reappearance at the conclusion of the sequence.

While this strategy organizes questions by focus and not by cognitive level, one can so classify these questions. Some questions in this strategy could even be classified as to affective level. While we can vary the sequencing of questions, we are not engaged in haphazard questioning. We have thought through our sequence; we have reasons for employing certain questions in particular orders. These are educative questions.

Spiral Cycle Strategy

Not all strategies arise from the academic setting; frequently, teachers invent their own methods. Todd Kelley developed a questioning strategy based on a spiral learning cycle. While designed primarily for the teacher, it can easily be taught to students. The Spiral Learning Cycle, representing a social interaction model of change displaying the dynamic interchange of student and student, student and material, contains four stages of cognitive processes: focus, explore, restructure, and refocus.

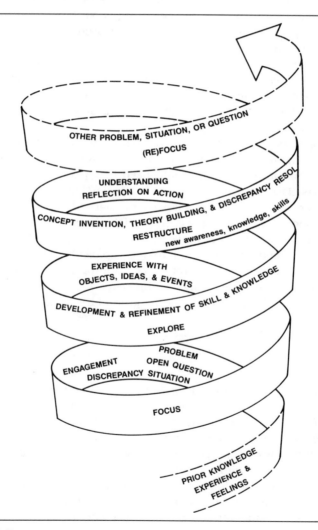

Figure 7–7
The Spiral Learning Cycle.[13]

Focus

The strategy commences with open-ended questions designed to focus students' attention, to set the stage, to make students aware of their levels of understanding, alert to their own expectations and cognizant of the teacher's expectations. In listening to these questions students start to organize their mind sets, information already possessed about the topic; they begin reflecting on their own potential questions.

While Kelley leaves to our imagination the specific kinds of questions to employ, it is not difficult to think of specific types of questions to get students' attention centered. However, the centering is on the general topic, not on a particular aspect of the topic. That is the reason Kelley identifies his questions as open-ended, divergent in focus.

If a lesson were only data gathering, focus questions could be at the knowledge level, or definitional level, or matter level, depending upon which classification scheme you employ. If you desire that students analyze the situation in focus, then initial questions might well be analysis, causal antecedent, or causal consequence.

In a writing class one might begin the lesson by asking the focus question, "How do we know how to begin a story?" A lesson in geography might commence with "What do you think influenced how people used the land?" In a language arts class the question, "What is a poem?" might serve to center students' attention. A social studies class might start off with "Why do we have neighborhoods?" while a science class might begin with the question, "Why do the earth's surface plates move?"

Besides getting students to attend to the topic, these questions ferret from students their feelings for the topic. The appropriateness of the questions can be determined by gauging the intensity and variety of students' responses. In dealing with such questions, the ground has been set for the next major stage: exploration.

Exploration

Exploration, the major part of the strategy, employs questions designed to trigger students searching data to gather relevant information, patterns, meaningful classifications. Here the teacher through questioning engages students in discussion, inquiry, and guided practice. In reflecting on exploration, it becomes evident that many of the generic strategies discussed in the previous chapters can be employed within this spiral strategy.

The exact nature of questioning and types of questions employed during exploration depend partly on the specific manner of exploration. If this phase is primarily discussion, students and teachers may engage more in statement making. *What* questions that we used may serve to guide the discussion along particular pathways, with the teacher assuming responsibility for keeping the discussion within certain parameters and furnishing examples when students become stymied. If exploration is primarily inquiry, then questions may direct students to reflect on steps required for processing information. Teachers might well ask procedural questions, such as, "How would you check out certain events to determine their validity?" For instance, students attempting to discover why certain metal strips curve in a particular manner when heated may hear the teacher ask, "What might you do to see how the metal strip acts under other circumstances? Does the metal strip react similarly when heated on the other side? What happens when you cool it? Have you ever before seen metal act in this manner? Perhaps we need to ask ourselves, 'Just what is metal?' What are its features? How is it distinguished from plastic?" Through such questions, students explore the problem before them.

In a writing class, questions might guide students in improving their writing of short stories. A common student statement in such classes is, "I don't have anything to write about." Here, the teacher asks the student, "Has anything happened to you this past week? How did you react to that event? What are some reasons for your reaction? You had none? Well, why do you suppose that you are so uninterested in those events?"

With a little probing, teachers usually can get students to admit to some interest in something: "Well, what would you like to say about that? If you would want to get me interested, or a new friend to participate with you in your interest, what would you say? Think of a sentence that would turn my head." Proceeding in this manner, the student quite likely starts to explore through the vehicle of writing.

Restructuring

Kelley's last major stage is restructuring. Good teaching is a process of getting students to structure their knowledge and then to challenge that structure and restructure it if necessary. This action results from thinking critically about what we are doing.

Restructuring occurs when students transform the understanding gained through exploration with previously held understanding; where students check out previous views made clear at the focus stage with current views resulting from the exploration stage.

At restructuring students make the information theirs. "Just what does this information mean now that I have employed this focus, engaged in this exploration?" Restructuring is a time for discovery, a time to synthesize information, to construct new knowledge, formulate new theories, invent new concepts, suggest novel ways of solving problems. In doing these things, students gain a more complete understanding and appreciation of the information.

Lessons do not need to end with restructuring. Ideally, information gained is available for continued thinking, continued questioning. Kelley's model shows this in the refocus stage. Students are now ready to apply gained information to other situations, to other problems, to other questions.[14] This stage is quite similar to Taba's application of principles stage.

SPECIFIC QUESTIONING STRATEGIES FOR STUDENTS

The strategies previously presented are essentially for teachers to employ to foster student processing of information in a thinking fashion. Certainly, students can be directly taught the various steps and literally become their own teachers. For instance, knowledgeable of Bloom's taxonomy or Taba's strategy, students can engage in self-study. Ideally, we as teachers should strive for this.

Notwithstanding this, there are strategies that are designed primarily for students; heuristics or algorithms that students can use when questioning. The term "algorithm" usually means "a precise, generally comprehensible prescription for carrying out a defined sequence of elementary operations (from some system of such operations); in order to solve any problem belonging to a certain class (or type)."[15] If the procedures noted in an algorithm are followed correctly, the user will attain the correct answer or the proper solution. The procedure for adding two digit numbers is an algorithm. If followed, assuming you know your number facts, you will always obtain the right answer.

Heuristics, similar to algorithms, suggest steps to be followed with the understanding that it is likely, but not guaranteed, that you will arrive at the correct answer or a useful solution. The general instructional methods discussed in Chapter 6 and the strategies discussed in the first part of this chapter are essentially heuristics, or what Landa terms quasi-algorithms.[16] The steps denoted are quite consistent; however, results cannot be guaranteed.

To elaborate a bit about quasi-algorithms, assume you wish your students to write well. You can construct a quasi-algorithm, or heuristic, for writing a paragraph. You can develop steps employing various types of questions designed to get students thinking of topics for the paragraph and contemplating interesting ways to start the paragraph, to develop the idea, and to conclude the paragraph. The quasi-algorithm presented might be (1) think of a topic, (2) ask yourself about the potential interest of the topic, (3) outline the key points, (4) write the topic sentence, (5) write the body of the paragraph, and (6) write the concluding sentence. While fairly clear cut, a student following the steps is not assured a quality paragraph. Even so, he or she has a better chance than a student without the slightest idea as to how to proceed. While the steps of paragraph construction may be kept constant, students need to know that it is not a true algorithm that guarantees them brilliant writing. It is not like a mathematical formula.

Despite this, students can come to realize that they can gain power in their information processing, their thinking, their questioning, if they view strategies as heuristics or quasi-algorithms, as means of obtaining results. Effective strategies have the characteristic of resultivity.[17]

Resultivity is reflected in the fact that these strategies always aim at a specific sought-for result; there always is a purpose. This result is always going to be obtained in the presence of an appropriate data set. For instance, if students are attempting to determine the validity of an historical event, they need to realize that they may need to employ a strategy different from one required for a mathematical problem.

In an algorithm, quasi-algorithm, or a heuristic, the steps suggested should elicit identical or very similar actions in response to identical or similar situations.[18] For example, if the step states exploration, then students confronted with a particular situation should initiate exploration. Students are not free to engage in some other function, such as restructuring. Phrased differently, when several students are directed to employ a particular strategy in a certain situation, each student must apply the process in a similar if not identical manner. The Taba strategy dealing with concept formation is a quasi-algorithm. Students confronted with listing information, must list; they cannot engage first in labeling. This holds true for all students using the Taba quasi-algorithm regardless of their level of expertise or the lesson content.

In summary, algorithms or quasi-algorithms are prescriptions for carrying out specified operations.[19] In the next section are prescriptions for processing questions in particular ways to gain desired answers, certain results. These prescriptions control how information is processed, evoking certain actions, certain modes of thinking, certain questions for consideration.

VAIL Questioning Strategy[20]

Most of the strategies for teachers have evolved from the analysis of teacher talk. In contrast, the VAIL Questioning strategy originated from analysis of the mental operations of question answering. Its name derives from Singer's work on the *V*erification of the *A*ssertions and *I*mplications of *L*anguage.[21] As with many strategies, the model does not specify types of questions students should employ at each step of the strategy; however, such questions are implied. The reader is invited to use any of the classification schemes already discussed: Bloom's, Hyman's, Lehnert's, someone else's.

While the strategy presented here is somewhat modified from the way Singer developed it, the steps remain true to its spirit: (1) question encoding, (2) assessing appropriate information, (3) case interrogation-comparison, and (4) response. An example should make the strategy clear. Assume that students in a language arts lesson face the following narrative: *The artist painted the picture. The teacher painted the room. The picture was painted with a brush.*

Assume further that students are asked, "Was the picture painted by the artist?" Before responding to the question, students are requested to arrange the narrative as points 1, 2, and 3. Rearranged the narrative appears:

1. The artist painted the picture.
2. The teacher painted the room.
3. The picture was painted with a brush.

Arranging the narrative in this manner enables the student to keep track of the narrative's key points. While this may seem unnecessary with this narrative, its value becomes evident if a narrative is quite long and students desire to identify the relationships between and among the various statements contained in the several sentences.

With the narrative so arranged, students are ready to employ the strategy.

Question Encoding

In question encoding, students view questions as verbal packages consisting of one or more propositions. Each proposition contains a predicate and one or more arguments. The *predicate* incorporates the primary verbal element in a clause. Nouns in the clause act as arguments, denoting agents and patients. The *agent* is the individual or thing that has executed the action; the *patient* refers to that person or thing receiving the action. While the language may seem a bit strange, the roles are fairly clear cut. Nouns are either *doers,* in which case we call them agents, or *receivers,* in which case we call them patients.

In responding to the question, "Was the picture painted by the artist?" students would encode the question as follows: (paint/predicate: agent/artist: patient/picture:). In this example, the student is to inquire about one particular concept, the artist. In encoding the question, students strive to distinguish between information given and new information suggested by the question. In our sample narrative, "Someone painted the picture" is the information given. The new information is imbedded in the request to determine if that someone is the artist.[22]

Prior to reading the question, students really are unaware of why they are reading the narrative. The question now makes that clear: they are to process the narrative to determine if an artist painted the picture. With this now clarified, students have the focus in mind and are ready to advance to the second stage of the strategy, assessing the appropriate information. It is obvious that students are not going to pick up this first stage on their own; they will need some direct instruction in decoding questions into their component parts. They will need to become familiar with the specialized terms of the question parts such as arguments, agents, and predicates.

Assessing the Appropriate Information

Here, students match the information presented in the question "painted by artist," with either information contained from memory or in the narrative just read. Essentially, students are to retrieve from memory relevant data. "Do artists paint pictures?" Was there anything in the narrative about artists? This step is fairly clear cut. This stage is similar to Christenbury and Kelly's external reality circle.

Case Interrogation-Comparison

In our sample question, "Was the picture painted by the artist?" the artist is the agent, the doer of the action. The question has demanded the reader to discover whether the artist painted the picture. At this point, students would ask whether or not the previous narrative includes any statements (statement node) about agents; statements (1) and (2) do. Which agent, however, addresses the question?

Students compare the question's new informational element "artist" with information presented in the narrative. Is there any information in the narrative about artist? In our example, artist is mentioned in statement (1), thus there is a match. Students can now advance to the fourth and final step in the strategy, creating a response.

Response

The response, the result, is the output of student action. Since in our example students found a match between element "artist" in the question and the agent "artist" in statement (1), they can reply "yes" to the question. "Yes, the picture was painted by the artist." But "Yes" is not the only answer possible from this narrative. If the question had been, "Did anyone beside the artist paint a picture?", students, employing the same steps, would have replied "No."[23]

Realizing that there are various types of questions possible at each step, students gain more power in following this quasi-algorithm. For instance, in question encoding, students knowledgeable of comprehension questions will easily find predicates and arguments (nouns). They will be skilled in asking themselves what they understand about the statements in light of information brought to their reading.

Case interrogation-comparison requires students to ask analysis questions centering on analysis of elements. Does the information in the narrative present any information that will match the new information in the question? Also, is the information relevant to the question? Again, analysis questions are required.

The response stage essentially requires students to pose synthesis questions. If using Lehnert's classification, the questions are concept completion. What is my response to the question or what is my conclusion to the question based on my reading? Here students process questions so as to meld the bits of information read into a meaningful answer.

The steps of the strategy are arranged in a flow chart in Figure 7–8.

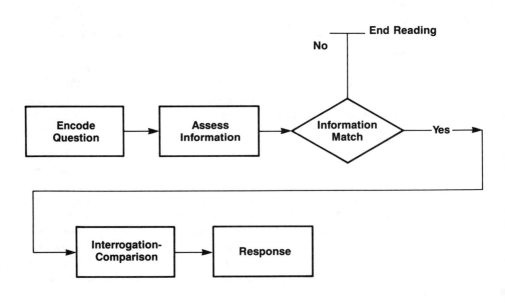

Figure 7–8
VAIL Strategy[24]
SOURCE: From "Mental Processes of Question Answering," by M. Singer, in *The Psychology of Questions* (p. 143), edited by Arthur C. Graesser and John E. Black, 1986, Hillsdale, N.J.: Lawrence Erlbaum Associates, Inc. Copyright 1986 by Lawrence Erlbaum Associates, Inc. Adapted by permission.

Activity

GETTING STUDENTS INVOLVED (VAIL STRATEGY)

There is a place for direct instruction. Plan a lesson to teach your students the VAIL strategy. Model how one would go through each stage of the strategy. Allow students to raise questions they might have about the particular steps in the procedure.

Remember that students will need time to practice this strategy. After they have been taught the strategy, have them try it out. It may help their practice if they have a sheet that identifies the steps. Eventually, the steps will become automatic.

After practice, schedule some debriefing, getting students to explain why they proceeded as they did. This is important for it allows students to become aware of and have control of their metacognitive approaches.

Question Answering Procedure

This question answering procedure has evolved from Arthur Graesser's work on how people actually answer complex questions.[25] A complex question is designed to elicit from an individual a high cognitive or affective level of functioning as opposed to one of simple recall of knowledge. However the procedure can be used to respond to simple questions.

Like the VAIL strategy, this heuristic contains four steps: (1) interpreting the question, (2) identifying the question category, (3) applying a question/answer procedure, and (4) formulating an answer. Figure 7–9 shows these steps in graphic form.

Evident from the figure is that each step requires students to access particular types of knowledge. In interpreting the question, students must draw upon linguistic knowledge. When determining question category, students must draw upon their knowledge of the various classificatory schema. When applying a question/answer procedure, various world knowledge structures are utilized.[26] However, the process is not that clear-cut. In actual use, students would most likely draw simultaneously information from several of these bases. For instance, when interpreting the question, students could well be drawing on world knowledge structures as well as linguistic knowledge of question sentences.

Interpreting the Question

What does the question ask of me? Essentially, this is the initial question students must pose when they confront a question in a narrative or hear one.

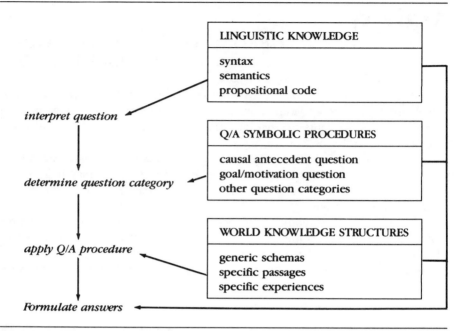

Figure 7–9[27]
Question Answering Procedure

Ideally, the teacher has informed students through direct instruction and modeling that the question in a linguistic creation possessing a certain semantic structure. Knowing this, students realize that a question is an expression that has a definite function, contains a statement and draws on a knowledge structure. They also appreciate that the question statement also suggests an answer. Assume in a language arts lesson in which students have read a story about children at camp that the teacher poses the question, "What made the children happy?" Students getting ready to interpret the question divide it into its semantic parts: function, statement element, and knowledge structure element. So divided, the question appears as follows:

Question function: What

Statement element: children made happy

Knowledge structure element: (?)

The students understand, from earlier instruction, that the *question function,* the interrogative function mentioned in Chapter 2, is usually determined by the first word of the question. Thus, this question serves the function of "what." Later, when dealing with the question/answer procedure, students will be more specific in identifying what kind of "what" question this is. We will assume that all students have been instructed that all questions contain within their structure a *statement element.* Students find this statement element by turning the question around to read as a statement. "What made the children happy?" becomes "The children were made happy by what?" This is reduced to "Children made happy."

The *knowledge structure* element refers to the context to which the question refers—what the actual situation is surrounding the question. It is the external reality circle of Christenbury and Kelly. At this initial stage, this may be left open. As students delve more into the lesson they start to grasp what the knowledge structure might be. However, if it is clear that the question refers to children in a particular story going to camp, then the students might note that the knowledge structure element is camp. In another story, it could have been school. If the question referred to students on holiday with their parents, the knowledge structure element might have been holiday.

What the knowledge structure element does is enable the students to commence thinking of possible answers to the question before them. For instance, if the question is about children at camp, then students might well contemplate possible things that we know about camp that make children happy, thus suggesting possible answers. If the question was about children on vacation, students would bring into attention what they know about vacations and possible joyful things. The knowledge structure element facilitates their setting the stage for their question processing. It channels their thinking.

The question in our example is a simple one and contains only one *statement element* (node). However, our questions and even those asked by students often contain more than one statement or statement nodes. Students might have been asked, "Why were the children so happy after the camp counselor left?" Here we have two statements (statement nodes).[28] The question can be broken down into "children were so happy" and "camp counselor left." Students first determine which is the key statement that should receive attention. Students employ the microthinking skill of interpretation to comprehend the question. In our simple example the primary question focus is on why the children were so happy. Sometimes, the placement of the statement node in the question clues students into the primary focus.

Identifying the Question Category

After interpreting the question as to its function, statement, and knowledge structure, students are ready to classify the question. Several of these categories have been presented in Chapters 3 and 4. However, this particular question processing procedure draws on question categories developed by Lehnert and modified by Graesser.[29]

In "What made the children happy?" the "what" type of question can introduce one of several categories of questions: causal antecedent (what caused something, what were prior events); causal consequence (what are the consequences of something, what events occurred later); enablement (what allowed something to occur); judgmental (what is your opinion or judgment); and feature specification (what is a key feature). In this second step, students analyze the question to determine which of the "whats" is really asked for. Interpreting this sample question, students realize that the "what" is requesting "what happened that resulted in the children becoming happy?" What caused the happiness? The type of question is causal antecedent.

Teachers may not actually use these terms in the classroom. At the elementary grades we might call this "a what question asking for causes." The function of the "what" is made known during this second stage, regardless of what terms we employ. Considering questions at this second stage results in pupils knowing the purpose of the question—this question is asking for the causes of something. I will search for these causes in my reading, drawing on what I already know about camps (world knowledge structure).

Applying the Question/Answer Procedure

This stage, influenced by the purpose of the question and by the relevant knowledge structure, has students confronted with the question "What made the children happy?" beginning to contemplate how they can process the question to result in an answer that identifies the cause for the event—children made happy.

Ideally, students have been introduced to several ways they can respond. Perhaps students decide that first they will think of the knowledge structure, the context of the question. It is about children who are at camp and are happy. Students might plot the following steps:

1. Think about camp situations, note all the possible reasons that children might be happy.

2. Read the material (remember this is a reading lesson). Check to see if there are any statements in the material that deal with the event suggested in the question statement. Here students are attempting to make a match between statement nodes.

3. Check the arrangement of the material to determine if the statements that seem to apply to the statement element in the question are arranged in an order that suggests cause. (Remember that the students have determined that the question is asking for what *caused* the students to be happy.) Students might be willing depending on their level of sophistication to make a conceptual graph of the material being read in which they note the sequence of events in the narrative.

A simple map breaks down the statements of the narrative into states, actions, and events—the three possible forms of a statement element of the question. Children made happy is an event. *Events* denote state changes in the physical world or social world.[30] *States* refer to the condition of an entity existing in the physical or social world. The camp had twenty-two children is a state of a particular social world. *Action* is a person or agent doing something designed to attain a particular state.[31] Actions direct an individual

---

State: *The camp had twenty-two children*

Event: *The wind was blowing*
↓

Action: *The counselor said, today we can go sailing*
↓

*Event: *Children made happy?*

(Students record the event first.)

Note: This figure refers to the particular story in question

Figure 7–10

toward a goal or goals. The counselor engaged in the action of saying that we are going sailing. In making this simple graph, students see that it was the counselor's action that resulted in the children becoming happy. The arrows denote areas that logically connect the story.

The actual arrangement of this figure may vary with different children, but there should be some integrity to the graph so it shows causal relationship. Students can be helped in their drawing of such graphs by starting with the question statement and placing it at the lower half of the paper and then working to connect the various statements encountered in the reading. It will become obvious to students that some of the statements will have nothing to do with this particular question, such as the camp had twenty-two children.

Formulating an Answer

In applying the question/answer procedure, students actually generate possible answers. At this concluding stage, students put into final words an answer to the question. They are actually making a judgment whether the suggested answers developed in the previous stage are really appropriate to the questions asked. In our case, students in the previous stage concluded that the counselor in saying that the children could go sailing resulted in making them happy. Thus the answer is "The children were made happy when told by the counselor they could go sailing."

At this juncture students query themselves if this answer suggests a cause—that was the original function of this "what" question. Students might also ask themselves, drawing on their world knowledge structure, if it is likely that children would be made happy with such news. The answer is yes; the answer has believability. This is important for students to determine; there may have been some other statements about what the counselor did, and students would have to choose the most likely one. There may even be more than one answer to the question. Perhaps the narrative noted that the counselor also said that there would be seconds on ice cream tonight.

The strategy can be arranged in a flow chart as in Figure 7–11:

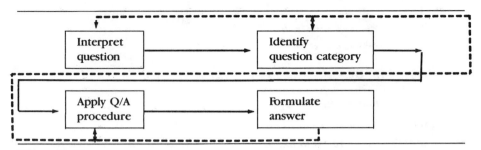

Figure 7–11

The dashed line shows that throughout the processing of the question, students can go back to previous stages, and when formulating the answer, they go back to the original question to see if there is a match between answer and question.

While there are many categories of questions with numerous functions, students can still follow this basic strategy, quasi-algorithm, in processing information. Students might find it helpful to use a planning sheet to keep them on task.

While this question/answer procedure may appear complicated, its level of difficulty can be adjusted to fit students' level of skills. The only part potentially complicated is Step 3, the application of the question-answer procedure. However, pupils at the early elementary grades can be given simple rules for seeking answers. The familiar SQ3R (skim, question, read, recite, and review) can be plugged into Step 3. At the upper grades, students can engage in rather sophisticated linguistic analysis of the information.

The key point is that this questioning strategy and the VAIL Strategy previously discussed are designed to be used by the student working alone or cooperatively. These are not strategies for the teachers. Teachers may wish to model them when teaching students to use them, but, primarily, these are procedures for students to command.

CONCLUSION

We teachers and our students really have a wealth of instructional procedures available to us, a rich resource from which we can draw specific questioning and thinking approaches. Ideally, teaching is the orchestration of many strategies, the placement of educative questions in specified sequences to advance student learning.

As evident from this chapter, educational discourse is not random conversation. Hopefully also evident is that all of this information should become part of students' procedural knowledge—their knowledge of how they should go about their business of learning, of raising questions, of seeking answers, of shaping their understandings.

Activity

PLAN SHEET FOR QUESTION ANSWERING

Topic:

Key Question:

Answering Procedure:

1. Interpret Question:

    Function

    Statement Element

    Knowledge structure

2. Identify question category

    _____

    _____

3. Apply Question/answer procedure:

    A. Think about context of question, what you know about this context, this world knowledge structure.

    B. Read material keeping in mind world knowledge structure, what the question is asking (function), and statement element.

    C. Arrange or rearrange the material in your mind or on paper that will show links (arcs) among states, actions, events read in relation to your key question.

4. Formulate answer:

    A. State answer

    B. Check answer against original interpretation of question. Is function addressed—did you find what question asked for?

Teachers who gain high levels of skill in these strategies gain executive control of their classrooms. Perhaps even more important, students who gain competence in these strategies attain executive control over their learning. Ideally, we want students to eventually function autonomously; that is, without undue reliance upon the teacher. Of course, learning and the raising of questions does not need to be done in a solitary manner; cooperative learning has its place. Much of life-long learning, however, is self-initiated and self-managed through metacognitive awareness.

Specific questioning strategies within the classroom can enable students to be true students. Such questioning allows us to be true teachers.

NOTES

1. Ronald T. Hyman, *Strategic Questioning* (Englewood Cliffs, N.J.: Prentice-Hall, 1979), p. xiii.

2. Bruce Joyce and Marsha Weil, *Models of Teaching,* 3rd. ed. (Englewood Cliffs, N.J.: Prentice-Hall, 1986).

3. Bruce Joyce and Marsha Weil, *Models of Teaching,* p. 18.

4. Benjamin S. Bloom, ed., *Taxonomy of Educational Objectives, Cognitive Domain* (New York: David McKay, 1956).

5. Francis P. Hunkins, *Questioning Strategies and Techniques* (Boston: Allyn and Bacon, 1972), p. 104.

6. Hilda Taba, *Teaching Strategies and Cognitive Functioning in Elementary School Children,* Cooperative Research Project No. 2404 (San Francisco: San Francisco State College, Feb. 1966).

7. Hilda Taba, *Teacher's Handbook for Elementary Social Studies* (Reading, Mass.: Addison-Wesley Publishing, 1972), p. 92.

8. Hilda Taba, *Teacher's Handbook for Elementary Social Studies,* p. 101.

9. Hilda Taba, *Teacher's Handbook for Elementary Social Studies,* p. 109.

10. Hilda Taba, *Teacher's Handbook for Elementary Social Studies.*

11. Portions of this section were adapted from F. P. Hunkins, "Students as Key Questioners," in William W. Wilen, ed., *Questions, Questioning Techniques, and Effective Teaching* (Washington, D.C.: National Education Association, 1987), pp. 153–72.

12. Leila Christenbury and Patricia P. Kelly, *Questioning, A Path to Critical Thinking* (Urbana, Ill.: National Council for Teachers of English, 1983), p. 13.

13. Todd D. Kelley, "A Teacher's Use of Questions," *Questioning Exchange* 1; 2 (May 1987); 119–23.

14. Todd D. Kelley, "A Teacher's Use of Questions," *Questioning Exchange.*

15. L. L. Landa, *The Algorithmization of Learning and Instruction* (Englewood Cliffs, N.J.: Educational Technology Publications, 1974).

16. L. L. Landa, *The Algorithmization of Learning and Instruction.*

17. L. L. Landa, *The Algorithmization of Learning and Instruction.*

18. L. L. Landa, *The Algorithmization of Learning and Instruction.*

19. L. L. Landa, *The Algorithmization of Learning and Instruction.*

20. A portion of this section was adapted from F. P. Hunkins, "Students as Key Questioners," in William Wilen, ed., *Questions, Questioning Techniques, and Effective Teaching* (Washington, D.C.: National Educational Association, 1987), pp. 153–72.

21. Murray Singer, "Mental Processes of Question Answering," in Arthur C. Graesser and John B. Black, eds., *The Psychology of Questions* (Hillsdale, N.J.: Erlbaum, 1986), pp. 121–56.

22. Murray Singer, "Mental Processes of Question Answering."

23. Murray Singer, "Mental Processes of Question Answering, p. 143"

24. Murry Singer, "Mental Processes of Question Answering."

25. Arthur C. Gráesser and Tamar Murachver, "Symbolic Procedures of Question Answering," in Arthur C. Graesser and John D. Black, eds., *The Psychology of Questions,* pp. 15–88.

26. Arthur C. Graesser and Tamar Murachver, "Symbolic Procedures of Question Answering."

27. Arthur C. Graesser and Tamar Murachver, "Symbolic Procedures of Question Answering, p. 17."

28. Arthur C. Graesser and Tamar Murachver, "Symbolic Procedures of Question Answering."

29. Arthur C. Graesser and Tamar Murachver, "Symbolic Procedures of Question Answering."

30. Arthur C. Graesser and Tamar Murachver, "Symbolic Procedures of Question Answering."

31. Arthur C. Graesser and Tamar Murachver, "Symbolic Procedures of Question Answering."

8

Techniques of

Questioning

In contrast to the previous two chapters, which presented information on generic and specific instructional strategies, this chapter addresses questioning techniques and nonquestioning options employable in the management of instruction. Often our instruction successes are determined by how we actually manage or implement teaching methods within the classroom social dynamic. Do we allow students sufficient time to process particular questions? Do we engage in actions that elicit from students deep searches for meaning? Do we challenge students to be clear in their responses?

While we must plan for good teaching, we must not neglect the planning necessary for managing our delivery of instruction. Several techniques or tactical moves exist that can trigger students optimally responding to particular aspects of instructional strategies or employing their own strategies efficiently. These techniques allow us as teachers to have some control of class lessons; not control in the sense of manipulating students but in the sense of allowing students to optimize their thinking and processing of information. Techniques enable us to shape lessons in particular ways, to raise lessons from mere fact gathering to sessions of productive thinking.

Compared to strategies which are carefully planned sequences of steps designed to attain particular goals, techniques usually are one specific behavior applied to a very narrow focus. Such specialized actions are designed not primarily to attain a given goal or general objective but rather to get students to improve their performance on a particular step or stage of an instructional strategy. For example, wait time is one technique crucial to good questioning. This behavior, waiting for students to respond to a question, is designed to facilitate students in thinking more carefully about a stage of a particular strategy they are at and to raise questions at higher levels.

Techniques might be called "tricks of the trade," tricks that allow us to maximize our and our students' actions. All professionals have procedural techniques. Actors employ the technique of changing the volume of their voices to make certain points, to set the stage for a particular audience reaction. As actors, teachers also utilize voice techniques to motivate students. Teachers draw on gestures, postures, and facial expressions to evoke from students thinking and questioning. In managing the classroom, teachers use techniques such as positioning themselves physically near students to get them to attend to lessons. Teachers also use eye contact to get students to pay attention.

While many techniques should comprise our teaching repertoire, the techniques discussed here are designed specifically for use with questioning and thinking strategies.

QUESTIONING TECHNIQUES

While the following questioning techniques are presented in an arbitrary sequence, it makes sense to begin this section focusing on the technique of wait time, a concept profound in its obviousness.

Wait Time Technique

Mary Budd Rowe identified the concept of wait time—specifically waiting for students to respond to questions. It takes time to think; however, Rowe discovered that teachers rarely wait very long for students to respond to questions, usually only a second. She informed us, and her research has borne this out, that we can obtain major results in the level of classroom discourse and thought solely from engaging in a three-to-five second pause after a question is raised.[1]

Actually, there are two wait times. Wait time 1, postquestion wait time, is the pause after a teacher poses a question and before a student answers. Wait time 2, postresponse wait time, is the pause present after a student answers and prior to the teacher reacting. Both are important in relation to students' thinking.

Allowing students time to respond and to think about their response has many beneficial effects. The length of student responses, suggestive of higher thinking, increases. Wait time 2 has been shown to promote effectively in students elaboration and evidence of thinking.[2] Wait time also encourages students to furnish relevant evidence to support inference statements. Diversity of student thinking also results from increased wait time. Even the number of student questions is augmented in those classrooms where wait-time is effectively practiced. More student participation, more cooperative student activity, heightened student confidence in their knowledge of the subject matter and their abilities to process information—such are the rewards of this remarkably simple technique. Wait time has also been shown to increase achievement.

Besides wait time benefiting students, it also affects us as teachers in positive ways. Engaging in wait time tends to make us more flexible in our dealings with students processing information. Actually, it encourages us to increase the diversity of our questions; it influences our questioning patterns or sequences. Our interchanges with our students become more conversational; we listen more carefully to our students' reasoning.[3]

Probing Technique

Often, we wish students to respond completely and thoughtfully to our questions or even to their questions. Probing involves a series of questions or comments usually addressed to one student designed to elicit a more complete or more adequate answer. Frequently, we probe to encourage students to think at higher levels, to support their statements.

Our probes can be directed to numerous things: vocabulary, more specificity in a response, additional data, theories to support statements, inferences, and procedures employed in thinking about data. We can probe for a student's intent in responding in a particular way, for predictions, for the generation of conclusions, for the application of principles to particular situations.[4]

The probing technique is usually a teacher response technique in that the teacher must first wait for the student to answer a question or raise a point before commencing a probe. There are exceptions, however. For instance, in a language arts lesson, teachers might begin the lesson probing for vocabulary, to ascertain if students know the meaning of a word. In social studies there may be times when the teacher might want to assess students' initial understanding and probe for students' understanding of perhaps the meaning of culture.

Sometimes, we probe when students express they lack the answer, when they say "I don't know." Perhaps they give an answer only partially correct. Sometimes, when one student replies, "I don't know," we go on to another. However, with probing we challenge the student to furnish a correct answer. We may start our probe relating the situation to what the student does know. For instance, a student might be unable to answer the question about the cultural interpretation of resources. In this case, the teacher might say, "Well, we have been talking about resources for the past week. We have also been discussing how people are influenced by their culture as they look at the

Activity

WAIT TIME

Sure, it is easy to wait for students to respond to my questions. I do that already. All right, let's see. Record a fifteen-minute lesson in which you do ask questions. After recording the lesson, check your wait time, either wait-time 1 or wait-time 2 or both. Your pulse usually operates on a one-second interval, so you can use it as a guide to see if you are waiting the recommended time length. How did you do?

If you do not wish to record your lesson, have a colleague visit and do the recording.

If you did wait the recommended length, good for you. Continue the good work. However, if you are like the majority of us, you have a bit of difficulty getting much beyond waiting one second. In your next lesson, make an honest effort to wait the three to five seconds, count to yourself after raising a question or hearing a response. Record this next lesson to see how near you get to your mark or have a colleague assist.

Examine your wait time for various content lessons. Do one a week. Plot your wait time on a graph for each content lesson to see if you are improving. You can compare your wait time performance for different content lessons. Record what conclusions you draw.

---

world around them. Does that give you some idea as to how you could answer this question?" Hopefully it does. If not, the teacher might furnish more clues to prompt student response. "Well, think of how you use your backyard as a resource. Do all people have backyards? Do all people with backyards use them in the same manner? Do all your friends use their backyards similarly? All right, now what seems to be the key reason that various people are using their backyards differently? Does this suggest then an answer to the original question, 'How does the culture of a people influence how they view their environment as a resource?' "

Sometimes, upon hearing students respond, we want to ask, "How come?" We wish students to furnish data to support their response, or we may desire them to explain a process. If students in a science lesson have made a statement that the ozone layer of the earth's atmosphere is being destroyed, we may want them to supply data to support the statement. "What information have you gathered to support that statement? What other information might you need to really have confidence in that statement?"

Probing's main function is *why.* Why do you say this? Why is this your answer? Why did you employ this method? Why do you make this prediction? Why is this theory appropriate?

Clarification Technique

At times we are not clear of the meaning of a student's response to a question; we do not understand what he or she is saying as fully as we would like. In such instances, we can engage in the technique of clarification.

Clarification can employ a question or several questions or statements to get students to engage in either restatement of information; or the furnishing of a definition, or a repeating of a statement or question. Sometimes the technique is solely the rephrasing of the student's response. The primary purpose is not to add other meaning to the statement but rather to determine exactly its meaning. It is a move to remove ambiguity.

For instance, in a science lesson, a student might respond to a particular question noting that certain mountains were being formed by the action of plate tectonics. Upon hearing this response, the teacher might seek clarification asking, "What do you mean by plate tectonics?" In a social studies lesson, students responding to a question might say, "The people are part of democracy," which might lead the teacher to reply, "I am not sure what you mean by the people being a part of democracy. Explain the word 'part?'" In an economics classroom dealing with marketplace, the teacher might seek clarification requesting, "I am not clear what you mean by market interdependency. Please draw on the chalkboard what you mean." Clarification is also used by the teacher to respond to a pupil's question. Perhaps a student in a language arts class asks, "Was our heroine completely free to choose that solution?" The teacher, seeking clarification, responds, "What do you mean by 'completely free'?"

No hard and fast rules exist for clarification. Talk is part of clarification when it is uttered to make clear the meaning of various statements. "Can you put that answer in different words. I am unsure what you mean." There will be times when we are unsure as to why students answer as they do. Rather than replying, "You are wrong," it may be more productive to seek the underlying rationale for the response.

Elaboration Technique

At times, it seems that students' responses are guided by the criterion of brevity. The fewer words the answer has the better. However, occasions arise when we want students to expand their answer, to elaborate, to extend their thinking to a higher level. When employing this technique, we pose open-ended questions or statements suggestive of additional directions to proceed with a response. Suppose the lesson is on social relationships that influence group dynamics. The teacher asks, "What makes an effective group?" A student replies, "Friendship." Wanting more from the student, the teacher asks, "What types of friendship might one find exhibited in a group? If friendship is a major factor in making the group run smoothly, what might be some other significant factors that would influence friendship? Would all of these types of friendships that you have just identified act similarly in the group? Would the purpose for the group's formation have anything to do with the types of friendship formed? Is it possible for a group to work effectively if the people are not friends?" Each of these questions would be followed by wait time to give students time to respond.

All of these questions ask the student to supply more than just the answer "Friendship." The teacher is requesting the student to consider the information, the response, from varying stances, not to converge prematurely on particular information. The student is to look for other reasons that groups work well. Elaboration requires students to engage in divergent thinking, in analysis.

In elaboration and in most of the other techniques, the teacher strives to engage student respondants in meaningful in-depth conversation. So often, intent on involving our class members in discussion or inquiry, we only allow one-word responses, neglecting to follow up when a student responds. Our classroom interaction takes on more of the look of recitation than actual processing of and thinking about information.

In Figure 8–1, *a* shows what occurs in a teacher's attempt to distribute questions evenly around the room. We get recitation. Figure 8–1 *b* shows an interaction that continues for a while between the teacher and one particular student and then another. There is even interaction between student and student. While not all students will verbally interact with the teacher on any given day, all students are interacting by being engaged in critical listening to the dialogue.

a *diagram on recitation*

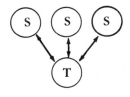

b *classroom with in-depth dialogue, questioning*

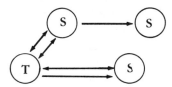

Figure 8–1

Redirection Technique

Figure 8–1 *a* shows the usual pattern of classroom questioning: teacher question-pupil response, teacher question-pupil response, teacher question-pupil response, and the like. Ben Harris in discussing questions identified that pattern as a controlled question response.[5] While not necessarily inappropriate, this pattern tends to contribute to teachers dominating classroom discourses.

Ideally, we want students to participate. A high degree of student involvement can be attained by balancing responses from volunteering and nonvolunteering students.[6] The ideal is that every student can make a contribution to class interaction. However, such involvement requires alertness on the teacher's part to verbal and nonverbal cues from students reluctant to participate. A perplexed look or even a head buried in a textbook clues the alert teacher perhaps to raise a question to involve that particular student.

The redirection technique is designed to do just that—to redirect classroom questions to distribute pupil participation more evenly. In using redirection, the teacher repeats the question, directing it to several students for their responses. The question need not actually be repeated or rephrased; rather, the teacher either through eye contact, head nod, or one word can involve additional students. For example, the teacher might ask students in an urban geography class, "What might be some ways in which we can solve the problem of grid lock?" One student responds, "Reduce the number of cars allowed in the city." The teacher responds, turning to the class, "Other ways?" Another pupil responds. The teacher replies, "What might be a third way?" A pupil responds, the teacher then sees Sandy looking a bit reluctant to respond, and says, "Sandy?"

Redirection can be employed when the teacher realizes that a question can trigger a number of response alternatives. Certainly, the question about grid lock does not suggest only one answer. If our questions are divergent, we will most likely have to engage in redirection. Certainly a question that asks for one specific answer does not need to be redirected, unless the pupil responding answers incorrectly. We would not need to go through much, if any, redirection with the question, "When was the Declaration of Independence signed?" There is only one answer.

There are times when our initial questions fail to draw a response. We may redirect our query to other students around the room. Perhaps we may have to go to several students before eliciting a response.

On numerous occasions, our questions generate differences of opinion among students. In such instances, we should engage in redirection. Perhaps Steven has stated that books with "obscene" words in them should not be allowed in classrooms. "Susan, assuming that we can agree on what obscene means, do you agree with Steven's viewpoint? What about the rest of you?"

Here, the teacher is attempting to facilitate student-student interaction rather than the usual teacher-student, teacher-student encounter.

Done effectively, redirection informs students that they are expected to participate, to think, to interact with not only the teacher but also classmates.

Supporting Techniques

Supporting techniques are those skills employed by the teacher to furnish cognitive and affective support to students. Such skills contribute to a classroom climate in which students feel comfortable responding to teachers' questions, classmates' questions, and to their own questions. Supporting techniques create a freedom to inquire, to question, to challenge, to think.

Perhaps the teacher behavior most contributory to positive classroom climate is that of accepting student feelings and ideas. Flanders in the early seventies identified the acceptance of students' feelings, praise, encouragement, and use of students' ideas as teacher behaviors supportive of positive classroom climate.[7] Essentially, teachers who accept students' feelings listen to students, use students' ideas. Furthermore, such teachers give evidence that they credit students with being capable of conducting much of their own learning. Presuming this, teachers encourage students to generate questions, to engage in processing information, to activate their thinking. Believing this, teachers often say, "Good, now you know what to do next. Fine, you almost have the solution to that problem."

Perhaps the highest compliment students can receive in a classroom is for teachers to employ their ideas in elaborating a point or directing further inquiry. Teachers drawing on students' contributions foster a feeling of joint inquiry, of cooperative learning. Perhaps a teacher records on the board the major student questions that will guide the focus of a lesson.

In employing the questioning techniques of probing, clarification, elaborating, and redirection in a caring, legitimately interested manner, the teacher is already engaged in supporting techniques. A place for praise exists in supporting techniques; however, it should not be overdone so that students come to consider praise statements as merely the teacher's verbal noise. Always saying "Fine" meaning "I hear you" really leads students to realize that there is no praise being given. However, there is a real place for teachers to praise the work of students. "That was an excellent paper, Frank. You raised significant questions and carefully developed your points." On occasion, we can say, "Leah, that question is most effective. It has the power to get us into a deep consideration of the issues."

When done well, the previous techniques enable students to process information more critically, to raise questions of significance. We also have non-questioning options available to us that we can employ in concert with our questioning strategies. These are discussed next.

Activity

REFLECTION ON TECHNIQUES

You have just read about several techniques: probing, clarification, elaboration, redirection, and support. Ideally, we should employ all in our classrooms. Using the following list, indicate with a slash mark how many of these moves you engage in during classroom discourse.

Class: _____   **Length of class in minutes:** _____

Technique	Number of times employed	Percentage of usage for total class*
Probing	_____	_____
Clarification	_____	_____
Elaboration	_____	_____
Redirection	_____	_____
Support	_____	_____

Total number of
techniques used: _____

*Figure from the total number for all techniques employed.

Your Reactions: *Did* you use all the techniques? Which technique did you use the most? The least? Not at all? What is your reaction to your use of techniques? Do you need to keep things the same? Change things?

Do this recording for several classes in different subject areas. Reflect on your findings.

NONQUESTIONING OPTIONS

Although questions are essential linguistic tools for engaging students in thinking and processing information, other linguistic means are available to elicit similar if not identical student responses. Dillon has argued that we as teachers have several meaningful alternatives for stimulating student thought and participation: declarative statement; reflective restatement, expression of state of mind, invitation to elaborate, and deliberate silence.[8]

Declarative Statement

Questions imply answers or statements; therefore, statements can suggest questions. When combined, statements and questions actually comprise the speech act. The number of statements and questions varies depending upon the complexity of the particular speech act. Dillon indicates there are times when the teacher makes a declarative statement instead of a question to register a particular thought in relation to what a student has said.[9] Perhaps the student has indicated that we get most of our coffee from Hawaii. Rather than the teacher asking, "How much coffee do we get from Hawaii?" the teacher mentions that the greatest amount of our coffee comes from Brazil. The statement is utilized to prevent students from spending time traveling an inaccurate route.

There are myriad instances when teachers make statements to furnish data, to present information directly. There is nothing wrong with this. Sometimes we get so enthused about involving students in their learning that we disparage the role of information giver that teachers can and must play. If a need for information exists, teachers certainly may address that need through statement making. Statements elicit from students responses, trigger in students thinking. In some instances, responses to statements may actually be more complex than responses to questions.[10]

David Ausubel has championed the use of advance organizers in teaching, setting the stage for particular learning. Essentially, an advance organizer presents, *through statements,* information that informs students what is coming in the lesson; it furnishes students with what Ausubel calls an "intellectual scaffolding" by which they can structure the ideas and facts to be encountered in the lesson.[11] The key characteristic of an advance organizer statement is that it is at a higher level of abstraction and generality than the material to follow. For instance, a teacher wishing students to understand a culture begins a lesson with the following statement (advance organizer): "The tools and machines that a people have created reflect in many ways the values of that people and the ways in which they view their environment. Realizing this, it is possible for us to 'read' the tools and machines of peoples at different time periods and develop a fairly good understanding of their cultural ways. These changes can be drawn from just determining the major machines of particular ages and the materials from which they are made." With these statements, the teacher informs the students that they are going to study in the upcoming unit on tools and machines—cultural readings. Students will keep these statements in mind as they respond to the material read or heard. These statements will also serve to channel their questions.

There is no doubt that statements can elicit responses from students. Since statements convey more information than a question, there is perhaps a greater range of responses possible. Also, statements may serve to help teachers refrain from giving students clear guidance as to how to respond, thus perhaps packing a greater surprise value. For this reason, a statement might trigger more elaborative thinking than a question about the same material. For instance, if the teacher in a science lesson utters, "Today, with our new knowledge in genetic engineering, we are for the first time able to begin to participate in our own evolution," it is quite likely that the surprise, even the shock value of the statement is very high. It is possibly higher than might be the case with the question, "Taking into consideration our knowledge on genetics, do you think that we will be able to participate effectively in our own future evolution?"

Certainly, we can debate which is the more powerful, statement or question. The central point, however, is that statements, just like questions, have a significant place in classroom discourse. Discourse would be artificial and limiting, if not impossible, if statements were eliminated. It is the skillful blending of statements and questions that comprise discourse of educational value.

While we have been discussing declarative statements, there are other statements declarative in form but pragmatically interrogative. For example, a teacher might make the statement, "That is the key reason for their poor use of their lands." However, through intonation and the context in which the statement is made, the statement is really a statement-question. The teacher wants students to answer the question, "Is that the key reason for their poor use of their lands?"[12]

In Chapter 2, mention was made that questions are demands for information. Specifically, imperative statements are demands. These demands we can consider as imperative statement-questions. For example, the teacher demanding the following, "Identify five major uses of wood fiber," is essentially asking students to furnish an answer. "Shut the door" is also a demand, essentially a request for the students to do something. So is "Tell us about the dilemma that confronted Mr. Jones in our story."

Statements are essential to classroom talk, enabling us to communicate information to students for their consideration. At times, however, students are unsure of what we are saying, and it is often the case that we are unclear as to what students are attempting to communicate. When such confusion exists, we can employ what Dillon calls reflective restatement.[13]

Reflective Restatement

In an atmosphere conducive to sharing ideas and raising questions, students realize that teachers hear what students say and also comprehend them. Dillon notes that we as teachers can employ in our discourse a second alternative to asking questions in the use of a reflective restatement.[14] This consists of the teacher stating his or her understanding of what the student has just said. It is designed to communicate to the student that you have heard what he has said, that you are attentive. Once this is established, you as teacher can then raise some questions.

As previously mentioned, there are times when you are not clear regarding a student's response. Rather than posing a question as part of a clarifying technique, such as "What do you mean, Samuel?", you attempt to rephrase in a statement what you think Samuel means. This may be a better move, for Samuel upon hearing your restatement can determine if you heard or interpreted him correctly. If Samuel, upon hearing your restatement, notes, "That is not what I mean," you can then ask Samuel to try again to communicate what he does mean. That may be more productive than just asking, "What do you mean?" at the outset, for Samuel has no clue from your question as to what you have missed in his response. Restatement informs Samuel of your private meaning.

Dillon notes several ways to phrase a reflective restatement. We might respond to a students' statement with "I get from what you say that..." or "So you think that...."[15] This move is not hard to employ. We can say "As I hear you...." or "Let me put what I think you said in my own words." Or "So you feel that if Mr. Tifdon had been more courteous, the situation would have been more pleasant."

There are times when we wish to restate what a student has said to support his statement. Thus, a pupil who has made a statement about "no smoking always" may elicit from the teacher, "Ann has stated that if the common good is to be protected, then laws should be passed to ban smoking in all public places."

Reflective restatement invites students to say more, to furnish more inclusive statements. It informs the student that he or she can add substance to his or her statement and enrich the depth of class conversation. When employed, reflective restatement promotes participation at both the speaking and listening level; it fosters student-student and student-teacher interaction.[16]

State of Mind

"Honesty is the best policy." This maxim is also useful in considering classroom conversation. There will be times when dealing with students when you are stumped and really have nothing to say. Rather than faking a response or asking a question for clarification, you can just share your current state of mind. Hopefully, in modeling this verbal response, students will come to realize that this is a legitimate move for them as well.

There are many states of mind and myriad ways of expressing them. Despite this, Dillon notes that the technique is very straightforward: "describe truthfully your state of mind, and none other."[17] If you are confused by what a student is saying, tell him, "I am confused about what you are saying," or "Sorry, I just don't get your point." Perhaps then the speaker or some other students can bring you back to focus.

Sometimes, we want to express to students what their statements mean to us. "You know, when I hear about the killing of seals, I get a real feeling of sadness and anger." This communicates to students your reaction to the situation. It also communicates that you are not yet ready to pose any questions regarding the topic.

However, your mind may voice questions indirectly. For instance, you might have said regarding the killing of seals, "You know, I wonder how people can bring themselves to killing these animals." It is certainly an indirect question; however, the key thrust of the statement is not interrogative but rather a communication to the students that you are unsure of how people can behave in such a manner. The statement describes your state of mind; it is not asking students to respond to a question.[18]

Invitation to Elaborate

This nonquestioning alternative resembling the elaboration technique previously discussed is simply informing students of your desire to hear more of their views. "I'd like you to expand on that point." Often, the invitation is presented in a declarative-imperative sentence.

Basically, this invitation is a type of probe. For this reason, it may be misleading for Dillon to have included "invitation to elaborate" as a questioning alternative. It involves the use of questions much of the time.

Silence

Wait time was discussed under questioning techniques. Silence certainly involves the technique of wait time, allowing three to five seconds to pass before expecting students to reply to your question or waiting a similar period before raising another question after a student has responded. However, silence is more than just three- to five-second breaks in conversation.

Silence can be consciously planned into a lesson following the presentation of an advance organizer. Perhaps five minutes is scheduled in which students contemplate that which they have heard. This silence can be introduced to the class as follows: "Class, take five minutes to reflect on this statement. Jot down any questions you may want to consider." It might be a good idea to have at the outset of any lesson a period of silence in which people can meditate on what they want to obtain from the lesson. There could well be a richness of questions and an increased quality in statement making from furnishing time to reflect, to consider complex thought, personal opinions, views, confusions.

At times, class discussions might get bogged down. Rather than continuing to raise questions, the teacher might inform the class, "Let's take some time to think this through." Before the concluding summaries of other lessons, the teacher might schedule silence to allow students to pull together their ideas.

Maintaining silence in a classroom is hard for us. We have been conditioned to speak. Even five seconds seems an eternity to some of us. Some of us may even feel that we are wasting time. Suggesting silence seems to be recommending that we go off task. Such is not the case. As Dillon notes, the need for silence is real, for time is required if students are to engage in deep thought, in indepth processing of information.[19]

Signals

Communication consists of both verbal and nonverbal moves. In dealing with students, we have options in the verbal realm other than questions or statements. Some of these signals are little more than what Dillon calls fillers such as "um-hm," or phatics such as "All right, Ok! Great!" These signals, usually done unconsciously, inform the student that you are listening.[20]

However, we may consciously plan signals into our lesson. We may wish to signal "we are attending" by a particular facial expression or keeping eye contact with the student. Perhaps, we may actually move closer to the student to signal that we are hearing what he or she is saying.

There may be times when we use gestures to indicate our response—a hand to the mouth, a dramatic covering of our ears or eyes. We may use gestures that say, "Go on," "Stop," or "Think of another point."

We may wish to use a video to record our behavior in the classroom to see how our signals are impeding or advancing our lesson. Having a sense of the dramatic will assist us in making our signals communicate what we desire. A glance properly placed may do more than a thousand words directed at a student.

CONCLUSION

We as teachers and our students as learners have available to us several techniques that can add power to our questioning strategies. Without doubt wait time and the nonquestioning technique of providing silence allow students opportunity for contemplating questions heard, questions raised, and information encountered. While both techniques are simple, requiring little skill, they are demanding for most of us as teachers have been conditioned to be the main verbal classroom performers. To wait for students to think, to furnish five or ten minutes for reflection we may find difficult. Even so, with practice, we can master these moves, and the results will be positive.

Classroom discourse requires cognizance of other questioning techniques. Probing, clarification, elaboration, redirection add richness to classroom conversation, informing students that they are going to be challenged—to think, to raise additional questions, to get beyond mere regurgitation of factual

Activity

YOUR NONQUESTIONING OPTIONS

We need not always raise questions to elicit students' questions or thinking. In this chapter, several nonquestioning options were mentioned. Consider the nonquestioning options you employ in your classroom. Have a colleague view a lesson and record the number of nonquestioning options employed. Have your colleague use a check sheet like the following:

Nonquestioning techniques

Technique	*Number of times used*	*Percentage of usage**
Declarative statements		
Reflective restatements		
State of mind		
Elaboration		
Deliberate silence		

General comments (also to be filled in by peer observer): _____

_____

_____

_____

_____

_____

_____

*Figured from the total number of all techniques used.

---

knowledge. Such techniques also testify to students our belief in their potential to do great things in their learning—to soar in their questioning and their thinking.

We must support students in their soaring, however. There are techniques to be activated that offer support to students, that communicate to students our acceptance of their feelings, that offer praise to students for their actions, that communicate to students that we value their ideas and realize their worth for further discourse and investigation.

Effective questions notwithstanding, we need not be limited to asking questions. Classroom discourse would be most difficult, if not impossible, if our only utterances were questions. Dillon provided us with nonquestioning options that can advance active student thinking and involved questioning. While the power of the declarative statement is evident, its value depends upon the particulars being communicated in the statement. The information presented in such statements should have worth to the students.

Other nonquestioning options are available to us. The reflective restatement enables us to generate a positive questioning and thinking classroom atmosphere. Such statements allow us to communicate to students exactly what we are hearing in attending to their comments.

Positive atmosphere is crucial if students are to feel comfortable in raising statements, in thinking, in generating questions, in conducting inquiries. An honest sharing of our reaction to a student's comments suggests to that student where we are coming from and also that such honesty in the students also will be appreciated. Sharing feelings demonstrates mutual respect.

Ideally, a classroom is a community of like-minded individuals engaged in learning; even a community of scholars, albeit scholars of differing levels of expertise. This sense of community, this accepting of students into the group of active questioners is relayed to students by the signals, both verbal and nonverbal, that we employ. Often our signals are little more than unconscious actions on our part. However, we can actually choreograph signals into our actions—a particular move that says, "I hear you, and I value your contribution." A move that says, "I have confidence in your ability to arrive at the answer." Great classrooms have a sense of theater about them, and good use of signals contributes to this good theater.

Much technical knowledge exists that when employed in classrooms maximizes the processing of information and that fosters learning in a thinking, questioning manner. This chapter has presented some techniques for the reader's consideration. The reader is invited to reflect further.

NOTES

1. Mary Budd Rowe, "Pausing Phenomena: Influence on the Quality of Instruction," *Journal of Psycholinguistic Research* 3; 3 (1974); 203–23.

2. Mary Budd Rowe, "Using Wait Time to Stimulate Inquiry," in William W. Wilen, ed., *Questions, Questioning Techniques, and Effective Teaching* (Washington, D.C.: National Education Association, 1987), pp. 95–106.

3. Mary Budd Rowe, "Using Wait Time to Stimulate Inquiry."

4. Ben B. Strasser, *Components in a Teaching Strategy* (San Anselmo, Calif.: Search Models Unlimited Publishers, 1967).

5. Benn M. Harris, *Supervisory Behavior in Education* (Englewood Cliffs, N.J.: Prentice-Hall, Inc., 1963).

6. Richard Kindsvatter, William Wi-

len, and Margaret Ishler, *Dynamics of Effective Teaching* (New York: Longman, 1988).

7. Ned A. Flanders, *Analyzing Teacher Behavior* (Reading, Mass.: Addison-Wesley, 1970).

8. J. T. Dillon, *Teaching and the Art of Questioning* (Bloomington, Ind.: Phi Delta Kappa, 1983).

9. J. T. Dillon, *Teaching and the Art of Questioning.*

10. J. T. Dillon, *Teaching and the Art of Questioning.*

11. David Ausubel, *The Psychology of Meaningful Verbal Learning* (New York: Grune & Stratton, 1963).

12. Robinson Schneider, et. al., *Papers from the Parasession on Non-declaratives* (Chicago: Chicago Linguistic Society, 1982).

13. J. T. Dillon, *Teaching and the Art of Questioning.*

14. J. T. Dillon, *Teaching and the Art of Questioning.*

15. J. T. Dillon, *Teaching and the Art of Questioning,* p. 31.

16. J. T. Dillon, *Teaching and the Art of Questioning.*

17. J. T. Dillon, *Teaching and the Art of Questioning,* p. 32.

18. J. T. Dillon, *Teaching and the Art of Questioning.*

19. J. T. Dillon, *Teaching and the Art of Questioning.*

20. J. T. Dillon, *Teaching and the Art of Questioning.*

9

Student

Questioning

Within the Classroom

"One of the simplest ways to permit student questions is to stop asking questions yourself."[1]

"The Good Thinker:
•Welcomes problematic situations and is tolerant of ambiguity.
•Is sufficiently self-critical. ...
•Is reflective and deliberative; searches extensively when appropriate.
•Believes in the value of rationality and that thinking can be effective."[2]

The information on questions and thinking is not just for you the teacher or you the administrator; it is also for students. For students to be intellectually independent, they require *knowledge that, knowledge how,* and *knowledge to. Knowledge that,* declarative knowledge, refers to those assumptions, alternatives, evidence, and arguments that contribute to one's knowledge base, enabling one to extend and revise his or her knowledge foundation. In contrast, *knowledge how,* procedural knowledge, refers to knowledge of process that expands one's understanding of information encountered. *Knowledge to* refers to being aware of one's commitment to act, to make one's knowledge manifest. *Knowledge to,* the realization and acceptance of the need to act, is perhaps the most crucial, for lacking it, students fail to initiate thinking and questioning.

A primary reason for our being teachers is to make students active learners, to enable them to learn how to learn, to be able to orchestrate their approaches to learning—to thinking and questioning. As Dillon notes, we can really involve students in their learning, their questioning, if we get out of the way, if we just stop asking most of the questions and allow students to assume this responsibility. In withdrawing from being the prime actors in the classroom, we facilitate students developing the characteristics of the good thinker.

This chapter presents ways to involve students in the total learning process, which entails a major planning stage, a major doing stage (the visible actions), and a major evaluation or assessment stage.

SETTING THE STAGE FOR STUDENTS' QUESTIONS, STUDENTS' THINKING[3]

"Give a student a question to answer and she will learn the passage she has just read. Teach her how to ask questions and she will learn how to learn for the rest of her life."[4]

We can teach students directly and indirectly how to ask questions, how to gain those competencies requisite for being autonomous learners for the rest of their lives. While teaching students to question and allowing them time to instruct themselves is challenging, our task is made a bit easier if we remember that students are natural questioners, commencing their educational experiences with high inquisitiveness. This natural inquisitiveness needs to be made more effective, however; students need to learn how to ask educative questions. They need to experience an environment that facilitates their raising of questions. Basic to creating and maintaining such an atmosphere is that both teacher and student express confidence in each other as people and as questioners.

Getting Students to be Key Performers[5]

An atmosphere conducive to effective student questioning is one in which persons respect the ideas and concerns of all. There is an openness to new views; students realize a freedom to raise questions at any level and a responsibility to allow classmates the same privilege. Everyone's question is legitimate. Questions are not to be viewed as admissions of failure or testimony to inattention. If students perceive teachers' questions as primarily asked to evaluate students and to manage the classroom, students will develop an adversion to questions and will fail to realize the power of questions. The productive atmosphere encourages the exchange of ideas and questioning in nonthreatening ways. Both teachers and students listen to each other—to each other's questions and statements. All class members exhibit a willingness to assist one another in active processing of information. Indeed, students and teachers alike possess an enthusiasm for learning, for thinking, for questioning, for helping each other to be involved actively in learning.

In a good atmosphere, all parties realize that questions and questioning are integral parts of the learning process. The teacher, in creating a good questioning atmosphere, informs and allows students to discover the nature of ignorance and the value of recognizing it. Accepting ignorance fosters a true spirit of inquiry; accepting ignorance allows students to appreciate the complexity of knowledge, its lure for the human intellect—the human spirit. Ignorance is a natural state of being uninformed, lacking knowledge. Recognizing and accepting being uninformed is prerequisite for engaging in inquiry, for raising questions. It allows one to set a baseline for dealing with awe and wonder; it defines an arena for open exploration.

Accepting ignorance as a necessary first step is done with the realization that it is not total ignorance. As noted earlier in this book, Miyake and Norman pointed this out in an article entitled "To Ask a Question, One Must Know Enough to Know What is Not Known."[6] Students come to realize the dimensions of their ignorance by drawing on their world knowledge structure that the question suggests. In raising their own questions, students identify those aspects of the information confronted that are not well understood by them or that require further attention.

In getting students to be key performers, the teacher must assist them in dealing with this apparent dilemma of having to be knowledgeable of their ignorance in order to question, to think. This initial awareness is crucial in setting the stage and will influence the entire direction of students' inquiries. Recognizing one's ignorance allows the generation of tentative hypotheses and questions for guiding one's investigation. This initial awareness influences one's perceptions of information, of reality. Such framing of initial ignorance will effect throughout inquiry an individual's judgments about the worth and validity of data encountered.[7]

Skillful teachers have myriad instructional approaches to assist students in dealing with this dilemma. Students can be informed that in dealing with entirely new areas of information, the questions of others can be utilized to direct attention to important information. Outsiders' questions furnish hints how the question should be processed. Students can be encouraged, indeed directed, to react to others' questions based on whether they know anything about the area questioned. Such consideration permits students to realize that they may already have some bits and pieces of information; they may certainly have various dispositions to react in particular ways to information or situations, and they definitely have interests likely to be addressed in dealing with a particular topic. Such consideration of outsiders' questions enables students to increase their information base about the material to be processed.

Another way for students to deal with this seeming dilemma is to realize that they can draw upon their incidental information, their shared cultural knowledge. Students do not live in a vacuum. In everyday living, they pick up vast amounts of information, albeit in bits and pieces much of the time. From their daily living students have accumulated much information about myriad issues and topics. In setting the stage, teachers inform students to reflect on their world, to take stock of information gained just from living. Teachers can make links between the new information of the lesson and some content or situations with which students are already familiar. For example, students might consider themselves totally ignorant of the various types of erosion, but all students have seen water running down the street on a rainy day. Many have seen hills by the side of the road with little gulleys. Drawing on such experiences, students come to realize that they can raise questions on this topic, even though they possess limited knowledge about the topic.[8]

Teachers can also take advantage of what some have called "incidental comprehension"—comprehension that results without much thought just from reacting to others' questions, either heard or read. Few among us fail to respond to what we hear or read. Even the reaction "I know nothing about that" is a statement indicating an initial assessment of the information in light of one's experience. Thus we have engaged in thinking at the evaluative level to assess that we do indeed lack information. Consummate teachers inform students that they have more information, more knowledge, about some topics than they at first realized.[9]

Essentially, a successful questioning environment furnishes students with tips regarding information to be investigated. Teachers make provocative statements designed to pique students' interests. Around the classroom, interest centers entice students to investigate further. Preliminary reading, using others' questions, can be assigned solely to generate questions rather than answers.

A positive questioning atmosphere reflects a certain leisure: there is no rush to complete assignments, to process questions rapidly. No academic race is to be run. Time is available for contemplation, and teachers and fellow students willingly cooperate, collaborate, and furnish encouragement for thinking and question asking.[10]

Students have opportunities to reflect on the focus topic, time to formulate questions meaningful to the search. Students have occasions to "get their own act of questioning" together. Students like to be independent learners. Van der Meij in his research has found that children seem to have developed an acceptance of an internalized norm of independence—"I like to-do-it-myself attitude."[11]

The good questioning environment allows students time to be playful with information, time to gather sufficient background data. A leisurely atmosphere is unpressured, affording students opportunities to generate questions.

There is time to synthesize the results of questions and to take a stand. A leisurely atmosphere informs students, "Savor your question formulation, relish your search, take satisfaction in the results of your investigation. Feel good about being the effective student, the effective questioner."

In a classroom atmosphere conducive to good questions and questioning, students realize a shared responsibility for their learning. While accepting an independence of functioning, students recognize that both fellow students and teachers possess competence to cooperate. Students will engage in cooperative learning only if they consider their fellow students competent, possessing those skills requisite for inquiry, for the search. Students only ask the teacher questions if they consider him or her to possess the necessary pedagogic skills and content background.

For students to share in the responsibility for their learning, they must feel good about themselves and realize that their fellow students like and respect them. Van der Meij has identified a concern of students called impression-making.[12] Impression-making refers to how an individual interprets others' perceptions of him or her for having raised a particular question or series of questions. Students can be anxious about the effect of their questions upon others. No one wants to pose a question and have other students laugh. No student wants to raise a question and lose points with the teacher or classmates. Skilled teachers receive student questions as legitimate requests for information or as valuable devices for processing information. Under the guidance of such teachers, students do not worry about being considered stupid, inattentive, or unmotivated.

In a classroom atmosphere designed for student involvement in questioning and thinking, students realize an independence of functioning and understand that they need not always wait for the teacher. They accept that it is often their responsibility, their privilege, even their enjoyment to map out their involvement.

A playful questioning atmosphere can arise when students play questioning games. Students can challenge their classmates to solve a problem a day. "Questions of interest to me" can be scheduled. Answers or statements can be written on the board with the teacher challenging students to discover the question. Teachers and students can place pictures around the classroom with the request, "What is my question?" Playful atmospheres address students' social concerns.

As already mentioned, students are concerned as to how their classmates and teacher view their competence. "I am not going to ask a question that will make people think I am stupid," is a thought common to students. Even adults are reluctant to reveal perceived deficits in knowledge and skill. "Nothing makes you feel worse than making a fool of yourself in front of others."[13] Shapiro expresses what frequently silences many of us. We all recognize our inadequacy, but we do not wish to announce it to the world. In a positive classroom environment, however, students realize that announcing not knowing something and a desire to inquire into it is not inadequacy but a recognition of the human condition and the prerequisite to learning.

In this informative age, it is impossible to be knowledgeable of and skilled in everything. Given the proper atmosphere, students realize that while they certainly will have deficiencies in their understandings they also have strengths; furthermore, their information gaps can be worked on both in and out of class. The lure of learning is made apparent upon recognizing that we do not know everything; that there still are things to investigate, books to read, questions to raise, people to talk to, places to go.

The effective classroom environment fosters productive student-student and student-teacher relationships. Students play both the helper and the one helped. Frequently, students will need help from teachers. In positive classrooms students do not feel threatened by the teacher's help. True, students will, upon obtaining help from others, recognize a certain degree of indebtedness; however, this indebtedness is offset by the realization that other students have similar feelings when they receive assistance. Realizing this is coming to comprehend human relationships more fully. We are all indebted to others; others are indebted to us. No person is truely independent; we all require interactions with others. Ideally, students in a productive learning environment become skilled in those personal human relation skills that make for meaningful relationships. Students gain a regard for the rights of others, esteem for the ideas and concerns of fellow students, and strength of conviction that they are capable not only of cooperative endeavor with others but also of self-study.

There are questions we can ask ourselves as teachers the answers to which will furnish us a picture of whether we have generated a positive questioning, learning environment; whether we have set the stage so as to involve students in their learning, their thinking, their questioning. The following list of questions was generated by this writer several years ago; the list is still appropriate:

- Did I provide an atmosphere that was nonthreatening and encouraged students to think about the questions they wished to ask?

- Did I schedule opportunities for students to discuss their questions with fellow classmates and with me?

- Did I encourage student discussion of the consequences of the questions they asked?

- Did I offer specific suggestions to students about how to plan, recognize, and implement particular question types into certain strategies for processing information?

- Did I provide students with opportunities to test their questions in role playing or simulation?

- Did I as teacher serve as an effective exemplar of the good questioner?

- Did I sit down with particular students or the class and discuss the dimensions of particular strategies and the place of the question in these strategies?
- Did I discuss with students the task of analyzing questions they encountered in written materials?
- Did I schedule opportunities for students to react cognitively and affectively to questions encountered or planned?
- Did I give guidance to students in judging their questions on cognitive and affective levels?
- Did I provide adequate time for questioning to take place?[14]

ENGAGING STUDENTS IN QUESTIONING, IN THINKING

Just as teachers need ways of planning their teaching, activating their teaching, and assessing their teaching, students require knowledge of and skill in ways of working with questions and questioning strategies so that optimal learning occurs. A useful paradigm students can employ consists of three stages: planning, implementing, and assessing.[15] The *planning stage* involves activities that assist students in preparing for some learning encounter or investigation. It is during this stage that students identify key questions they wish to consider and map out procedures to deal with those questions. The *implementation stage* involves the actual application of questions and procedures identified during planning. It is the doing phase of working with questions, the enactment of questions and questioning procedures. This stage allows students to employ in the manner intended that which they have planned. It permits them to monitor themselves as they process information. The final stage, *assessing,* has students engaged in critically thinking about the results of their investigation, evaluating the data gathered and the conclusions reached. It also directs students to evaluate the question and questioning strategies employed.

The Planning Stage

It is axiomatic that good planning leads to good instruction. Few teachers enter the classroom feeling that there is no need to plan, and to plan carefully. "You get out of it what you put into it" is a truism. Likewise, students need to realize that the quality of their questioning and thinking strategies will be influenced to a major degree by the quality of their planning. For students to employ what has been presented in the previous chapters, they need time to plan their questions and thinking strategies and time to apply what they have learned. Students must generate plans that will get them ready to carry out their own learning.

Activity

Such planning need not be rigid, it need not back them into a specific action that cannot be altered. Rather, plans that students generate are suggestive, giving them an idea as to what questions they might employ and what strategies they might utilize. Plans are not to be followed blindly, ignoring new data that might arise or new situations that might result. In the planning stage, students make estimates for action based on initial interests, concerns, questions, and perceptions of world knowledge. Students realize that as they actually carry out their plans, they may uncover new interests, concerns, and questions; they may indeed alter their perceptions of the world. Such new information should foster in students a willingness at least to entertain making adjustments in their plans.

While planning may appear specific, the actual teaching and learning encounter is diffuse, dynamic, with gaps in the logic of delivery. There are emotional factors that can and will arise; surprises that will result from the interactions of student-to-teacher and student-to-student.[16] James Macdonald compared education to a controlled accident.[17] We, and our students, have to realize that in our planning we know that certain things are likely to react with other things; ideas are likely to cause responses; questions are likely to stimulate answers; materials are likely to elicit responses from students. We and our students will fool ourselves, however, if we think that we can always be precise in anticipating the consequences of our plans. Students might do well to realize that they are participants in what may well be improvisational theater. There is a general story line, but the actual scenes and dialogue emanate from unique mixes that arise. Good planning makes allowances for good things to arise from the moment. Good planning anticipates good things and allows for alternatives and following up the consequences of alternatives. Students' plans for their questions should show a prizing of the uncertainty of the lesson. Students who gain skill in planning their questions constantly think about their world experiences, their experiences as humans, and how such experiences have educational significance.[18]

There are numerous specific ways and activities for involving students in planning questions and questioning strategies. From the several discussed here, one should not conclude that these are *the* activities for involving students in planning. The activities presented are suggestive of the *kinds* of activities possible.

Planning Activities

Planning Activity: Brainstorming Question Types—Brainstorming, familiar to us all, is a fairly open activity in which people are encouraged to raise many points without them being initially evaluated. In brainstorming, students in teams can generate lists of potential questions addressing a particular focus or several foci. This activity pays dividends for it not only allows students time to work cooperatively to generate questions but also informs students of their right and power to generate their own questions.

Students by brainstorming questions and strategies recognize that they have a major responsibility for their own learning and that this includes planning the means of their learning. Students in generating lists of potential questions and ways to sequence them begin to see upon discussion of such lists the value of questions in focusing their investigation and suggesting productive avenues for inquiry. Brainstorming questions allows students to discern the emphasis of the types of questions they prefer. In many cases, students realize their need to modify their questions to correct an overemphasis on certain question types. Most likely, students will discover in initial brainstorming activities their fondness for knowledge-level questions—specific fact questions, closed questions.

Students involved in brainstorming questions must have received some direct instruction in types of and nature of questions and the nature of questioning and thinking strategies. In debriefing a brainstorming session, students may require direct teaching on questions or may need to engage in class discussion on the nature of questions and questioning. Students' learnings regarding questions must not be considered complete, either by the teacher or by the students. Each time students plan their questions through brainstorming, they should gain new insights into this linguistic device.

The Activity—Brainstorming can be introduced in several ways. One approach indicates to the class the importance of questions to any type of investigation and notes that time must be scheduled for considering possible questions for processing information. Allow fifteen minutes, or even an entire class period if one is at the beginning of a unit, informing students that they are to generate as many questions as possible about the particular topic of the lesson. They should not try to determine whether the questions are good or bad, or their cognitive level; rather, they are just to record questions as they come into their minds.

After the allotted time, students share their questions with classmates to determine the appropriateness of the questions to the topic. Students can organize their questions by cognitive level, affective level, or some other classification. They can note the intent of their questions, the answers suggested, the directions implied for the investigation.

Students engaged in brainstorming can employ a form such as in Figure 9–1 on which to record the results of their actions.

EXAMPLE

Assume that a teacher selects for a lesson the topic, freedom in our lives. The teacher might introduce this topic using an advance organizer, presenting a general statement or statements about the topic that sets the stage. The teacher might say, "Over the next several days, we are going to investigate the topic of freedom in our lives. Most of us realize that we are a nation of free people and that freedom influences many of the things we do and the manner in which we do them. But, many of us take our freedoms for granted and do not really understand the nature of our freedoms or the consequences of freedom in our lives. In this lesson we will discover the variety of our freedoms and will uncover how a people's concept of freedom influences the quality of life, even on the everyday level."

The teacher continues, "I am going to schedule a fifteen minute period in which you can write any question that comes to mind that relates to freedom. Do not judge the value of the questions, just record them. After you have

---

Brainstorming Session # _____

Topic: *Possible Questions*

_____   _____

_____   _____

                                               _____

                                               _____

General Reactions to Questions Generated

_____

_____

Figure 9–1
Brainstorming Record Sheet

BRAINSTORMING SESSION #1

TOPIC: Freedom in our lives.

POSSIBLE QUESTIONS

What is freedom?

What is my emotional response to the term freedom?

What freedoms do I think I have?

Are my freedoms unique to me?

What examples of my freedoms can I list?

What have I read about freedom?

What are some examples of people who do not have freedom?

Do such people realize that they lack freedom?

Does freedom produce problems for the people who have it?

What is the opposite of freedom?

GENERAL REACTIONS TO QUESTIONS GENERATED

From these questions, I should get a definition of freedom. I also will get a feeling for some of the freedoms I have. I may be able to create a hypothesis regarding freedom in peoples' lives that I can later test.

engaged in this brainstorming, with your fellow students judge the worth and appropriateness of your questions in light of the lesson topic."

Given this introduction and directive, students working alone at first and then cooperatively might produce a brainstorming record like in Brainstorming Session #1.

The brainstorming activity gives students something to work with—their questions. Realizing that these are their questions is important, for it informs students that they are being given the responsibility for determining the nature of the lesson on freedom and even the directions that the lesson will take. Hopefully, students come to realize that it is their responsibility to assume some risk in shaping their investigation of freedom in people's lives. Certainly, the teacher is also mindful of the risk—the risk of allowing students to play a major role in determining the direction and nature of the lesson. Of course, the teacher can maintain a major control of a lesson even if he or she does employ this activity. In most situations, it is beneficial to have a shared responsibility for the lesson.

Planning Activity: Preparing Reaction Avenues—What will be the direction or route of our investigation of a topic? Customarily, the teacher has determined this. However, if we want to empower students to assume command of their learning, we must furnish them opportunities to learn procedures and skills for mapping out where they will go with their questions.

An activity to allow students to determine suggestive routes for investigation is the reaction avenue. A reaction avenue is basically the recording of various questions deemed worthy of investigation and graphing such questions on paper to make apparent various directions or routes of investigation these questions can take. It is also a recording on paper of the tentative or likely responses such questions might generate. Besides recording the major routes that questions can take, side trips of interest, even if not directly related to the major thrust of the planned investigation, can be charted. In creating reaction avenues, students may realize that there are or can be several major routes to the investigation planned, all leading to an anticipated conclusion.

Essentially, a reaction avenue is a type of relevance tree, denoting a definite hierarchy of events, in our case questions, sequenced logically. It reveals to students that in following their questions as noted on their reaction avenue, they will most probably attain their investigative goals.

If a reaction avenue created for a potential lesson denotes several possible avenues, each avenue or branch can be considered a decision tree. Decision trees are implied in the relevance tree methodology. The route or branch of a decision tree is a distinct pathway or avenue of investigation. While there certainly may be branches along one of these alternate routes, these branches relate primarily to the alternative, not the main route. Of course, these alternate routes all relate back to the major initial starting point of the investigation.

The basic rationale for creating reaction avenues, relevance trees if you will, is that students need to comprehend that the types of questions they generate will influence greatly the nature of their answers and the overall direction of their investigation. Appraisal of the consequences of their questions is important, for such awareness provides data useful in determining the worth of a potential direction of inquiry and the productivity of their questions. Furthermore, it makes students cognizant that there are indeed alternative routes of questions that will enable them to investigate the topic from varying directions resulting in differing insights into the topic being studied. Often we and our students get into a rut in our questioning, tending to always take the same route when confronted with our learning. We tend to ask the same questions, follow the same sequence of question asking, and engage in the same activities. Frequently, we teachers by undertaking total class direct teaching foster this sameness, this oneness of routes to investigation. All students come to realize that there seems to be only one way to approach a problem. Creating reaction avenues encourages students to determine their own routes to a lesson topic.

Reaction avenues serve as road maps. Students will not make meaningful maps, however, without some prior knowledge—mainly that there are numerous types of questions possible, each having the potential to elicit particular cognitive, affective, and perhaps even psychomotor responses. Ideally, before students commence creating their own reaction avenues, they will have received some formal lessons on the nature and purpose of questions, the types of questions possible, and information about instructional strategies. Knowledge of particular strategies will suggest to students possible ways to structure their reaction avenues.

The Activity—To introduce this planning activity one can inform students that not only is it necessary to comprehend how to formulate questions but it is also essential to determine the direction particular types of questions might take. Specifically, we need to know where we want to go. To encourage students in this, we might select a topic for consideration and request the class to think of a central question for investigation. After the question has been noted, we can have students indicate anticipated responses or answers to this central question. Students might then be asked to suggest possible questions of value in light of the expected responses. What answers can be anticipated from these possible questions? Responding, students map out the routes that particular questions could take in light of the topic, also suggesting probable replies. With students at the upper school levels, one might want to note that creating reaction avenues is essentially generating decision trees, and a complete reaction avenue containing several decision trees comprises a relevance tree.

To get students facile in creating such avenues, have them engage in some safe risk taking. Request that they plot an avenue that would seem to lead them down an uncertain route, a route that is very different from a route they normally would take.

Reaction avenues can be created by student teams of two or more students. One might want to do this to take advantage of the benefits of cooperative learning.

The teacher should encourage students, whether working alone or cooperatively, to raise questions as they create their reaction avenues. Students should query themselves as to whether the questions being plotted have the potential to enable attainment of the destination. Do all the questions and responses along one route in the reaction avenue sheet belong in that route? Are there junctures where one could proceed to another avenue or route? Are there two or more main routes that can be followed in dealing with the topic in question? Will the questions mapped provide data to answer the major concern or hypothesis of the lesson?

Suppose a teacher has planned an economics lesson as part of a unit on the economy of Washington state. In this lesson students are to identify the major types of economic activity in the state to generate a conclusion about such activity. Students have been directly taught the planning process of creating reaction avenues. In this lesson, they are to get an opportunity to apply their knowledge.

Assume that the students are working in teams of three. On p. 239 is an abbreviated version of one team's reaction avenue to the central question, "What are the major types of economic activity in Washington state?"

The example of the reaction avenue is not complete. Only the avenue or pathway for high-tech light industry is expanded for the example. The R stands for response. One might inquire how students can know tentative responses and even suggestive directions if they have not previously studied the topic. You may recall that students bring to most school situations a lot of incidental knowledge, world knowledge if you will, that can suggest possible responses and potential avenues of action. Certainly, most students have enough world knowledge to know that when they pose questions about major economic activities, they at least have sufficient incidental information to think of two or three major ways to group such activities. In this planning activity, students begin to realize that they already may know a great deal about the lesson topic and that the lesson actually is going to add depth to their understanding, not just fill an empty vessel.

Planning Activity: Mapping Investigations—The planning activity, creating reaction avenues, noted possible directions that the logic of the lesson might take one. Mapping investigations is similar. However, it differs in that it is guided by the actual steps of particular questioning or thinking strategies. For this reason, students can make the most of this planning activity if they have had some direct instruction in types of questioning strategies and thinking approaches. Students can be introduced to playing with this planning procedure early on before any formal instruction in questions and questioning strategies. Students come to school with an intuitive sense of questioning. They can employ this feel for questions in mapping out questions they would want to ask regarding topics of interest. When this occurs, there is not much if any difference between planning through mapping investigations and planning doing reaction avenues. Having said this, it still should be noted that mapping investigations is an attempt to note particular questions that would be raised at particular questioning or instructional strategy steps. It is possible that students might actually have a major map denoting the key steps of perhaps the VAIL strategy and then do a reaction avenue for the questions that would be raised at each step. The same could be done for any of the strategies noted in Chapters 6 and 7.

REACTION AVENUE FORM

Name: Co-op. team: James, Patricia, Ann

Lesson: Basic economic activities in Washington state.

Objectives: To generate questions that will allow one to arrive at some conclusion or conclusions regarding the types of economic activity in the state of Washington.

Date: _____

(Key Heuristic Question: "What are the major types of economic activity in Washington state?")

↓	↓	↓
(R) farming	*(R) light industry*	*(R) heavy industry*
↓	↓	↓
What types of farming?	*What types of light industry?*	*What types of heavy industry?*

(R) farming
↓
What types of farming?
↘   ↘
(R) truck   Livestock
* farming*

(R) light industry
↓
What types of light industry?
↓
(R) High-tech   Low-tech
↓
What are some types of high-tech light industry?
↓
(R) examples
↓
How do these examples actually contribute to the state's economy?
↓
Are any light industries on a growth pattern?
↓
Where are these industries located in the state?
↓
What percentage of the work force is involved in these industries?
↓
What percentage of salaries statewide is paid to these workers?

(R) heavy industry
↓
What types of heavy industry?

Figure 9–2

This planning activity affords several benefits. First, it forces students to make a strategy choice. "Why do I prefer this particular approach to the lesson topic? What is my rationale for selecting this strategy? Could I achieve the same results with another strategy?" In most classes, these are unusual questions for students to ask themselves. In raising such questions, students frequently realize that they really have never inquired of themselves if they have certain preferences for particular types of questions or not; if they have any rationale for employing definite questioning strategies.

Second, students, from engaging in this activity, begin to reflect on the consequences of their planned questions and line of questioning. They begin to realize that it is valuable to anticipate likely consequences of processing information along certain lines. Cognizance of potential consequences enables students to ascertain if they really wish to employ certain questions and questioning strategies before actually becoming involved in doing their learning. Perchance, a student might look at his strategy mapped out and decide that it will not take him where he wants to go. Realizing this, he or she decides to generate a different map, to employ another strategy. Students employing this planning approach become managers of their own learning, taking or beginning to take executive control over their learning.

The Activity—Essentially, the activity is little more than the teacher informing students that they are going to investigate a topic, either selected by the teacher, by the students or jointly, and that they are going to employ their knowledge of various questioning strategies in mapping out a particular strategy for this lesson. Students are informed that it is their choice as to which strategy to map out. An important point is that the various steps of the strategy selected need to be identified and reflected upon to uncover preferences, rationales, and awareness of functions.

EXAMPLE

Consider a language arts class studying forms of literary writing. Students armed with knowledge of the various types of strategies are given time to map out how they are going to consider genre of literary writing. In this class, some students might prepare a plan sheet similar to the one on p. 241.

The plan sheet on p. 241 can be used with any of the strategies suggested in this book or with any other strategies one might create. From engaging in mapping, students force themselves to reflect on key questions and to relate them to a particular strategy. Not all questions to be asked are noted on the plan sheet. Rather, the questions on this sheet are samples designed to trigger additional questions of a similar type.

Three planning activities have been presented to involve students in preparing to investigate, to question, to think. Numerous other planning activities

Plan Sheet

Strategy: Bloom's strategy

Topic: Forms of literary writing

STAGES OF STRATEGY	POSSIBLE TYPES OF QUESTIONS	MY QUESTIONS
Stage one	knowledge	What is the meaning of literary writing?
Stage two	comprehension	How does literary writing differ from other forms of writing?
Stage three	application	How can I organize the various forms of writing that I may experience in this class?
Stage four	analysis	What are some of the underlying assumptions behind the various forms of writing?
Stage five	synthesis	What conclusions can I generate about literary writing?
Stage six	evaluation	Would authorities agree with my conclusions about forms of literary writing?

Reactions to my questions:

_____

_____

_____

_____

can be generated. It is important for students to realize that by planning care-fully, there is a greater likelihood that ensuing learning activities will be qual-ity ones, allowing students to attain their objectives and goals most propitiously. Now students are ready for engagement—the actual carrying out of their plans, the active employment of particular questioning and thinking strategies.

The Doing or Involving Stage

The second major stage of involving students in questioning and thinking is the *doing* stage. Here the plans made in the previous stage are enacted. As with the activities for planning, there also are myriad doing activities possible.

Activity

> ## REFLECTING ON PLANNING TO INVOLVE STUDENTS IN PLANNING
>
> This section has presented three ways in which to involve students in planning their own questions, their own approaches to processing information. However, you as teacher need to plan ways in which you will involve students in such planning. You certainly can employ some of these activities for your own lessons.
>
> Select one or make a planning activity that will get students actively involved in their planning. Indicate why you are using this approach, the benefits you anticipate, and the feasibility of your approach.
>
> Get a colleague to review your plans. Discussing our plans with a colleague forces us to think a bit more carefully about our intentions.
>
> Record the results of such colleague discussion regarding your plans.

Doing or Involving Activities

Employing Various Questioning Strategies—Essentially, this activity engages students in enacting particular strategies planned. The activity is not just one activity but rather a basic grouping of activities in which learners apply particular questioning and instructional strategies to specific topics.

The Activity—This doing of a strategy does not have a specific format to which students must adhere. They are free to create their own formats. Important for students to understand is that this activity provides them with means of identifying the strategy being employed, the reason or reasons for its use, and some means of assessing their reactions to its employment.

One possible form is provided in Figure 9–3.

Using this monitoring sheet a student commencing an investigation would note the subject area, central topic, name of strategy selected, and reason for selection. The key question(s) to initiate the strategy would be drawn from a planning sheet done previously. The student would fill in the general perceptions regarding strategy use during the actual application of the strategy and at the end of its employment. The type of information is recorded during strategy utilization. Conclusions are noted after strategy use. Judgment regarding the strategy is done both during and after employing the strategy, involving the student in both formative and summative evaluation.

Students can create their own doing sheet on which to record their actions. So involved, students are mindful of the technical steps they are using as well as the rationale behind the strategy steps. Essentially, students are

Subject Area _____

Central Topic: _____

Strategy selected: _____

_____

Reason for strategy selection: _____

_____

Key question/s to initiate use of the strategy: _____

_____

_____

_____

General perceptions regarding strategy use: _____

_____

Type of information, conclusions derived with strategy: _____

_____

_____

_____

_____

My judgment regarding my use of the strategy: _____

_____

_____

_____

Figure 9–3
Strategy Use Monitoring Sheet

engaged in metacognitive analysis of their actions. Cognizant of their thinking and questioning, students gain a rich understanding of process and content being studied.

EXAMPLE

Currently, increasing attention is being directed to the development of civic responsibility among students. Assume that a teacher is going to engage his or her students in investigating the concept of civic responsibility. The teacher wishes students to employ the Taba strategy. Students are allowed to plan their questions following the Taba approach. After planning, students commence their study employing the strategy use monitoring sheet. The following is a possible example of one student's sheet.

Strategy Use Monitoring Sheet

Subject area: Civics

Central topic: Civic Responsibility, Its Implications for Me

Strategy selected: Taba Strategy

Reasons for strategy selected: My focus is to get a handle on the meaning of civic responsibility. This strategy will allow me to raise questions to foster a definition of civic responsibility. I can then apply that definition to my own and others' actions.

Key question/s: What is civic responsibility? Do I demonstrate such responsibility?

General Perceptions Regarding Strategy Use

I began the strategy by posing questions that asked me to list behaviors appropriate to the category of civic responsibility. What activities do I see? What activities belong together? I raised questions that directed me to analyze various writings on civic responsibility.

Type of information derived with this strategy

During my investigation, the strategy enabled me to categorize information related to civic responsibility. I used my questions to focus on the diversity of peoples' public and private actions. I discovered that the term civic is open to some interpretation. Also, a diversity of views exists as to what responsibility is.

My judgment regarding my use of the strategy

I think that I followed the spirit of the Taba strategy. I gained some insights into the concept civic responsibility. At the interpretation stage of the strategy I saw that people's interpretation of the concept influenced what they considered as behavior appropriate to civic responsibility.

I also gained more comfort in using this strategy with this content.

―――――――

The monitoring sheet can give students a procedural profile of their learning approaches. Students can see, over a period of a school year, how their use of strategies changes and their understanding of questioning and thinking matures.

If students work cooperatively the profile can depict their team efforts.

In keeping a record of their strategy use, students can gain a greater understanding of strategies employed and can also realize which strategies are productive in particular situations. Furthermore, students can appreciate that questions are integral parts of all strategies greatly influencing the quality and type of information obtained.

Analyzing Questions in Materials—Effective teachers want students to have an extensive understanding of and awareness of their questions and others' questions, whether written or oral. Analyzing questions in materials is directed toward fostering in students such critical mindedness towards questions encountered in written materials. Learners often assume that questions incorporated in written materials, essentially textbooks, have high cognitive levels and will always lead to worthwhile answers. They are frequently surprised, upon analysis, to discover that many textbooks and trade books employ few questions and those that are present often stress just knowledge and comprehension. Of course, students should not jump to conclusions that a heavy emphasis of such questions is necessarily bad. Most current textbooks are designed with some attention to questions and seem to have questions within the prose at lower cognitive levels, questions at the end of chapters at higher levels, and questions at the end of units at even higher levels. Still, students need to study textbook questions. From such analysis, students can discern the quality of the questions and determine if modification in the questions is required to address more closely the goals of a particular lesson.

In analyzing questions in materials, students can compare questions in materials with their own questions. Textbook writers, when putting questions into material, assume that not only are students able to process such questions but such questions have value and address students' interests and needs. When comparing questions in textbooks and other materials, students can see where there is a need for modification of the questions in light of their interests and needs. Students will sometimes scrap their questions in favor of the textbooks'. However, students should view questions in materials not only as demands for particular answers but as prompts for generating additional questions.

The Activity—While the activity is simple to do, it does require students to possess some understanding of questions and questioning strategies. The sophistication of the analysis of the questions encountered depends upon the students' level of understanding. The teacher should provide students with various types of written materials to analyze. Certainly, textbooks can be the major type, but other written material such as reports or newspaper articles contain questions.

Students record on a form the types of questions encountered and indicate their judgments of worth. Students should gain practice in employing several question classification schemes to refine their understanding of the various ways to identify and group questions.

Students can create their own form for recording the questions encountered, or they can use one furnished by the teacher. The form might resemble the one presented in Figure 9–4.

EXAMPLE

A class is studying communism and has just been presented with an article written by Barbara Ward. The teacher informs the students that before they actually read the article, they are to scan the article to identify the questions in it. They are then to list these questions on their "questions in materials form" and classify them as to type. In this instance, both Bloom's cognitive domain and Krathwohl's affective domain are to be used.

Only a portion of the article is presented for this example.

> What are these presuppositions? Perhaps before I outline them, I should allow for one possibility. Are we conceivably living in the final decades of pure communist orthodoxy? The appearance of Titoism on the world stage and the current discussions of "different roads to Socialism" may presage the beginnings of a whole spectrum of communist faiths, allied yet different, as the sects of Christianity. We can still talk of communist orthodoxy today. But in twenty years time, shall we be able to say so emphatically what communism is?[19]

Source analyzed: _____

Pages analyzed: _____

Subject of source: _____

Questions Listed	**Pages**	**Type of Questions**
1. _____	_____	_____
2. _____	_____	_____
3. _____	_____	_____

General reactions to questions present in this material: _____
_____
_____

Figure 9–4
Questions in Materials

Questions in Materials

Source Analyzed: *Five Ideas that Changed the World,* Barbara Ward
Subject of source: Social studies, communism
Pages analyzed: 22–39

Questions listed	*Pages*	*Types of Questions*
1. What are these presuppositions?	25	Comprehension, (cog.) Responding (affect.)
2. Are we conceivably living in the final decades of pure communist orthodoxy?	25	Comprehension Responding
3. But in twenty years time, shall we be able to say emphatically what communism is?	25	Analysis

In this sample list, a student has noted the questions and indicated their levels. There are two comprehension questions also coded by affective level. The final question is analysis.

In completing this form, students determine the types of questions the material requests be considered. However, students decide a match of these questions with their questions. Engaging in this activity students develop a critical eye for questions in materials. It "informs" them that questions are of equal if not greater value than statements. Statements may only require acceptance or rejection; questions, at least at the upper levels, require reflection, a thinking about material confronted.

A variation of this activity is the analysis of questions employed by speakers. Students can start by analyzing the questions of the teacher and classifying them. Upon gaining skill, they can analyze the questions posed by other speakers, either those invited to the class as resource persons or speakers in the local or national community.

The Assessing Stage

The final stage of actively working with questions is the assessing of questions and questioning strategies, either one's own or those of others. Assessing activities emphasize to students that being active requires not only taking some responsibility for planning and carrying out of plans but also making judgments as to whether the actions carried out, the questions asked, the strategies utilized, did in fact enable one to attain one's goals.

Activity

DOING YOUR OWN PLANS

Activity 9–2 had you creating your own plan for involving students in their plans. In this activity, carry out what you had planned, using some means of monitoring your approach. You can use one of the doing activities that have been presented for the students or create your own.

It is important to try your plans focusing on getting students planning their questions. You can share with students that you are doing a bit of risk taking yourself in taking a role of getting them more active in their learning.

As with the previous two stages, students need to understand the nature and reason for assessment. They need to realize that assessment involves values as to what is important and as to preferences of ways to approach the processing of information. While assessment is suggested as the third and final stage of the overall processing of information, it is essentially a fluid activity in that one would engage in it in the previous two stages, performing a type of formative evaluation. Notwithstanding this, the assessing activities presented in this section are basically employed after a lesson has been processed, questions having been raised and strategies having been utilized.

Assessing Activities

Judging One's Questioning Strategies—It has been argued that students need to be knowledgeable about the nature of questions and various questioning strategies in order to gain information about realms of knowledge and about themselves. In order to gain skill and competence in the use of process, however, learners require means of assessing their questions and their questioning strategies. This activity furnishes such a means for self-assessment and also instructs students as to the essence of evaluation in relation to process learning.

The Activity—For students to make their own evaluations, they require either audio or videotapes of themselves employing questions in a particular strategy or a critique of their questions as recorded in their notes. Again, the quality of the activity depends upon the level of understanding students have of questions and questioning. As a variation of this activity, classmates can assist in judging the questions of their fellow students.

Students can create their own assessment forms or use one furnished by the teacher. A sample is presented in Figure 9–5.

Questioning Strategy Utilized: _____

Questions used in strategy:	Judgment of Questions	Reason for judgment
_____	_____	_____
_____	_____	_____
_____	_____	_____
_____	_____	_____
_____	_____	_____
_____	_____	_____

Rating of strategy as to its appropriateness for the particular topic investigated: _____
_____

Elements of the strategy to be maintained: _____
_____

Elements of the strategy requiring improvement: _____
_____

Figure 9–5
Judging Questioning Strategies

EXAMPLE

Consider learners in a fourth grade class studying the concept of neighborhood. The teacher has directly taught the students the questioning circle strategy of Christenbury and Kelly in which there are three major types of questions that can be asked: matter, personal reality, and external reality. Furthermore, students realize that other combinations of questions can be generated by melding these three main question types.

In this class, students have had the opportunity to plan their questions and to work in teams of two. Questions have been recorded on the plans and students have noted on paper when and if they used the questions suggested. At this final stage, they assess whether their questions were of value with regard to this lesson focus.

Employing the form just presented, a student team might generate a completed form as follows:

Judging Questioning Strategies

Strategy Used: Questioning Circle strategy

Questions Used in Strategy	Judgment	Reason for judgment
1. How does the author define neighborhood? (matter)	Appropriate question	It allows me to get a definition on the matter in focus.
2. Based on my understanding of my neighborhood, is my definition of neighborhood in agreement with the author's? (personal reality)	Effective question	Allowed me to consider my view of neighborhood.
3. How many neighborhoods are there in my community? (personal reality)	Probably not appropriate	Did not really furnish data that enabled me to develop a deep understanding of neighborhood.
4. In other countries, how are persons organized by where they live?	Good question	Allowed me to consider other regions of the world. Got a world view of this concept.

Rating of Strategy: I think the strategy was appropriate. It helped me to ask and organize my questions so that I arrived at a formation of the concept neighborhood.

Elements to be maintained: I would retain all elements of the strategy.

Elements of strategy requiring improvement: No major improvements required, but I can be a bit more careful at the outset in thinking of questions to ask. I can try to reduce the number of questions that are really not on target, such as "How many neighborhoods are there?" This question really did not advance my inquiry.

The actual form for the assessment can vary, depending upon the needs, skills, and interests of the student who creates it. Important is not format but that students be afforded opportunities for assessing their questions and questioning strategies. For students to function independently, they require opportunities within the classroom to take charge, to judge the quality and effectiveness of their work, to be charged with suggesting how they might further improve their thinking, their processing of information. One educational goal is to make independent learners; this activity contributes to that goal.

Judging One's Own Questions—The previous assessing activity focused on the evaluation of one's use of various questioning strategies. There are times when one just wishes to critique one's questions. The assessing activity of judging your own questions serves this purpose. Students address the major questions: just what types of questions do I use most often: Why do I ask the questions I do? Will the questions I raise provide me with meaningful results?

This activity enables learners to take stock of their questions to develop critical mindedness.

The Activity—The activity is simple. Students can participate in it in response to the teacher requesting that they take time to contemplate their questions to determine if questions employed are really effective or ineffective in relation to the topic. Did their questions assist them in proceeding in meaningful directions; did their questions just center on facts; did they "demand" processing information at higher cognitive levels?

In engaging in question assessment, students can use a form similar to the one illustrated in Figure 9–6.

EXAMPLE

Consider a language arts class at the secondary level in which students are studying the use of metaphor. Students have read about metaphors and have created their own and discussed their purposes. Students have gone through the planning stages and have used several strategies in reflecting on this linguistic form.

At this juncture, the teacher informs the class that they are going to take some time to reflect on those questions they used in studying this topic. Students are given a form such as the one presented and instructed to work either alone or with a class colleague in judging their questions.

Such critiquing by a student might produce a format sheet filled in as follows.

Assessment Sheet, My Questions

Topic: Metaphors

My Questions:

1. What are the uses of metaphors?
2. What are my uses of metaphors?
3. Indicate the assumptions behind the use of metaphors.
4. How have my favorite metaphors influenced my entire manner of speech?

Topic of Lesson: _____

Questions raised in this lesson:

1. _____

2. _____

3. _____

4. _____

5. _____

_____

_____

Reactions	Level	Importance	Effectiveness in getting desired information
Question 1	_____	_____	_____
Question 2	_____	_____	_____
Question 3	_____	_____	_____
Question 4	_____	_____	_____
Question 5	_____	_____	_____

Overall reactions to my questions: _____

_____

_____

Figure 9–6
Assessment Sheet Format

5. How might metaphors be dangerous to my thinking?

Reactions	Level	Importance	Effectiveness
Question 1	Knowledge, definitional	Yes	It allowed me to see the uses of this language form.
Question 2	Valuing, feature specification	Yes	It allowed me to personalize my study of metaphor. I also got some idea as to whether I really valued this linguistic form.

| Question 3 | Analysis, causal antecedent | Yes | This question caused me to get behind the use of this form. I also began to think of the bases of some of the metaphors I used. |
| Question 4 | Instrument, analysis | Yes | This question added to my awareness of my entire speech patterns, also got a glance at how I view the world. |

Overall Reactions to my questions:

I am very pleased with my questions. While the first one just focused on facts, the others really got me thinking, affording me some appreciation of the complexity and richness of language and an understanding of how I use language.

This example shows a student with a very good grasp of questions. From looking at the comments under level, it is evident that she knows several question classification schemes: Bloom's, Lehnert's, and Krathwohl's. This would not be unusual for a student at the secondary level who had received direct instruction in questioning.

The example only gives four questions, but a lesson certainly can have more. Most lessons, however, are not going to have forty questions in forty minutes. If they do, there is scant time for reflection, and the questions would essentially be at the knowledge of specifics level. Effective questions at the upper cognitive levels take time to process, so that in a regular class period of approximately fifty-five minutes, students might actually only raise four or five major questions.

The activity has no format that must be followed in a specific manner. Students and teacher are free to design their own sheets. What is important about this activity is not its form but the fact that it informs students that it is important to reflect on one's questions and assess them as to their effectiveness in relation to one's goals. Assessing one's questions is part of the total process of learning; it completes the process and furnishes data that will allow one to modify one's learning approaches.

Several variations of this activity of judging one's own questions exist. One can engage in a question self-analysis in which students tape their questioning responses in class. At designated periods, they listen to these tapes, noting and classifying questions raised and responded to. Students can tape five-minute segments of their questioning behavior over a period of a week to get an indication of the types of questions being asked and those actually being responded to in class.

Another variation has students recording the dominant type of question raised at particular times. A dominant use of a question type would mean that it comprised fifty percent of the total number of questions asked. The time periods can be the dates the class meets. The information is recorded on a chart so that the student can draw a line denoting a profile. A form such as in Figure 9–7 can be employed.

The student puts a point beside the dominant question level for each date checked. The resulting graph line informs students where their questions are and whether the questions are getting more sophisticated as time progresses or remaining rather flat regarding cognitive level.

The sample sheet in Figure 9–7 has used Bloom's categories for the question types, but any classification scheme can be applied.

The students can employ this profile check as long as they find it useful. At first, students might be surprised to discover that they do not ask questions at the level they assumed they did, and then they may be surprised from analyzing their profiles that their questions at first do seem to be consistently at the lower cognitive levels.

Students will improve their questioning behavior if time is taken to discuss the results of this profile. It is essential that students not just do these assessment activities but engage in analyzing, in thinking about these assessment results in order to gain awareness of and additional skill in questioning, in thinking.

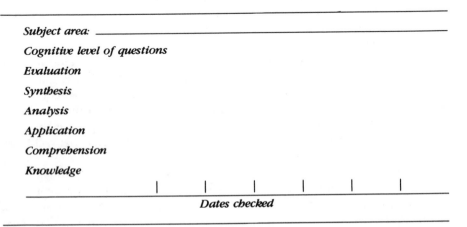

Figure 9–7
Profile Question Check

Activity

TURNING THE CRITICAL EYE ON YOURSELF

Well, you planned, you did what you planned, now how did you do in doing your plans? The section just completed discussed the importance of assessing one's actions. What is good for our students is good for us.

Turning the critical eye on yourself is just that—assessing how well you delivered what you intended.

In doing this activity for the first time, you can just reflect back on how you think the lesson went. To get more precision, prior to actually carrying out your plans, arrange to have the lesson either audio or video-taped. That way, after the lesson, you can watch yourself and play the role of supervisor. It is sometimes surprising that upon looking at ourselves as an outsider, we gain some insight that could be easily missed from viewing ourselves and our behaviors from the inside.

Note what you need to maintain or change. Remember that in attempting new strategies, you will be a bit clumsy at first, but you will get better with practice.

CONCLUSION

It is the student who is to be the prime actor in the classroom. This point is repeatedly stressed in this chapter that has presented involving students in planning, doing, and assessing their questioning. This does not diminish the need for students learning content, declarative knowledge but rather emphasizes that along with declarative knowledge they also must master procedural knowledge.

Both teachers and students have a wealth of procedural information possible for utilization. Part of the challenge for students is not only building their base of procedural knowledge but gaining skill in deciding when to employ such knowledge, when to formulate particular questions, and when to place such questions in certain strategies.

Gaining such competence takes time. At first, students will not be very good at it, but they need time to mess around with their questioning. When afforded such time in an environment in which all members say, "I value you and your questions," students will develop consummate skill in questioning and in thinking.

The activities suggested in this chapter can empower students to be autonomous learners—to take executive control of their learning. When given opportunities to learn ways of managing the totality of their learning, students readily take to the task. Most students relish being given opportunities to decide the avenues of their investigation. As mentioned in this chapter, students come to school with a natural ability to question and also a desire to do it themselves. We can facilitate productive learning environments and activities to go in them if we remember the quote that introduced this chapter: "One of the simplest ways to permit student questions is to stop asking questions yourself."[20]

NOTES

1. J. T. Dillon, *Teaching and the Art of Questioning* (Bloomington, Ind.: Phi Delta Kappa, 1983), p. 37.

2. Allan A. Glatthorn and Jonathan Baron, "The Good Thinker," in Arthur L. Costa, ed., *Developing Minds, A Resource Book for Teaching Thinking* (Alexandria, Va.: Association for Supervision and Curriculum Development, 1985), pp. 49–53.

3. Portions of this section were adapted from Francis P. Hunkins, "Students as Key Questioners," in William W. Wilen, ed., *Questions, Questioning Techniques, and Effective Teaching* (Washington, D.C.: National Education Association, 1987), pp. 153–72.

4. James R. Gavelek and Taffy E. Raphael, "Metacognition, Instruction, and the Role of Questioning Activities," in D. L. Forest-Pressley, G. E. MacKinnon, and T. Gary Waller, eds., *Metacognition, Cognition, and Human Performance* (Orlando, Fla.: Academic Press, 1985), pp. 103–36.

5. Portions of this section were adapted from Francis P. Hunkins, "Students as Key Questioners."

6. N. Miyake and D. A. Norman, "To Ask a Question, One Must Know Enough to Know What is Not Known," *Journal of Verbal Learning and Verbal Behavior* 18 (1979): 351–64.

7. M. Snyder, "Seek and Ye Shall Find: Testing Hypotheses about Other People," in E. T. Higgins, C. P. Herman, and M. P. Zanna, eds., *The Ontario Symposium on Personality and Social Psychology* (Hillsdale, N.J.: Erlbaum, 1981).

8. N. Miyake and D. A. Norman, "To Ask a Question, One Must Know Enough to Know What is Not Known."

9. James R. Gavelek and Taffy E. Raphael, "Metacognition, Instruction, and the Role of Questioning Activities."

10. H. van der Meij, *Questioning* (The Hague, the Netherlands: Foundation for Educational Research in the Netherlands, 1986).

11. H. van der Meij, *Questioning,* p. 44.

12. H. van der Meij, *Questioning.*

13. E. G. Shapiro, "Embarrassment and Help-Seeking," in B. M. DePaulo, A. Nadler and J. Fisher, eds., *New Directions in Helping, Vol: 2 Help-Seeking* (New York: Academic Press, 1983), pp. 143–63, cited in H. van der Meij, *Questioning.*

14. Francis P. Hunkins, *Involving Students in Questioning* (Boston: Allyn and Bacon, 1976).

15. Francis P. Hunkins, *Involving Students in Questioning.*

16. Zvi Lamm, *Conflicting Theories of Instruction* (Berkeley, Calif.: McCutchan, 1976).

17. James Mcdonald, in conversation with Macdonald many years ago.

18. Zvi Lamm, *Conflicting Theories of Instruction.*

19. Barbara Ward, *Five Ideas that Changed the World* (W. W. Norton, 1959).

20. J. T. Dillon, *Teaching and the Art of Questioning,* p. 37.

10

The Questioning

Attitude

"As we question, so do we act."[1]

Without awareness of questions there is little likelihood of commitment to them; without commitment, there is little possibility of learning questioning ways of action; without a learning of the ways of action, there is little chance for meaningful action; without meaningful action, there is less than optimal living. Bringing students to an awareness of questions is requisite to the learning process; however, it is only the first step. Students must be encouraged and facilitated to get beyond recognizing that there are various types of thinking and particular types of questions and questioning strategies.

This book has furnished information that when used by both teacher and student will allow for learning ways of action—ways of questioning and thinking that will advance one's knowledge base and enable that knowledge to be employed so as to live life in optimal ways. Along with learning these ways of questioning and thinking is the development of an overall questioning attitude: a disposition to pose questions and to reflect. This questioning attitude is central to the literate person, pivotal to what the Club of Rome, an international think tank, has called innovative learning, in which individuals besides receiving information participate in planning the nature and direction of their learning, in generating questions and thinking about these questions.

This group described innovative learning as

> problem formulation and clustering. Its main attributes are integration, synthesis, and the broadening of horizons. It operates in open ... situations or open systems. Its meaning derives from dissonance among contents.

257

It leads to critical questioning of conventional assumptions behind traditional thoughts and actions, focusing on necessary changes. Its values are not constant, but rather shifting. Innovative learning advances our thinking by reconstructing wholes, not by fragmenting reality.[2]

QUESTIONING WITHIN INNOVATIVE LEARNING

Notice that the subtitle for this section is questioning within innovative learning, not within innovative teaching. Certainly, innovative teaching is essential, but the thrust of this book is to furnish teachers with those understandings and skills of questioning and thinking so that such understandings essentially become the domain of students.

Questioning and thinking within the context of innovative learning has the student as both scientist and artist. The various strategies presented in this book can allow students to be neophyte scholars, but if students reflect on the nature of questions and thinking they will be more than technicians—they will be artists in touch with their curiosities.[3]

Louis Rubin talks of the artistry in teaching, but his comments can easily be related to artistry in "studenting."[4] He posits that all artists possess the ability to conceive and execute tasks with consummate tact, judgment, and imagination. Such persons demonstrate great skill, originality, flair, dexterity, ingenuity, and virtuosity to such a degree that others notice, admire, and value the resulting actions or products. Ideally, we want students to be artists, to reflect and to question with such applaudable skill, originality, and flair that they will be known for their creativity and zeal in learning. Artistry connotes human accomplishment unusual in both its proficiency and cleverness.[5]

Many might argue that while artistry in learning as well as teaching is certainly laudable, artists are born, not educated. Few students can become artists of the question, great masters of thinking. But are artists of the world only those born with hereditary talents?

Certainly, in earlier times in this century, the answer might well have been "Yes." Today, however, many of us are changing our views. We are not denying the impact of heredity; however, we are coming to agree with Howard Gardner's notion that what we have considered prodigy and attributed to the luck of heredity is more often than not a talent "nurtured through a shrewd educational invention."[6] Teachers are essentially in the business of nurturing talents and motivating students to develop their many gifts—to develop their intelligence.

Today there is much talk of developing intelligence. In the last century such talk might well have been considered nonsense by serious scholars of learning. We are now coming to know more about our brains, our minds, our thinking processes, and our questions. With such knowledge, we are realizing that we have not maximized the marvelous capabilities of our brains; we have not enabled students truly to tap their unused brain potential. Leslie Hart talks of making the school environment compatible with the way the brain functions. He notes that creating a brain-compatible ambiance in the classroom calls for deliberately identifying and eliminating sources that threaten students—those actions that inform students that to succeed they must sit still, obey, and uncritically accept.[7] Many of Hart's points were discussed in the previous chapter on setting up atmospheres conducive to good questioning. Questioning within innovative learning occurs in an atmosphere of joy and adventure, with sufficient time allowed for maximizing such feelings.

We can make our students smarter, better questioners and better thinkers. Gardner refers to the national effort in Venezuela in which the entire country is working to raise the intelligence of its citizens. He refers to Luis Alberto Machado, a Venezuelan politician who is in the unusual role of first minister in the world for the Development of Human Intelligence. Machado has noted that

> Einstein learned intelligence in the same way that a person learns to play the piano "by ear"; government should be, then, engaged in the teaching of intelligence. The development of man's intelligence allows him to rationally direct the biological evolution of his own species and to eradicate chance and need from the entire process of that evolution.[8]

Few now discount such statements as foolishness uttered by the unknowing. Today we can participate in our own evolution. We can create smart environments that stimulate and form our intelligences. We experience a time in which students can engage in innovative learning of ways of questioning, of thinking.

To accomplish such learning, certain skills are required. Knowles has furnished a list that should prove helpful to students in increasing their skills of questioning and thinking.

1. The ability to develop and to be in touch with curiosities.
2. The ability to *formulate questions,* based on one's curiosities, that are answerable through inquiry (in contrast to questions that are answerable by authority or faith).
3. The ability to identify the data required to answer the various kinds of questions.
4. The ability to locate the most relevant and reliable sources of the required data (including experts, teachers, colleagues, one's own experience, printed material . . . and the community).
5. The ability to select and use the most efficient means for collecting the required data from the appropriate sources.

6. The ability to organize, analyze, and evaluate the data so as to get valid answers to questions.

7. The ability to generalize, apply, and communicate the answers to the questions raised.[9]

In all of these skills, the question is central.

Approaching Artistry in "Studenting"

The artist student has learned to maximize the interplay between "good" questions and effective thinking processes, has developed the questioning attitude. This interplay is learned; few of us are born with it. Buying into many of the strategies of questioning should furnish students with those understandings and skills requisite for artistry in learning.

Often, upon hearing of a good idea or cluster of behaviors that will reward us with quality teaching or learning, we tend to reduce it or them to a magic formula. To do so is dangerous, for human action is complex. And added to the mystery is that it can be interpreted differently depending upon which learning theory we employ to interpret human action and which philosophical orientation or orientations we engage.

Rubin has given us a list of behaviors that characterize great teachers.[10] With little modification, the list can be applied to great students. Great students are those who:

1. Focus on the subtleties of learning, the place of motivation and the formulation of wonder, the pacing, and the control that initiate and maintain basic learning approaches. Great students realize that just knowing content and technique will not result in innovative learning. Rather, it is the way in which one thinks about content and the manner in which technique is employed that fosters such learning. Artist students understand that they must develop ways of sustaining their incentives, of keeping constant a degree of awe and wonder for the mysteries of the search. They appreciate that they must manage schemes to attend consistently to their learning and grasp when to continue to raise questions and when to relax a bit anticipating fatigue.

2. Draw upon myriad means of raising questions and processing information, employing diverse approaches to thinking. There is a major element of surprise in most if not all learning situations. Students need to recognize that in planning their approaches to learning, they need to accept that there will be surprises that will require attention. Artist students anticipate alternatives, taking pleasure in engaging in divergent thinking when contemplating possible avenues of investigation.

Great students constantly work both alone and cooperatively with their classmates in devising contests, exercises, and learning games, and great artist teachers allow such actions. Constantly considering alternatives makes for more exciting, more innovative learning.

3. Seize opportunities to clarify ideas and reinforce concepts. Artist students understand that there is a degree of spontaneity in learning and that such "sparks" bring not only enjoyment to the activity but creativity to questioning, to thinking. All teachers have heard of taking advantage of the teachable moment. Students as well need to grasp that they also need to take advantage of the learning moment—the moment for raising dynamic questions, for thinking.

These are times when students can jump into dealing with conceptual diversity, indeed creating conceptual diversity. Here students with spontaneity enthusiastically greet the challenge of dealing with things radically new. Students who seize opportunities are sensitive to situations, aware of factors that can interact. This is central to metacognition.[11]

4. Employ intuition and hunch in modifying actions. Bruner talked of getting students to engage in "intuitive leaping."[12] De Bono speaks of lateral thinking.[13] Certainly, the artist student realizes that one does not always need to be coolly rational. Intuition has its place; some of the best questions result from following a feeling, a hunch, as to what avenue of inquiry to take, what behavior to initiate.

Students reflecting on their own learning are quick to realize that engaging in learning is replete with surprises. Things do not always proceed as planned. Surprises do occur, and when they do, one often cannot take extended time for reflecting what to do. One must act with some alacrity. Innovative learners skilled in questioning appreciate that there will be times when spontaneous action is more productive than deliberative pondering.

5. Take advantage of temporary digressions on related topics to enrich learning, foster interest, and heighten pace. This characteristic of artist student is related closely to that of seizing opportunities to clarify ideas and concepts and employing hunches and intuition. There are times to follow plans and times to put aside such plans. The artist student, as well as artist teacher knows when to do both. There are times when the answer to a question appears as a system break in one's plans. Take advantage of it. The reaction avenues planned should allow for digressing down side roads. Such detours will reward us with village squares, road side stands, picnic tables by bubbling streams, and interesting people. As Rubin states, "adroit additions add blossoms to the bare limbs of a lesson."[14]

6. Determine efficient and expedient ways of getting things done. This appears to oppose the previous two characteristics. However, there is a time for divergence, for detours; likewise, there is a time or are times to proceed efficiently to our goals. While the artist student knows when to dream, he or she knows when to attend directly to the task. The artist student comprehends that there are certain questioning strategies that allow for a direct focusing of the topic under investigation and that there are times to activate them.

Artist students accept that it is their responsibility to justify in a broad sense the processes of knowledge acquisition and conceptual change. Students understand that questioning strategies are justified at various levels of application. One level deals with the adequacy of questions for themselves as students—how do my questions relate to my learning styles, my views of the world, my personality?

Another dimension of adequacy ties it to the social and institutional modes of concept use. This is efficiency in light of established forms of processing information as determined by the various disciplined fields of study.

A third dimension of adequacy relates to its contribution to one's overall procedural knowledge. Does one get from employing particular strategies a greater understanding of process as well as product?[15]

7. Believe in oneself. Master students believe in themselves; they have confidence in and respect their convictions. Students recognize that it is healthy to individualize their approach to learning, guided by their beliefs. Ideally, students who gain executive control of their learning nurture belief in themselves. Controlling their own learning and managing their own questioning attitude supports the growth of self belief. "I can do it; I have done it; I can do it again." Armed with such an attitude, students strain to take risks. While recognizing uncertainty as to outcome, artist students possess confidence that they can manage the uncertainty; they can move with the flow, reacting to the nuances of the evolving situations.

Learning is personal. Good students and good teachers prize and nurture it. These are my thoughts; my questions; these are my attitudes, my dispositions to act.

8. Take joy in the learning process. Joy is crucial to learning. The artist student takes joy in his or her questions, thinking, processing of information, and contemplating particular content. Students with some degree of control over the content they will study and the ways of investigation assure themselves of satisfaction. They are drawing from their encounters contentment for jobs well done; they are receiving from their questioning the thrill of the search, the excitement of the

uncertainty, the pleasure at solving puzzles, the delight of inventing new ways of looking at the world and at the content organized about the world.

Ideally, artist teachers allow artist students opportunities for not only fostering such joy but for sharing such joy with others. Many a student has become interested in a particular content listening to an excited classmate run on about what great fun has been had in learning about this topic.

Students who take joy in their educational actions and believe in themselves take a reasonable pride in being students. Teachers certainly play a role in fostering student pride and contributing to positive self-concepts. Allowing students to assume much control over their learning informs students that they are worthy of the teacher's trust.[16]

Approaching artistry in "studenting" has the student dealing with self-schemata. It is axiomatic that a student's personal beliefs, motivations, perceptions, and attitudes will influence the ways of approaching learning. These are person variables, and those who have studied metacognition realize that they are crucial to innovative learning.[17] We all have views of our capabilities and limitations. Artist students realize that they possess capabilities to deal with their limitations; to stretch intellectually, socially, emotionally; to work toward a total self-actualization; to strive toward perfecting a questioning attitude that both excites and delights one in learning and in inquiry.

QUESTIONING AND THINKING WITHIN THE CONTEXT OF CONTENT

While one can directly teach questioning and thinking, such teaching should be woven into the total content of the curriculum. It is not an either/or option that confronts us—either teach process, procedural knowledge, or teach content, declarative knowledge. Both are essential; in fact, the reason for learning procedural knowledge, process, is to better understand declarative knowledge and to employ our procedures to advance the various realms of content.

Students are not to be passive receivers and storers of knowledge. Rather they are to question, to reflect, to interact with knowledge encountered.

To grow is the goal of all life. To be human is to strive to maintain and nurture one's own growth. One's outlook on life is an incredibly complex and always changing, configuration of perceptions, impulses, habits, values, ideas, strategies, and hopes.[18]

To *grow* means to grow in all domains: academic, physical, social, and personal. This book on questioning and thinking has primarily addressed the academic goals of the school, although one could argue that a person who questions well and thinks effectively will also master the social and personal realms.

Knowledge as Organizer of World Knowledge

Throughout this book mention has been made of world knowledge. A dimension of a question's structure, noted in Chapter 4, is world knowledge structure. When students identify the world knowledge structure of a particular question, putting the question into a proper context, they are well on their way to effectively processing the question. For example, a student only hearing the question, "Why did the woman yell fire?" first perceives the question to lack a focus. However, if the lesson has been about famous women in battle, then the student can draw on his or her world knowledge structure about battles and hear the word "fire" in a very different light. "Fire" in the question might again be considered differently if reading a story about fire fighters. The context of the question is most important to questioning and thinking.

The knowledge students possess and their views and organizations of such knowledge greatly influence how they will raise questions about that knowledge, how they will think about that knowledge. For this reason, knowledge, organized as school content, is presented both to provide grist for perfecting questioning and thinking processes and also so that students will truly understand such knowledge; that they will grasp primary associations within and among various knowledge domains.

A term presently with much currency is "paradigm." Patton notes that a paradigm

> is a world view, a general perspective, a way of breaking down the complexity of the real world. As such paradigms are deeply embedded in the socialization of adherents and practioners; paradigms tell them what is important, legitimate, and reasonable. Paradigms are also normative, telling the practioner what to do with the necessity of long existential or epistemological consideration.[19]

The various disciplines of knowledge can be perceived as paradigms— world views somewhat formalized by scholars working within such fields. The strength of such disciplined world views is that they allow scholars, really anyone interested in the discipline, to have a certain focus on the world, to place a lens with a particular optic on the world, to raise particular types of questions, and to process such questions in definite ways, following accepted procedures and agreed upon proofs. This strength is also a potential weakness, for while a particular disciplined lens lets us see certain wave lengths of light, it may also blind us to other wave lengths. We may never question the assumptions of the paradigm for we do not see them.

Considering disciplined knowledge and even nondisciplined knowledge as created organizations of information makes one aware that each of these content areas represents a definite and particular way of viewing the world and of mapping what is viewed. Each of these knowledge organizations has specific approaches for investigations, ways of raising questions and analyzing the information resulting from such questioning.

Students possessing questioning attitudes realize the nature of knowledge and that there are various realms of knowledge each organized in special conceptual ways. These students understand ways that each of these knowledge cores is dynamic, with new ways of conceptualizing its content being generated and of processing its content being applied.

Organized Knowledge as Schemata

Students with a questioning attitude realize that organized knowledge can be viewed as specialized schemata, a type of prototype or mental model to influence our actions and thoughts—our questions. Schema theory indicates that we employ our organizations for linking new information with existing information, mindful of the potential ways of organizing knowledge. New knowledge is not deposited in a vacuum; rather it is assimilated into existing structures or paradigms. Thus, students who are questioners constantly build upon what they already possess, reflecting upon their actions. Essentially, they are engaging in metacognitive action as they process new information.

Students should grasp that as they process new information and raise questions about such information, they are using schemata to enable them to determine the pertinent, the important. Questions are employed to elaborate incoming information and generate new forms of knowledge, new understandings. Their organizers can be used to search their memory banks to bring up information deemed relevant to the particular situation under consideration. Also, this allows students to generate conclusions and to evaluate such conclusions as to worth. Engaged in questioning with definite schema allows students to view information gathered and to identify gaps in information. Furthermore, students with such an attitude can generate hypotheses to close recognized gaps.[20]

Students knowledgeable of and skilled in questioning realize that schemata can exist at various levels of generality. Considering a realm of study such as history or mathematics is holding schemata at a most general level; however, within each realm are also schemata that refer to segments of that knowledge organization. One might well argue that there is a schema around each concept we possess. We apply past schemata to each concept encountered in processing information. Upon reading a story of Halloween, we bring to bear specific schema relating to holidays, mystery, witches, ghosts, and bobbing for apples. Upon hearing of St. Patrick's Day, we might still bring forth the schema for holiday, but we adjust our schemata to the specific occasion, bringing in the notion "wearing of the green," leprechauns, and perhaps parades.

Armed with the questioning attitude students realize at which level they should process information; which level of schemata is appropriate for the situation confronting them. With increased skill in questioning, many of these processings of schemata become automatic. This is fine, for students need not ponder every word or utterance they hear. If they did, they would never get on with the task of advancing their learning; they would be stuck with asking themselves about some specific. For instance, in reading, students need not consider deeply every word encountered. Students can read the sentence, "The leader said, 'Do not fire until you see the whites of their eyes.' " Students do not need to consider every word to get the meaning. Likewise, students upon hearing one say, "The robin was singing a beautiful song," do not need to reflect on the schemata "bird" or the singing. Each student reading the word "robin" certainly brings unique visions of the bird into his or her mind's eye depending upon past experiences, but there is enough general background information about birds and particularly robins for students to know what the sentence means. Nevertheless, there are instances when students may need to ponder the meaning. If the student hears the sentence, "The cockatoo wobbled nicely," he or she may have to first determine if a cockatoo is a bird. Once done, the meaning of the sentence is fairly straightforward.[21]

Essentially, students who apprehend that knowledge is organized into clusters, into paradigms, into schemata, not only formulate meaningful conclusions but also create knowledge themselves, structuring it in personal ways.

Organized Knowledge as Specialized Procedures

Students striving to master ways of creating knowledge appreciate that when engaged in such action they are mimicking scholars' procedures; however, not all specialists act similarly. Mathematicians, biologists, and novelists think of their subject matter in diverse ways, influenced by particular paradigms. Such knowledge is important to the student with a questioning attitude. Students realize that while they have various heuristics for questioning and thinking, they may indeed need to modify them when working within particular subject fields. Certainly, one questions in biology and in mathematics, but sometimes fine tuning is necessary. Proofs in history differ from proofs in mathematics.

Mathematicians engage in processes primarily deductive, raising questions essentially at the analysis level. In contrast, a biologist engages in processes primarily inductive, in which observed reality is investigated and questioned to generate a conclusion with broad applicability. Students with questioning attitudes realize the commonness of processes among various knowledge realms as well as differences.

Effective questioners and thinkers become skilled in the numerous procedures for processing information. They possess conditional knowledge. In addition to knowing the various questioning and thinking strategies, they comprehend why certain questioning and thinking strategies work. Furthermore, these students grasp when to employ particular strategies, when to bring up certain paradigms. These students also apprehend why certain strategies of questioning and thinking are more appropriate in particular situations.[22]

Realizing that organized knowledge comprises specialized procedures to the world also means that effective students also understand the various camps for approaching knowledge, for processing it, for viewing reality. Indeed, students at the upper levels of schooling should realize that while we are in a positivist emphasis currently, there are scholars advancing a post-positivist posture to knowledge. We teachers need to realize both the positivist and post-positivist postures and what such postures mean to questioning and to thinking.

QUESTIONING ATTITUDE WITHIN POSITIVIST CAMP

Positivism refers to those families of philosophies that adhere closely to following the scientific method, indeed believing that through science and its methods we will come to know reality precisely. Much of our teaching assumes that the positivism posture is the one that should guide our teaching and our students' learning. Certainly, the positivists have added greatly to our knowledge. One might argue that the acceptance of this posture, which started with Newton's work and that of Francis Bacon in the 16th century, characterizes modern western culture.

Positivism, as discussed by Wolf, has the following assumptions:

1. Things move in a continuous manner. All motion, both in the large and in the small, exhibits continuity.

2. Things move for reasons. These reasons were based upon earlier causes for motion. Therefore, all motion was determined and everything was predictable.

3. All motion could be analyzed or broken down into its component parts. Each part played a role in the great machine called the universe, and the complexity of this machine could be understood as the simple movement of its various parts, even those parts beyond our perception.

4. The observer observed, never disturbed. Even the errors of a clumsy observer could be accounted for by simply analyzing the observed movements of whatever he touched.[23]

Accepting these assumptions, students raise questions about a reality both observable and predictable. They realize that the world in which they live, indeed the universe in which they exist, resembles a big clock running smoothly. Our questions are posed to discover how the clock works, to observe its working, and then to draw conclusions. As investigators, we are not really involved in the clock's workings; we are only objective observers of the phenomena.

The empirical method, a hallmark of this century, is part of this positivist tradition. That one can process much of the information of this book can be viewed as testimony to the value and significance of this posture. Hesse presents some statements about the empirical method that furnish additional insight into this positivism posture.

1. In natural science, experience is taken to be objective, testable, and independent of theoretical explanation. . . .

2. In natural science theories are artificial constructs or modes, yielding explanation in the sense of a logic of hypothetico-deduction: if external nature were of such a kind, then data and experience would be as we find them . . .

3. In natural science, the lawlike relations asserted of experience are external, both to the objects connected and to the investigator, since they are merely correlational. . . .

4. The language of natural science is exact, formalizable, and literal; therefore, meanings are univocal, and a problem of meaning arises only in the application of universal categories to particulars. . . .

5. Meanings in natural science are separate from facts.[24]

Perhaps the key for us to remember is that experience is taken to be objective, testable. Students with this questioning attitude take as truth or at least as useful that experience is out there. Experience can be seen, quantified, tested. Reality exists even prior to our questions; it is to be discovered. Phrased another way, "The acorn *does* make a sound in the forest even though there is no one to hear it."

QUESTIONING ATTITUDE WITHIN POSTPOSITIVIST CAMP

Much emphasis on thinking draws from the positivism camp. This is not inappropriate provided students realize that there exists another questioning paradigm that can be applied to reality—postpositivism. This new view, postpositivism, has made some major inroads into the natural sciences. Postpositivism is the opposite of positivism. Hesse presents five major points of postpositivism to support this claim.

1. In the natural sciences, data are not detachable from theory, for what count as data are determined in the light of some theoretical interpretation and the facts themselves have to be reconstructed in the light of interpretation.

2. In natural science, theories are not models externally compared in nature to a hypothetico-deductive schema; they are the way the facts themselves are seen.

3. In natural science, the law-like relations asserted of experiences are internal because what we count as facts are constituted by what the theory says about their interrelations with one another.

4. The language of natural sciences is irreducibly metaphorical and inexact, and formalizable only at the cost of distortion of the historical dynamics of scientific development of the imaginative reconstructions in terms of which nature is interpreted by science.

5. Meanings in natural science are determined by theory; they are understood by theoretical coherence rather than by correspondence with facts.[25]

A student accepting this attitude toward the world also raises questions but realizes that as questioner he or she cannot be an objective outsider solely looking in at the world desiring to describe and then to manipulate its parts. Rather, the very things one sees in the world will be influenced, in a way created, by the internal views one possesses. We create our experiences invented from the chaos of the world; it is not out there to be discovered.

Students with a postpositivist questioning attitude realize that they and others are essentially human primary data gathering instruments. Actually, it is impossible to create a nonhuman instrument, for all instruments are created by persons and only an individual is capable of comprehending and assessing the meaning of the interactions the instrument is intended to measure. Students realize that they cannot raise objective questions, questions divorced from their person. "These are my questions, influenced by my prior and present experiences, my views of the world, my judgments as to what is worthwhile and worthy of investigation. My questions come from an interaction that I have with my world. As I discern my world, my perceptions and my questions will change just as I change and grow.[26]

"In phrasing my questions, I will draw upon my intuition as well as prior knowledge I have recorded and received from others. I will tune into the nuances of the multiple realities experienced. I will reflect deeply, engage in in-depth processing of information, aware that I am part of my world, and the world is part of me. I am cognizant that my values, while expressions of me also serve to mold me."

Students with this postpositivist attitude realize that one's inquiry, one's questions, depend upon the structure and quality of interactions between the inquirer and perceived knowledge. One negotiates the meaning of the data uncovered. Much cooperative learning can allow students to experience the negotiated aspects of knowledge production.[27]

Since all conclusions are tentative, students are cautious about making broad applications of findings resulting from employing particular questioning and thinking strategies. This is because findings to a certain degree are dependent upon the particular interaction between the investigator and the respondents or objects that have been the focus of the inquiry. Such interactions may be situation specific, not applicable to other situations. For this reason students accepting this posture are inclined to consider interpreted data as idiographic. Despite such a consideration, however, students appreciate that there will be conclusions that have some degree of generalizability to other situations of like kind.[28]

In this book, there is no stand taken that one camp is correct and the other incorrect. We teachers and our students as innovative learners all must realize that these two major attitudinal positions exist and that we can employ both in our questioning and our thinking. Some teachers and students will be unwilling, wishing only to accept one of these postures; that is fine providing these individuals realize that they are making a choice aware of both the limitations and benefits of their choice to process and think about information in that manner.

The important point is that all of the information presented in this book is applicable to both major positions. A person questions in both camps; an individual thinks and processes data in both camps. A student arrives at conclusions and employs them in both camps.

Students should have *a* questioning attitude; they need not have *the* questioning attitude. *The* questioning attitude assumes that we currently possess sufficient data or can obtain sufficient data to indicate without equivocation that there is just one questioning attitude that will advance active inquiry. There may be as many attitudes as there are individuals, at least regarding the particulars. What we want for our students is that they have *a* questioning attitude—that they realize that questions are central to gaining understanding and that those of us who think deeply about and with our questions, who take responsibility for our questions, are most inclined to arrive at conclusions, however tentative, that have worth. Such conclusions should advance us in our journeys toward a greater understanding of ourselves as humans within a dynamic and ever changing world.

CONCLUSION

Having a questioning attitude is more than just enjoying asking questions. It is having a disposition toward experiencing what Mezirow defines as a kind of "perspective transformation" in which new learning transforms learning rather than just adding to it.[29]

Activity

ATTITUDE CHECK

This chapter has discussed the dimensions of the questioning attitude. It is evident that having a questioning attitude is a complex cluster of knowledge, feelings, values, and accepted norms for behaving.

If we as teachers are to foster in students awareness of their questioning attitudes and appreciation of the power of positive attitudes, then we must also have cognizance of our questioning attitudes.

Reflect on this chapter's content and write down your emotional or affective responses to the content presented. Study your comments and then write a brief statement that would sum up your questioning attitude and your feelings toward possessing this attitude.

Is your attitude positive? If so, good. If not, then you certainly need to map out ways in which to make it so. As teacher, one must value questions to ignite a love of questions in our students.

Most likely, we cannot directly teach a questioning attitude; we can only plan for educational encounters in which students can learn of the ways they can think about and relate to questions and questioning. We can only schedule time in which students can reflect on their questions and how they can inquire within the various realms of organized knowledge. We can only furnish situations in which students can realize the myriad ways in which to process information and that the question is central to each of these ways.

We can directly teach process, procedural knowledge, but the questioning attitude is *knowledge to,* a commitment to action. While we can inform students that it is essential to realize the primacy of being skilled in questioning and thinking, we can not tell students how they must feel, what dispositions they must have; that is for students to decide. We do need to inform our students, however, that there are numerous points regarding a questioning attitude about which they do need to reflect and about which they can question.

Getting in touch with one's attitudes toward questions and thinking is prerequisite to becoming a truly competent and caring individual.

NOTES

1. Francis P. Hunkins, personal comments, Oct. 1987.

2. J. T. Botkin, M. Elmandjra, and M. Malitz, *No Limits to Learning; Bridging the Human Gap: A Report to the Club of Rome* (Oxford: Pergamon Press,

1979), p. 9. Cited in Howard Gardner, *Frames of Mind* (New York: Basic Books, 1985).

3. Bonni Pitman-Gelles, "Museums and Schools: A Meaningful Partnership," in Mario D. Fantini and Robert L. Sinclair, eds., *Education in School and Nonschool Settings,* Eighty-Fourth Yearbook of the National Society for the Study of Education, Part 1 (Chicago: The University of Chicago Press, 1985), pp. 114–39.

4. Louis J. Rubin, *Artistry in Teaching* (New York: Random House, 1985).

5. Louis J. Rubin, *Artistry in Teaching.*

6. Howard Gardner, *Frames of Mind, The Theory of Multiple Intelligences* (New York: Basic Books, 1983), p. 368.

7. Leslie A. Hart, *Human Brain and Human Learning* (New York: Longman, 1983).

8. Cited in Howard Gardner, *Frames of Mind* (New York: Basic Books, 1985).

9. Malcolm S. Knowles, "Lifelong Learning in the Museum," in *Museums, Adults, and the Humanities: A Guide for Educational Programmers* (Washington, D.C.: American Association of Museums, 1981), pp. 134–35; cited in Bonnie Pitman-Gelles, "Museums and Schools: A Meaningful Partnership," in Mario Fantini and Robert Sinclair, eds. *Education in School and Non School Settings*, Eighty-Fourth yearbook of the National Society for the Study of Education Part I (Chicago: University of Chicago Press, 1985), pp. 114–39.

10. Louis J. Rubin, *Artistry in Teaching.*

11. J. H. Flavell, "Metacognition and Cognition Monitoring: A New Area of Cognitive-Developmental Inquiry," *American Psychologist* 34 (1979): 906–11.

12. Jerome Bruner, *The Process of Education* (Cambridge, Mass.: Harvard University Press, 1960).

13. Edward de Bono, "The CoRT Thinking Program," in Arthur L. Costa, ed., *Developing Minds, a Resource Book for Teaching Thinking.* (Alexandria, Va.: Association for Supervision and Curriculum Development, 1985), pp. 203–9.

14. Louis J. Rubin, *Artistry in Teaching,* p. 21.

15. Hugh G. Petrie, *The Dilemma of Enquiry and Learning* (Chicago: The University of Chicago Press, 1981).

16. Louis J. Rubin, *Artistry in Teaching,* pp. 20–22.

17. J. H. Jenkins, "Four Points to Remember: A Tetrahedral Model of Memory Experiments," in L. S. Cermak and F. M. Craik, eds., *Levels of Processing in Human Memory* (Hillsdale, N.J.: Erlbaum, 1979).

18. William H. Schubert, *Curriculum Perspective, Paradigm, and Possibility* (New York: Macmillan, 1986), p. 421.

19. Michael Q. Patton, *Utilization-focused Evaluation* (Beverly Hills: Sage, 1978), p. 203.

20. Robert J. Marzano, et. al, *Dimensions of Thinking* (Alexandria, VA: Association for Supervision and Curriculum Development, 1988).

21. E. D. Hirsch, Jr. *Cultural Literacy* (Boston: Houghton Mifflin Co., 1987).

22. Robert J. Marzano, et. al. *Dimensions of Thinking.*

23. Fred A. Wolf, *Taking the Quantum Leap* (San Francisco: Harper and Row, 1981), p. 56; cited in Yvonna S. Lincoln and Egon G. Guba, *Naturalistic Inquiry* (Beverly Hills: Sage Publications, 1985).

24. Mary Hesse, *Revolutions and Reconstructions in the Philosophy of Science* (Bloomington: Indiana University Press, 1980), pp. 170–71; cited in Yvonna S. Lincoln and Egon G. Guba, *Naturalistic Inquiry* (Beverly Hills: Sage Publications, 1985).

25. Mary Hesse, *Revolutions and Reconstructions in the Philosophy of Science;* pp. 172–73; cited in Yvonna S. Lincoln and Egon G. Guba, *Naturalistic Inquiry* (Beverly Hills: Sage Publications, 1985).

26. Yvonna S. Lincoln and Egon G. Guba, *Naturalistic Inquiry* (Beverly Hills: Sage Publications, 1985).

27. Yvonna S. Lincoln and Egon G. Guba, *Naturalistic Inquiry.*

28. Yvonna S. Lincoln and Egon G. Guba, *Naturalistic Inquiry.*

29. I. Mezirow, "Perspective Transformation," *Adult Education* 1978, 28, 100–110.

INDEX